THE FLIGHT OF THE BROKEN PHOENIX

OTHER PEOPLE'S LIVES
published by the Larks Press

⌐⌐⌐

Diary of an Optimist – Mary Barnard

Is this you, Nurse? – Brenda Sayle

The Mill House and Thereabouts – H.C.Harrison

Miller's Daughter – Nancy Potter

The Boy at Willows End – Frank Wrigley

*The Life that Jack Lived – Jack Troup

Memoirs of a Shannock – May Ayers

The Strange Family at Yorke's Hill – Katherine Yorke

Pavements to Ploughed Fields

The Gamekeeper's Boy – Mike Cringle

The Seventeenth Child – Ethel George

From Crow-scaring to Westminster – George Edwards

Mother of Necton – Mary Nichols

When I was Your Age – Sheila Upjohn

A Boyhood in the Fleggs – Jimmy Leggett

The Flight of the Broken Phoenix – Derek Dix

*Out of print

THE FLIGHT
OF THE
BROKEN PHOENIX

Derek Dix

The Larks Press

Published by the Larks Press
Ordnance Farmhouse
Guist Bottom, Dereham, NR20 5PF
01328 829207
Larks.Press@btinternet.com

British Library Cataloguing-in-Publication-Data
A catalogue record for this book is available
from the British Library.

ISBN 978 1 904006 63 3

FOREWORD

An active little boy is struck down with polio just before his fifth
birthday. He lies unconscious for six weeks and wakes to find
himself totally paralysed. The doctors tell his distraught mother
that all of his muscles have been severely damaged, or destroyed,
and that he will be bedridden for the rest of his life. She prays
fervently for him to die.

The doctors may have thought that the boy had no future, but
Fate had other ideas.

I was that small boy and, lying on my back, unable to move, I
could never have guessed what was in store for me.

This is an account of my long and eventful journey through life,
and of some of the interesting people that I met on my way.

Derek Dix

Derek at eighteen, happy and confident

CHAPTER 1

A Promising Beginning

My life had started full of promise. Born on a beautiful sunny day on the first of September 1932 and weighing in at a robust ten pounds, I was the third child of Bertie Albert Arthur Dix, of Great Yarmouth and Ivy née Kingham from Coddicot in Hertfordshire. I had a brother Albert and a sister Ivy, my seniors by seven and five years respectively.

We lived in a small terraced house at Caister-on-Sea, a small fishing village just two and a half miles north of Great Yarmouth. My father had been badly wounded in the First World War and was carried off the battlefield minus his right leg, his right hand smashed into an almost useless claw and the rest of his body holed and torn. But for all that, he was a tall well-built man with a warm nature and good humour. We all survived on his total disability war pension. This amounted to only twenty-five shillings a week, since the grateful government decreed that, as he was unmarried at the time of his injuries, he qualified for a single man's allowance only. We managed, but no one can say that I was born with a silver spoon in my mouth.

The family just after our fateful move to Great Yarmouth

At that time our next door neighbours were Arthur and Nellie Norton. My mother and Nellie, who were good friends, had both been pregnant at the same time. Unfortunately Nellie, who was forty and childless, had a stillbirth just before I arrived. I suppose to console her in her grief, my mother allowed Nellie to share me and I spent almost as much of my young life with Aunt Nellie as I did with my mother. In a way this was a wonderful arrangement as I had two mothers, but it led to some confusion in my young mind. I well remember demanding to know who my real mother was, and even after positive assurances, accepting the information with some suspicion.

Aunt Nellie played a major role in my life. When I was a small child it was she who insisted on scrubbing me clean and dressing me smartly to be taken on the beach or along the Yarmouth Road to feed crusts of bread to the horses at the field gate. As I became a little older, it was she who sat me on her lap in front of the fire and read stories to me or helped me to cut out pictures and paste them in a scrap book. She also taught me my first prayers, hymns and little songs. Aunt Nellie was a wonderful pastry cook and I was encouraged to assist her. I was also taught how to dust and clean the house. Nellie was kind and loving, but meticulous about cleanliness and good appearance. Quietly and gently she demanded absolute obedience and good behaviour. So, on the one hand I had the attention of an only child, on the other I had the rough and tumble of family life with my parents and siblings. My brother played with the local children and by the time I was three I joined in some of their wild escapades, such as sailing a large bath tub across a flooded marsh. Once they constructed a rickety bridge of old tin cans and clods of earth over a large dyke at the rear of our terrace. As the smallest and lightest of the group, I was instructed to cross the bridge first to test its strength. Needless to say, half way across the whole construction collapsed, tossing me into three feet of muddy water. It was all very normal.

Sometimes my father took me to visit my grandmother at Albion Road in Great Yarmouth. She was seventy-six when I was born and to me, she always appeared very old indeed. Her house was unchanged from the time she had furnished it as a young woman. It was full of antique furniture. Pictures and plates filled the walls and valuable ornaments, that must not be touched, were everywhere. My brother called it 'the museum'.

'Sit there!' my father would indicate a chair or the end of the couch in the kitchen. I sat. The horse-hair covering had sharp little ends that pricked the back of my knees unmercifully. 'Sit still and stop fidgeting,' my father would say. Any thought of disobeying my father never entered my head. He and my grandmother talked about people I did not know and things that I did not understand but I just had to sit still and listen. If I spoke at all there would be the sharp rebuke, 'little boys should be seen and not heard.'

It was better on the Saturday visits to grandmother's, when the whole family was there, for then my brother would go out to play and take me with him. Our visits were so frequent that we were as much at home playing with the children around Albion Road as we were with the Caister children. Football was the major activity. I loved football. My brother taught me how to 'dribble' and 'shoot for goal'. One of the boys was called Roy Hollis. He thought he was good but I could get the ball past him. Sometimes we played in a wide passage and sometimes we ventured onto St George's Park, when the park-keeper was not about.

It was on our way to the park one day that, passing along a passage at the rear of a terrace of houses, one of the boys noticed through an open door a man shaving in a wash-house. He was small, stripped to the waist, his face covered in thick white lather highlighting his flaming red hair. Leaning over the little wicket gate the boys began to chant. 'Ginger you're barmy – you ought to join the army.' Without more ado, the little man, with a howl of rage, came for us. At first I thought he was just driving us away but he was quickly out into the passage and pressing home his attack. We ran and he followed. He was very fast. I took one look at this demented, half-naked fiend with his white face and flaming hair, swearing and brandishing an open cut throat razor and ran for my life. His heavy hob-nailed boots thudded close behind me. I ran as fast as I could and eventually outran him. My mother was always saying that I could run like the wind. That run was exhilarating. I remember it vividly, with pride and nostalgia. A feeling perhaps akin to a mountaineer who, just once in a lifetime, climbs and stands on the summit of Mount Everest.

In 1936 Aunt Nellie moved to Yarmouth so that Uncle Arthur could be nearer to his work place and within a month or two, we also moved to a larger terraced house in the town on Alderson Road. I soon had new friends and played happily with them in the roads and passages in the area.

Auntie Nellie and Uncle Arthur and Jock

We visited my grandmother more often now. It was on one of these visits, when I was about four and a half, that I was playing on the road with several children. We were doing nothing in particular, except making a lot of noise and 'showing off' as one might say. An old lady came along the pavement on the opposite side of the road. She was small, thin and dressed in black. She hobbled along painfully because one leg was much shorter than the other. On this leg she had a big boot with a sole some six inches thick. On impulse, to show off to my friends, I began to ape her funny walk. Their laughter attracted her attention and she saw the cause. She pointed at me angrily and said,

'It isn't funny. I hope that one day you will have to walk like me.'

I had not meant to be unkind. I had just not thought about it. I did not know what to say and just stood there feeling guilty and ashamed.

Sometimes we were visited by Aunt Maud, my father's sister and Uncle William. Aunt Maud was painfully thin, sallow-skinned with dark hair and dark brown eyes. She was always pessimistic, always looking for the bad in everything and highly critical of everyone, including my father, who she said ought to know better than to have children when he had no means of supporting them. It was not that I disliked Aunt Maud, it was perhaps some mischief in me that wanted to shock her out of her starchy attitude, but shock her I did. Once it was by cunningly showing her drawings I had done, among which were graphic illustrations of large fat naked women peeing into chamber pots. When she came to those she was suitably disturbed and at a loss for words. I felt that in some small way I had punished her for what she had said to my father. My mother said I was a naughty little boy for drawing rude pictures and a very bad boy for upsetting Aunt Maud. I felt unrepentant.

The summer we moved to Yarmouth, my mother like most people on the road, offered lodgings to holiday visitors. They were accommodated in the front room and the front bedroom. One week three young ladies came to stay. I suppose they were in their late teens. They were all big, well-built girls. When they came in for the midday meal or at teatime, they laughed and talked to me while waiting for meals to be served. One of them picked me up, holding my hands and feet and swung me face up between her open legs, singing 'one, two, three, four, five, once I caught a fish alive, six, seven, eight, nine, ten then I let it go again. Dead or alive?' If I said 'alive,' she flicked me onto my feet, if I said 'dead,' she laid me on the ground. As she swung me backwards and forwards, I gazed up at those massive bare thighs, towering above me, watching the muscles ripple rhythmically under the motion and weight of my body and was overawed and fascinated by their sheer strength and beauty. When one girl tired, another carried on the game. When they had finished with me I was intoxicated with a wild excitement that I had never experienced before. I thought they were magnificent.

Now that we lived in Great Yarmouth we often went to play on the recreation ground. On one occasion the whole family went there and my brother and I were kicking a ball around. My father, who had been a keen footballer and swimmer in his youth, watched with smiling approval. 'He is going to be a great footballer,' he said to my mother, 'look how strongly he can kick the ball with either foot.' Yes, I thought, I am going to be a champion footballer just like my dad.

The summer of 1937 was long and hot. Every day I played outside. Life was good. That is until people started talking about me being nearly five years old and having to go to school in September.

'I don't want to go to school,' I repeatedly told my mother. 'I am not going.'

'Everyone has to go to school when they are five,' she said.

'Well I'm not going, I would sooner die.'

'Don't be such a wicked little boy. You are going to school and that's an end of it.'

I brooded about this and raised the matter several times but always received the same reply.

In July the schools broke up for the summer holidays. I suppose with my brother and sister being at home my mother must have been grateful that Aunt Nellie should have me for a couple of weeks. I was glad to go. My father had been getting irritable with me lately.

'Why do you keep making that silly little cough?' he kept asking. I explained that it was something tickling the back of my throat. 'Have a drink of water' he suggested. I did, but the tickle remained. So I kept on giving a little cough to clear my throat. 'You are developing a silly little habit with this cough' he said. 'Just stop it. It's very irritating.'

The tickle in my throat did not go away but Aunt Nellie said nothing about it. She took me shopping in Gorleston and we went to the beach and had a lovely time.

I had been at Aunt Nellie's for only three or four days when I had a headache and began to feel unwell. 'You are getting feverish' she said. 'I am going to take you home.' I protested that I was alright and did not want to go home but she insisted and took me back to my mother.

My father's verdict was that I had caught a chill, eating ice cream on Gorleston beach. For a day or two I felt unwell but was not ill enough to go to bed. But the morning came when something seemed to be wrong with my legs.

'Come on, get up' my mother said coming into my bedroom.

'I can't get up, Mummy,' I said 'my legs won't work.'

'Nonsense,' she said briskly, throwing aside the bedclothes and lifting me out of bed. As she stood me down my legs just folded under me and I collapsed to the floor. Once she realised that I was not playing the fool I was put back to bed and the doctor was sent for. He examined my legs. Taking a penny from his pocket, he held it above my foot.

'If you can touch the penny with your toe you can have it,' he said. I tried desperately to raise my leg but it refused to move. He tried the other leg but that would not move either. He said to my father 'It is infantile paralysis (poliomyelitis).'

1937, a few weeks before polio struck

Later in the day the pains started. My legs and arms ached dreadfully. 'Rub them for me Mummy,' I cried. She rubbed my legs and arms but the pain was undiminished. The doctor had said I was not to sit up and my mother fed me with fluids, using a doll's teapot. I felt helpless and embarrassed at having to be treated like a baby.

I discovered much later that my father was at the time doing everything possible to get me into hospital. He visited the Town Hall to see the Medical Officer of Health. The response was that he should keep quiet about my illness as, if it came out that the disease was in the town, it would panic the holiday makers and that would be a financial disaster for the resort. Whereupon my father threatened to hire a loudspeaker van and tour the seafront to make sure all the holiday-makers were aware of the situation. This must have triggered some action. I recall nothing of my last few hours at home, but through the haze of semi-consciousness I heard, fleetingly, the persistent and urgent ringing of a bell and felt a frantic rocking motion beneath me. Vaguely I was aware of being in an ambulance on my way to hospital. There was a brief few seconds when I heard the crunch of gravel and realised that I was being handled by a bustle of people. Then there was nothing. I had slid behind the black curtain of unconsciousness.

I am told that this state of unconsciousness lasted for six weeks.

CHAPTER 2

Hospital

I awoke to find myself in a large bed with a tall metal canopy rising above me draped with muslin curtains. The room was spacious, with big windows and a high ceiling and light green painted walls. A metal trolley with white, enamel dishes upon it was just visible. Everything seemed to be cold, functional and austere.

The door opened and a small woman came into the room and up to the bed. She was dressed in a greyish overall, had black rimmed spectacles and short, frizzy hair. She lifted back the bedclothes and rolled me over onto my side. 'What is this?' she shouted angrily. 'You dirty little boy.' Then she began to slap my bottom hard. It went on and on. All the time she was shouting 'dirty little boy' with each slap. Although I could not feel the blows I was frightened and upset. I had never been hit before. My parents and Aunt Nellie had never smacked me. Then another woman came into the room. She wore a dark blue dress with a stiff white apron and a white cloth folded over her head. She spoke sharply to the woman and took her away. Only when they were gone did I start to cry. Then two younger women came in. Both had pale blue dresses with white aprons. 'I want my Mummy, I want to go home,' I cried. They said nothing. Their faces seemed expressionless and it was just as if I had not spoken. They washed me and changed the sheets and then left. Unable to move, I lay in that big bed in that miserable big room in total silence. The women came only to feed and wash me. They did not speak and ignored all my questions. My body was there but it was just as if I did not exist.

My parents were told that I had returned to consciousness but I was totally paralysed and would have to spend the rest of my life on my back. My mother told me much later, how she had been devastated by this news and prayed fervently that I might die.

Lying there helpless, in total isolation, was soul-destroying. Days seemed like weeks. Visits from the nurses were infrequent and brief and brought me little spiritual comfort. My tears, pleas for my mother and all the questions were ignored. There was no human contact. In the end I resigned myself to my fate and became just a passive lump of flesh. When I was alone, relief was gained only by the release of tears, until I had sobbed myself to sleep.

Then one day the routine was broken. A large trolley was wheeled into the room and placed next to the bed. Deftly they lifted me onto the trolley and wheeled me off, through the door, along a corridor and into a large room full of beds and children. Their voices seemed as sweet as music. I was placed in the third bed from the door on the left hand side of the ward. I took in my new surroundings with mounting excitement. It was like a return from the grave. Two boys, fully dressed, came up to the bed.

'What's your name?' one asked.

'Derek' I said.

'What's wrong with you?'

'I don't know. I can't move.' They accepted this information with the same equanimity that might have been expected had I said it was just a cold. Once they had established my age, where I came from and similar basic details, they must have decided I was not going to be much fun and wandered off to join other boys. I did not mind. It was enough just to have life, movement and the presence of other children about me.

Every day seemed much like any other. We were woken early in the morning, about 5.00 a.m. and, half asleep, were washed. Then a trolley came round with a milky liquid which they said was tea. This was followed by breakfast. Then all the beds were made and everything tidied up ready for the doctor's round. No one was allowed to move in their beds, so that the crisp white sheets and covers looked immaculate. Even during the day, beds had to stay looking uncrumpled, otherwise the lady in the dark blue dress would order two nurses to remake the bed. They did not like this and would be angry with any child who disarrayed a bed. Just before midday, dinner was served with another drink and then the nurses gave out big orange blankets, laid out on top of the beds, for those children who were not kept in bed and everyone had to lie in or on their beds for an hour. Teatime was at 3.30 p.m. At 4.00 p.m. everyone in bed was washed and the others taken away for a bath. By 5.00 p.m. everyone was in bed for the night, after having the medicine they needed. It was the same routine day after day after day.

I knew that all the women looking after us were nurses but I was surprised that they were all from the same family, because there were so many of them. I mentioned this to an older boy who came to talk to me. He looked puzzled.

'Of course they are not from the same family' he said.

'They are,' I insisted 'they all call the older one in the dark blue dress Sister and she bosses them about like my sister bosses me. If she is sister to all of them, they must all be sisters to each other!'

He fell about laughing. 'You idiot' he said, 'the Sister is not their sister, she is a nursing sister. That is what she is called because she knows more than the others and is in charge of them. It is like all the men being called 'Doctor'. Although,' he added thoughtfully, 'the very best doctors are called Mister.'

'My dad is a Mister,' I said hoping to regain some credibility. He grinned pityingly.

'You are ignorant, you don't know anything.' I was not sure what ignorant meant but had a fairly good idea. 'Don't you think some of the nurses are pretty?' he asked. 'I like the one with the curly blonde hair.'

After he had left, I thought about it. What did he mean by pretty? They all frightened me. In fact everything about this place frightened me. I wanted my mother. Once, in reply to my request for my mother, a nurse broke her silence. 'You can't see your mother until you are better.' I knew then that I just had to get well.

A day came when, while being washed, the nurse stopped what she was doing and looked at my hand. 'Did you move your finger?' she demanded.

I said 'No.'

'Move it again' she commanded. Looking at my hand, I concentrated hard. The index finger moved just ever so slightly. She said nothing and put my hand back on the bed and went away. Within seconds she came back with the Sister who held my hand.

'Let me see you move your finger' she said.

I tried and again the finger moved slightly. When the doctor came on his round the performance had to be repeated. They seemed quite pleased and smiled. The doctor said 'Good boy.' A little while later a plump lady, like my mother, dressed all in white, came to see me. She smiled and seemed to be different from the other nurses. She talked a lot, asking my name and wanting to know about where I lived and my brother and sister and our house and everything. She took out from her bag a wooden box with a wire, which she plugged into the wall. In the box was a long metal rod that slowly wagged from side to side, like the pendulum in my grandmother's big clock. Then she plugged into the box two stick-like things with a piece of gauze at the ends formed into little pads. These were dipped into a basin of water. She put one on my arm and the other on my hand.

'Can you feel anything?' she asked.

'Yes,' I told her, 'it's like pins and needles.'

'Good, good,' she said. She tried moving the little sticks all over me. The tingling sensation was very strong in my arms but much weaker in my legs. She did this for a little while and then put some powder from a tin on my arms, first one, then the other. This she rubbed in very gently, bending my elbows, wrists and fingers. She visited me every day. The nurses said she was a masseuse.

Within a few days I could move all my fingers in both hands. 'Keep moving them all the time but have rests in between,' she told me. She was nice. Not as nice as my mummy and Aunt Nellie but she was nice. Within no time at all I could move my hands at the wrists and my fingers were becoming much stronger. Slowly but surely life returned to my arms and, perhaps waveringly, I could reach up to touch my face. It was exciting.

'Am I getting better?' I asked her.

'Yes, but we have a long way to go yet.' I knew what she meant. My legs lay at the end of the bed like two dead sticks.

The hospital routine was shattered one day. Nurses appeared with balloons, paper chains and a tree in a pot. Everyone seemed excited.

'It will soon be Christmas' the nurses said as they decorated the ward. 'Father Christmas will come and bring you all presents.'

I was not too sure about this. Last year Aunt Nellie had written to Father Christmas for me on a small piece of thin paper, telling him what presents I wanted. This she held over the fire until it was sucked up the chimney. There was no fireplace here and nobody to write a note. Anyway, I had a little doubt in my mind because my brother had said Father Christmas did not exist and it was just a story everyone told small children.

At night, there was just one nurse on duty. She sat at a little table in the middle of the ward, with a very dim table lamp. It produced just sufficient light to make everything in the room visible, without causing disturbance. It was very quiet in the ward when I awoke. Everyone was asleep. There was a slight sound from the corridor and I turned my head towards the doorway. Then the door opened and I could not believe my eyes. There he was, Father Christmas. He was huge, dressed in a bright red jacket edged with white fur, red trousers, big black boots, a broad black belt and a red hood fringed with white fur. But what I noticed most was his large white beard and bushy white eyebrows. He pulled behind him a large rubber-wheeled trolley loaded with sacks. I could not breathe for excitement as I watched him stop and place a sack at the foot of each bed. By the time he had gone round the ward and reached me my eyes felt as if they were popping out of my head. For a moment he was about to pass on, then he looked me straight in the face. Realising I was awake, he put a finger to his lips to warn me to be quiet, then he came up to the side of the bed and bent over me.

'You must be a very special little boy,' he said in a deep voice, 'because only very special little boys can see me. I am magic! Now you must be very quiet and go to sleep.'

He put out a very big hand and stroked my head gently. Then he moved on delivering his sacks to the remaining two beds. I watched, mesmerised as his huge frame disappeared through the doorway.

My excitement was intense. My brother was wrong! Father Christmas did exist. I had met him! I went over the event again and again in my mind until, exhausted by the wonder of it, I fell asleep.

But it was not for long. Shouts and screams of excitement rang throughout the ward as the children discovered their sacks of presents and eagerly tore off the wrappings. A nurse brought my sack to the bedside and helped me to unwrap my gifts. There were little picture books, a model racing car and other small presents but then she withdrew from the sack a beautiful boy's size, real leather, stitched football, a real leather pair of boxing gloves and a pair of roller skates. I looked at them sadly. Father Christmas must have left me the wrong sack or he did not know I could no longer walk. When the Doctor came round he saw my presents.

'Excellent,' he said 'just what you need.' He picked up the boxing gloves and put them on my hands. Holding up a pillow in front of him, he said, 'Come on, punch it out of my hands.' I made a tentative punch. 'Harder,' he said. I punched as hard as my wavering arms would permit. Laughing, he told the Sister that I had to punch a pillow for five minutes every day. From then on a nurse made me indulge in this one-sided fight every morning, until the day came when my punches were so strong that they decided that further punching was unnecessary.

On Christmas day we had jelly, blancmange and cake for tea and the nurses helped everyone to pull crackers. But with Christmas behind us, the hospital routine returned.

One day two nurses brought a trolley, lifted me on to it and wheeled me out of the ward and along the corridor.

'Where am I going?' I asked. As usual there was no reply. They had that expressionless look again and I feared the worst. The journey was short and I was pushed into a room with a large couch covered in a white sheet. On the couch lay a girl, much older than myself, with long blonde hair. She seemed to be asleep. There were two doctors and several nurses present. They lifted me onto the couch to lie next to the girl. I began to tremble with fear as they removed my gown, and produced a length of tubing.

'What are you going to do?' I asked, not expecting a reply. As they put something round my upper arm, I was surprised when one of the doctors said,

'This girl has the same disease as you. Your body has killed the germs and we are going to let some of your blood flow into her body to see if it can kill her germs.' There was no pain and I laid there very still. After some time, one doctor said,

'It is no use, she has gone.' They all looked disappointed. I knew the girl had died.

They disconnected me from the tube and returned me to the ward. I felt very sad for the girl. I asked a nurse what was a germ. 'It is a little creature, so small that you cannot see it,' she explained, 'and if it gets into your body it can make you ill.'

'Did I have a germ get into my body to make me ill?' I queried.

'Yes.' How did a germ get into your body, I wanted to know.

'You probably breathed it in' she told me. For several days I tried holding my breath to avoid getting germs but it was no use. I had to breathe after a second or two, so soon gave up the idea. When I asked the masseuse about germs, she told me the germs that attacked me had travelled in the blood stream injuring all the muscles they reached. But my body had produced cells to attack and kill the germs and now they were all dead. The damaged muscles now had to be repaired.

I thought a lot about germs. If you were attacked by big animals you could shoot them or run away. But because you could not see germs, there was nothing you could do to protect yourself. It seemed that the world was a much more dangerous place than I had thought. If the germs were in the air and could not fly, then they would drop on the ground and be in the soil. I concluded that Aunt Nellie must know all about germs and that is why she was always on about washing my hands all the time. The thought of the germs was very frightening. I wanted to tell the other children to watch out for germs but it was not easy to talk to them. Many children were very ill in bed and those not in bed went and played together. Anyway, they were generally only there for a few days and then went home. Most of the very sick ones did not go home. Sometimes the nurses put screens around a bed and then the next day the bed would be empty. A boy told me that the screens were put up when they were dying. I was awake one night when the nurses removed the screens from five beds and wheeled the children out of the ward on trolleys. I think they were all dead. After that I kept a sharp watch when the nurses wheeled out screens, in case they put them around my bed.

One could not be sure but it seemed unlikely that I was going to die. Day by day my arms became stronger and when the masseuse put the little pads, which she called 'electrical treatment', on my legs, the tingling was so strong that it made one of the muscles in my legs jump. She said this was a good sign.

It was about this time that a new girl came into the ward. She was much older than the rest of us and was tall, dark-skinned, with her long black hair in plaits. The other children said she was a gypsy but I liked her, even if she was bossy like my sister. She used to sit on my pillow and read comics to me, like Aunt Nellie used to read me stories. One day I asked her to read to me but she refused. 'Oh read it for yourself,' she snapped.

'I can't read, I haven't been to school,' I explained.

'Can't read!' she exclaimed. 'It's easy. I'll soon teach you how to read.' Perched on my pillow, with her leg under my head to raise it up, so I could see, she held the comic in front of my face. After explaining the sound of the different letters, she started to read through the comic, accentuating each letter individually before pronouncing the complete word. Within a few days I was reading the words with her and in no time at all I could make out most words, needing her help only occasionally to master the difficult words. She was only in hospital a few weeks before she went home. I was very sad when she left. I cannot recall her name. She may even not have mentioned it, as there was no formality or normality in hospital. But I remember her vividly with great gratitude, for she, perhaps unknowingly, laid one of the major foundation stones that was to support my future life. She gave to me that greatest of gifts – literacy. Once I could read there was no looking back. Comics, fairy stories, nursery rhymes, any piece of printed material, were all grist to the mill. I read avidly.

With my arms now much stronger, I was able to heave myself about the bed and lever myself into a near sitting position, propped up by my arms. Noticing this, the nurses lifted me out of bed for a short time each day to sit in a wheelchair. This was a much better view of the world than from a prone position on my back and much more comfortable for reading.

Out of the blue, when all my hopes had faded, the Sister said I could see my parents, but there was one condition she told me firmly. 'There must be no crying to upset your mother. One tear and you will not see them again.' My mind was in turmoil. Emotion was already sweeping over me misting my eyes with tears but I had promised not to cry. A short time later the Sister put me in a wheelchair and took me down the corridor into a small room. A solid plate glass screen stretched from floor to ceiling and I was placed next to the glass. A door opened the other side of the screen and my parents came in and stood the other side of the glass. Apparently they had also been threatened by the 'no tears' rule. For a second or two we looked at each other through the glass. I knew who they were but had difficulty in recognising them. I put out my hand and touched the glass. My mother put her hand on the other side of the glass next to mine. The distress on her face as she struggled to control her tears, is impossible to describe. A lump grew to the size of an orange in the back of my throat, painful and choking. We hung on for a few seconds more before removing our hands. Simultaneously we waved, as they were escorted towards their door and I was wheeled away. Whoever devised this arrangement must have been a sadist. The mental agony was excruciating. I was to see my father, just once, under normal visiting conditions, but my mother just could not face the ordeal a second time. Her distress could not have been helped by the information that she received from the hospital that, although I was able to sit up, I would definitely be unable to walk again. Back in my bed, a whirlwind of emotions passed through me. For the first time I experienced a terrible sense of isolation, mixed with grief and disappointment. The promise to see my mother had conjured up the vision of being cuddled up close in her protective arms and being, after so long, back with someone who loved me. Nobody here loved me. Instead I had but a fleeting, almost surreal, glimpse of a very sad, almost forgotten face, viewed through a watery mist. They had cheated me. Slowly my grief turned to real anger. I now realised I hated them and resolved never to put my trust in anything they promised.

A few days later, two nurses came to my bed and started to wheel the whole bed, with me in it, out of the ward. I was now very suspicious of any change in the routine. In reply to my question about where they were taking me, they said that it was to the isolation ward because I had scarlet fever. I was not sure what that was but felt pleased, in the hope that I might die.

As it turned out, the isolation ward was not too bad. I was in a small room on my own, attended by two nurses, who were quite friendly. The whole atmosphere was relaxed and quite different from the regimented routine of the ward. There were no books or toys because, they said, everything I touched eventually had to be destroyed to get rid of the scarlet fever germs. I understood this and it reinforced what I already knew about these terrible germs. But they gave me some plasticine and I spent my time making models. The two nurses did not seem to have much to do and laughed and talked. Mainly they talked about two people they knew. I liked to listen to them talking, it reminded me of my mother and Aunt Nellie who were always talking. I gathered that one of them had met somebody who was a 'cheeky devil' who was always after 'you know what', but was a good laugh. What they were talking about was not always clear to me, although it was interesting to hear about the dances they went to and the pictures they had seen. This seemed to be the only part of the hospital where the people were normal and for me the days spent in isolation were very happy. All too soon I was sent back to the ward.

My legs were improving all the time. It was possible to move my toes and feet and bend one knee, but if I wanted to move my legs to a different position I had to lift them with my hands.

It was not long before they moved me again. This time it was out of the main ward onto what they called the veranda. This led out of a door halfway down the ward and was a narrow room with about eight beds, placed head to the wall. There was just enough room to pass along the bottom of the beds. The outer wall was only as high as a bed and then the remainder of the wall was windows which folded back, so that the whole space of the windows was open. This looked out onto a lawn and beyond that trees and shrubs. This was lovely. It had been a long time since I had seen the sun and the sky. The only disadvantage was the cold at night. I slept with my head under the bedclothes. Sometimes, if it was very windy, they closed the windows but I remember waking one morning to find snow on the bottom half of the bed.

It was soon after being moved onto the veranda that they took me to a room where they encased both my legs in plaster of Paris, from my thighs to my toes. I asked, as usual, what it was for, and as usual, they made no reply. My legs must have been in plaster for some time because, when they finally cut it off with large shears, both legs were stiff. After that a very big, powerful man in a white jacket came into the veranda. A nurse said something to him and left. As he came towards me it was clear that he was completely blind. Without a word he took hold of my left leg and with his arm under my upper leg above the knee, he forced the bottom of the leg down. There was a fierce stab of pain in my knee, a cracking sound, and then a dense aching pain. I started to cry with the pain. He then took my right leg to repeat the process. This time the pain was excruciating. I screamed in agony. He became desperate in his attempt to bend the knee, trying again and again. Now I just screamed continuously. Suddenly there was a very loud crack as the knee bent. He went away. Nobody came to see me as I lay crying. The pain in my right knee was truly terrible. I never knew what he did to my right knee that day but, thereafter, I was never able to lock the joint properly and my right leg grew slower than my left leg. At the time I was ignorant of this and only glad when the pain stopped.

With my legs out of plaster I commenced seeing the masseuse again. She carried on with the electrical treatment on my legs and massage. One day she said thoughtfully, 'I wonder,' then lifting me up she stood me down saying 'hold on to the couch.' I clutched the couch in some trepidation. Gradually she eased her support of my body and for the first time in nearly a year, I found myself standing on my feet. It was exciting but frightening. She quickly lifted me back onto the couch with a smile of great satisfaction.

'Good boy' she said 'now you can stand.' I thought this was very doubtful. However the same performance was repeated each day and, each day, she left me standing just a little longer before returning me to the couch. I had just about felt confident that this was alright, when one day she put me down about two feet from the couch.

'Now walk to the couch when I let go of you' she said gently. Blind panic gripped me.

'I can't walk' I yelled.

'You will have to, won't you?' she said. 'Ready?' My legs took the weight as her support eased. 'Go' she said.

In one superhuman effort I managed to move one leg forward and threw myself towards the couch, grasping at it like a drowning man clutching at a life-belt. Immediately her hands were there steadying me. I leaned on the couch breathless. I had not fallen. And so it continued. The electrical treatment, the massage and her holding me, teaching me to walk as if I were a small baby. But each day was easier. Slowly but surely my legs grew stronger, my balance returned and soon I was able to take several steps unaided. Then things progressed by leaps and bounds and I was able to walk about. It may have been slow and difficult but once again I was mobile. For the first time I was able to walk slowly into the grounds and play on the lawn with the other children. On the farther side of the lawn, close to the shrubbery, was a large summer house which housed a huge rocking horse. Enviously I watched the children having rides and wanted to join in.

Eventually they helped me up onto the back of the great horse. At first they rocked me gently but then one boy started rocking it violently, the head dipped lower and lower in an alarming fashion until, at last, I could hold on no longer and shot clean over its head, diving straight through the window, to end sprawled on the grass. A little girl ran to me but I was not hurt.

'You were lucky,' she said. I did not think it very lucky. She continued 'If there had been glass in the window, you would have been cut into little pieces'. This philosophical thought intrigued me. Had I, or had I not, been lucky being hurled out of a window that had no glass in it?

There was another time when we discovered a small door in the outside wall at the end of the veranda. We opened it and entered. Inside there was just enough room to stand up and, as far as we could see by the light from the open door, large metal pipes stretched away into the darkness. One boy said they were the central heating pipes under the hospital. Then we saw a large oblong wooden box. Cautiously we lifted the lid and in great excitement pulled out the contents, four large wooden hammers, some balls and some metal hoops. Some of the children said they were a croquet set. We carried them outside and were having a lovely time until one of the balls hit my ankle and made it hurt. After a while we had to go in for tea. We never saw the croquet set again.

Sometimes I explored the shrubs and was thrilled to find one bush full of beautiful chocolate-and-white speckled caterpillars. Another time I found a huge bee. I watched in total fascination for a long time. But my greatest find was a large mushroom at the edge of the tennis court at the back of the hospital. With delight I picked it and was carrying it carefully to show to the other children when a man in dark blue overalls came up to me. 'Give me that mushroom' he demanded gruffly. I refused. But my moments of pleasure in possession of my wonderful trophy were short-lived. Coming across the lawn I was called by a large, stout woman who took me into the main entrance of the hospital and ushered me into a room with a desk, which I supposed was her office. The man in the overalls stood there holding his cap in his hand. 'Give the man the mushroom' she demanded severely. 'No, it is mine. I found it,' I said. She looked annoyed then, picking a tomato out of a bag, she said 'you give me the mushroom and you can have the tomato'. I did not want a tomato. My mushroom was much more exciting. She then seized my arm and shouted 'Put the mushroom on the table.' In the struggle the mushroom broke in two and fell on the floor. I was then thrust into the corridor. They had stolen my beautiful mushroom. The man was frequently about the hospital grounds, cutting the grass. I kept in the bushes out of his way. I did not like him.

We spent much of our time out of doors that summer. Even our meals were served on the lawn. Dinner was nearly always the same, a soggy mass of brown, green stuff, which they said was cabbage, potatoes and a thick brown stew with little white bits in it like little maggots. Then a thick, glutinous, white lump, which they said was rice pudding. It was after dinner one day when two nurses appeared. One carried a large white enamel dish. The other one took what looked like a glass rod from the dish, took hold of a girl and pushed it up her nose. The girl wriggled and cried out in pain. Then they moved on to the next child and the next. It quickly became apparent that we were all in for this treatment. Deciding from what I had seen that this was something best avoided, I set off as fast as I could for the bushes. But the nurses were soon in hot pursuit, crashing through the bushes behind me. I was, of course, soon captured, but put up such a determined fight that they were unable to put the tube right up my nose and finally gave up the struggle. I never did have the treatment, whatever it was for.

Now that I was up and about I was taken every evening for a bath. It was a very large bath that would accommodate several children. On one occasion we were being bathed by a very big nurse with black hair. For no apparent reason she forced my head forward, down into the water and held it there. Then she let me up, spluttering and gasping for air. She did it again and again. I began to get very frightened and started to cry. But she just laughed and pushed my head under the water again. Reaching out in desperation my fingers found a heavy metal soap dish. As she let me up again I threw it at her head. It missed and crashed into the door. I was now in a very distressed state. But then the door opened and the Sister came in. 'What is going on?' she demanded. 'She keeps holding my head under the water,' I sobbed. The Sister ordered the nurse out of the bathroom and we never saw her again. That was the second time the vigilance of the Sister had saved me. I felt very grateful.

The 1st September 1938 arrived – my birthday. I had been in hospital over a year. A young doctor on his round in the ward heard that it was my birthday and persuaded the Sister to let him take me out for a treat. So it was that, after dinner, with three other children, I was put in his car. It was a very big car with huge headlamps. It was a beautiful afternoon, with brilliant sunshine. My excitement and wonder knew no bounds as we passed along the busy roads with cars and buses and people and horses and houses. I had almost forgotten what the real world was like. Then we were out of the city, drifting down winding country lanes with fields, hedges and trees, houses with gardens full of flowers and the wind blowing our hair. We all laughed with glee and the young doctor laughed. At last we stopped at a big house with a large lawn at the front and an even bigger lawn and flower beds at the rear. We were met by a large lady in a grey dress and with snow-white hair. We had a wonderful tea on the lawn. There were all sorts of different sandwiches, jelly, blancmange, cake, ice-cream and more sweets than we could eat. We played games on the lawn and then went into the house. It was beautiful. Eventually we all climbed back into the car and waved goodbye to the lady. 'You will

have to hold on tight. I shall have to go fast because we are late' the doctor told us. The trees and hedges rushed past as we sped along the lanes and we were thrown about as we went round corners. It was exhilarating and exciting. We arrived back at the hospital about 6.00 pm, well past bedtime. Sister was waiting at the door and spoke severely to the doctor about being late. In bed that night I reflected how different my birthday had been to the previous year. I really was very lucky.

During the summer I had a visit from my father. Of that I can be sure because

Unable to stand, but happy to see my Dad

there is a photograph of me in a pushchair with him standing behind me. But my memory of that visit is extremely vague.

The hospital regime had finally crushed me. I had given up all hope of going home. The hospital was now my life and I would have to make the best of it. It was a hard lesson, but now well learnt, that it is no good crying for what is unattainable. To compensate for the monotony of my restricted environment I started to create a fantasy world. At night it was possible to create, in my imagination any situation and play out the most exciting actions the mind could conceive.

The electrical treatment and massage continued but there seemed no significant improvement in my performance. The masseuse explained that many of the muscles had been killed. Gone were the stomach muscles and the leg muscles that would have enabled me to sit up from a lying position or raise my legs up from the bed. In the left leg it was possible to stand on my toes, straighten the leg from the knee but not raise the leg from a lying or sitting position. 'You will have to learn to manage with what you have' she told me. I soon found ways to overcome some of the shortfalls. By locking my left leg and pulling on it with my left arm it proved easy to lever myself into a sitting position. Similarly, it was possible to move one leg with the other, or move my legs with my hands. I was to become so adroit at these manoeuvres that they became instinctive and were performed with such precision and speed, that the trick was not apparent to the observer. This all helped to minimise the impact of my disability.

As summer and autumn receded it became a bit bleak on the veranda. Just before Christmas, I was awake one night when a man climbed in the window and made his way to the cupboard at the end of the veranda where all the toys were kept. He began quickly to put all our toys into a sack. I shouted for the nurse. Two nurses came quickly and we all watched the man running across the lawn into the shrubbery. It was puzzling. Why would anyone want to come and steal battered toys and books from children in hospital?

Christmas 1938 was a non-event. I think that because hope of getting really better and leaving hospital had faded, I had started to withdraw into my own little world, so that even the Christmas celebrations failed to raise any interest. What did register in my memory was the change in the atmosphere early in 1939. The hospital seemed to be moving into a new era. There was more bustle, an air of tension and excitement pervaded the wards and nurses started talking to each other in animated tones about someone called Adolf Hitler, who I gathered was a German and who was going to start a war. As new children came into the ward they brought with them an updated version of what was happening outside. We were all soon seized with speculation about planes, bombs, guns, warships and soldiers. What we did not know we invented and that fed the rumours. Whether the hospital was preparing for war or not we did not know, but they did seem to be emptying the wards. But it came as a total surprise when one day the Sister said that I was going home that afternoon. The date is uncertain but it must have been during April or May 1939. I had been in hospital for over a year and a half.

The Sister took me to my parents in the reception area. I was in a daze. She said I was to choose a leaving present from a big cupboard of new toys. I did not want a present, but the easy option was to take something. I chose a large, bright red, clockwork racing car. The Sister waved as I left and gave me a big smile. The journey across the city and on the train, cuddled close by my mother, was just a kaleidoscope of new sounds, sights and smells, that completely confused me. Everything had happened so quickly that I was unable to adjust. I hardly recognised our home. The room was so dark and small, and there seemed to be so many people crowded into that small space, that it became claustrophobic. I just took in the fact that I had a new baby sister, nearly one year old, called Dorothy. Then it all became too much for me. The recoil was like piano wire snapping under tension. To get what I had been seeking so long and never expecting to achieve, the build-up of emotion was suddenly released and burst like a dam in my heart. I just sat under the table and cried.

'I want to go back to the hospital,' I wailed.

My mother took me to bed and I fell asleep in her arms.

CHAPTER 3

Facing the World

The next morning I woke to find myself in my old bedroom. Everything was familiar but not quite as I had remembered it. On the mantelpiece of the little fireplace were two pennies, the ones the doctor had left there all that time ago, when he had offered them to me to raise my legs from the bed. In the morning sunshine the house seemed brighter and there was my new little sister. She was blue-eyed, blonde and beautiful. She is not very strong, my Mother told me sadly, and I understood there was something wrong with her heart. Later Aunt Nellie came to see me. She hugged and kissed me. She cried, my mother cried and although I did not know why they were crying, it made me cry.

My father talked to me a lot about how difficult it was going to be for me with my legs being so weak. He advised that I should avoid crowds of children when they were playing and should stand close to a wall if possible, so that they did not knock me down.

I could not wait to get outside. To see once again all the scenes that had been but memories was exciting. The passage at the back of the gardens, that had been the main play area, was disappointing. It looked much narrower and dirtier than before. Within a day or two it seemed to revert to what it had always been. But it took much longer to reach the end of the passage. Walking was very slow. No more running like the wind, I thought ruefully.

Two doors down the passage there now lived a little girl, who had not been there before. She had straight, black hair, with a fringe and wore little white socks and very shiny, black shoes.

'What is wrong with your legs?' she asked sympathetically.

I hesitated, realising how difficult it would be to explain all about germs and not wishing to say those dreadful words 'infantile paralysis', which I hated. So I just said I had been ill. She seemed quite happy with that explanation and the subject was not mentioned again although we played together often. Next door to her lived a boy about my age. He was not allowed to play in the passage but we could play with him in his garden. He had a very battered little model bus. Most of the paint had been scraped off long ago and it had no clockwork to make it go. Swapping my big, new, red racing car for the little bus seemed a good idea. My father was not pleased, however, and told me to take the bus back and get my car. This was achieved with some difficulty but I did not want the car and put it at the back of the sitting room cupboard, where I would not have to see it. It reminded me of the hospital and I was trying to forget everything about that awful place.

When I was tired or not concentrating on walking, my legs often just collapsed and my knees would smash onto the concrete. Dark red blood would ooze down my legs and onto my socks. My mother showed me how to fold a big white handkerchief to tie round my leg to cover the wound after falling and always ensured that my jacket top pocket contained a neatly folded clean white handkerchief. People used to notice the handkerchief and laugh, saying I was a proper smart little gentleman. I did not bother to enlighten them that it was my emergency bandage.

It seemed that much had changed while I had been in hospital. My brother was much older now and did not want to play with me, and my sister was always out somewhere with her friends. All the children that lived near my grandmother seemed to have vanished. Nobody played football in the passage any more. The only thing that had not changed was Aunt Nellie's. We did all the things we used to do when I was small. There were never children to play with at Aunt Nellie's. She had always said they were too rough and it was much better to be neat and clean and go for proper little walks. These walks usually resulted in being stopped in the street by women who knew Aunt Nellie, to talk about other people who were unknown to me. They usually asked how I was 'getting along' and saying what a 'brave' or 'happy' little boy I was. They did not know that when I was alone, I cried.

Any hopes that might have been entertained about escaping the clutches of the medical establishment by leaving hospital were dashed, when my parents were told that arrangements had been made for me to have treatment three times a week. So on Monday and Wednesday morning and Friday afternoons my father took me to the Melton Lodge Clinic, which was a large building, nearly opposite the Wellington Pier at Great Yarmouth. We went whatever the weather, taking a bus to the pier and then walking the rest of the way. Sometimes the

the wind was so strong that we were nearly blown over and often we were soaked, waiting for the bus in the open, in driving rain. The treatment was similar to that in hospital but I also had to sit with my feet in a bowl of salt water with an electric current passing through it for about half an hour. One day my brother took me. While I was having the electrical treatment and the nurse was out of the room, he said 'Would you like a sweet?'. I reached out with one hand to steady the bag while looking for a sweet. As our hands touched he was immediately thrown back and gave a yell of pain. The nurse rushed in and realised what must have happened. 'You must not touch him,' she warned my brother, explaining that although I felt only a tingling sensation, it was because my body had become accustomed to the strong electrical current. My treatment seemed mild compared to that of a small girl who had a leather harness strapped round her head and was then hoisted on a rope to hang dangling by her head. Dad said they were trying to straighten her neck but it looked like torture to me.

What I disliked most was having to see the orthopaedic surgeon every three months. We would have an appointment for 10.00 a.m. and sit in the crowded waiting room. At 11.30 staff would start rushing around, like ants on an anthill, passing the news that Mr Brittain had arrived. A quarter of an hour later he would stride in with a flutter of nurses and other staff around him. At 1.00 p.m. he left with his entourage. 'Gone to dinner,' my father would observe, drily. The procession would return about 2.30 p.m. If we were lucky we would be summoned to his presence about 4.30 p.m. He usually looked at my legs, twisting and turning my ankles and knees, make one or two technical comments to his secretary and then we would be ushered out. The whole inspection lasted about two minutes. Mr Brittain was a big, florid-faced man. I did not like him.

When the weather was fine I liked to be outside as much as possible. But there was plenty of entertainment indoors. We listened to the radio, mainly news broadcasts about Adolf Hitler and Mussolini and war. But when my father was out, my sister tuned in to dance music and sang all the popular songs. And then there were the books. The large cupboard in my bedroom was full of books, and the cupboard in the sitting room had shelves of books and I read anything that took my fancy: *Tales of Robin Hood, Legends of Greece and Rome,*

Robinson Crusoe, the daily paper (the *News Chronicle*) and of course all the comics. Then there were all my toys, long unused, like my fort and soldiers, my farm animals and wild animals, horses, carts and all sorts of little cars and trucks. It was while foraging in the cupboard for toys that I discovered a large wooden box. After man-handling it into the light I opened the lid. There were four small wooden cages with wire fronts. They were painted shiny black on the outside and wires, while the inside was a greenish-blue colour. I had never seen them before but they seemed vaguely familiar, like a long-distant memory. My contemplation of them was interrupted by my mother coming into the room. She told me they were my father's canary cages and I learned that he had not kept canaries since before my birth. 'That is all that is left,' she said, 'just the cages, some award cards and his book.' My ears pricked up 'a book?' Another rummage in the cupboard produced a huge, heavy, leather-backed book, *Canaries – British Birds and Hybrids* by J. Robson. It was printed on shiny paper and illustrated with photographs and coloured plates depicting every variety of canary. Fascinated, I ploughed through this massive tome from start to finish. When my father asked what I would like for my seventh birthday there was only one choice – a pair of canaries. In due course my father gave me my present of three border canaries, a clear yellow pair and a green hen. They were kept in a large cage in the kitchen.

My pleasure in my birds was marred only by the fact that I had to start school. The Northgate School was at the end of our road and my father delivered me to the headmistress, Miss Thacker, at the start of the autumn term. Just two years late, I was at last 'present'.

Miss Thacker was very stern and all the children were awed by her. Our class teacher was Miss Grice, who was quite nice but strict. She kept a large bottle of black liquid on a high shelf and said that anyone who used a bad word would have to wash out their mouth with the black liquid. We all made sure that we used no bad words.

When we went out at playtime several children asked about my legs. I just said I had been ill and they never asked any more questions. On one large wall of the school building were painted round targets to throw balls at. Several of the children played with me throwing at the targets and kindly ran about gathering the balls for me so that I did not have to walk to get them.

None of the children could read as well as I did but they could all write and do sums, which I could not do. But there was a strange difference between me and them. It was nothing to do with my crippled legs, but a different level of perception, for I had experienced things beyond their imagination.

The declaration of war had caused great excitement. My brother took me out one day and from the sea wall, near the Wellington Pier, we watched a plane attacking a small cargo ship just off shore. The plane dived over the defenceless ship again and again. For the first time I heard the real chatter of machine-gun fire. Men came and erected Anderson air-raid shelters in everyone's back garden. The first time the air-raid siren wailed I was out of bed, down the stairs, through the house and garden and into the shelter well ahead of anyone else. But there were no air raids at that time and life continued as normal.

The visits to Melton Lodge for treatment seriously interfered with my school work. Writing became easy and I soon caught up with the rest of the class but my absences seemed to coincide with arithmetic lessons. I never did learn to chant the multiplication tables like the other children; on the other hand my arithmetic advanced well ahead of theirs because my brother taught me not only the sums being taught at school, but arithmetic way beyond that level.

In the spring of 1940 my canaries began to breed. Watching the hens build their nests with moss and cow-hair in wooden boxes hung on the back of the cage was fascinating. The sight of the first shiny little green-blue egg, speckled with brown held me spellbound. The first nest of small, squirming, naked little chicks was viewed with apprehension. But they developed quickly and in no time at all, were flying about the cage fully feathered. However, all the happiness of the past few months was soon over.

At the beginning of May, Dorothy became ill. For a few days she lay feverish in her cot, which had been brought downstairs into the living room. It was clear that she was very ill. My father looked haggard, grey-faced and sad. My mother cried quietly all the time. Then Dorothy was dead. It was just a week short of her second birthday. Never again would we hear her happy laughter or watch her dance or be warmed by her smile. She lay in her small coffin on the table in the front room, like a large, beautiful doll. My father would not let me go to her funeral. But I overheard him tell the lady next door where she had been buried, between two large, white crosses. Without telling my parents, I went to the cemetery and soon found Dorothy's small grave. I lay on the ground to be as close to her as possible and cried bitterly for that wasted little life, her shining personality and a happiness that was gone forever.

As the months passed everyone became absorbed by the war. We were told constantly about the terrible Germans and Italians, who were not real human beings. Soon the talk was not of air raids but the real possibility of invasion. People said that if the Germans invaded they would kill all old people and cripples. This frightened me. In an air raid there was a good chance of survival and if you were killed it was just bad luck. But to be rounded up by soldiers would leave no avenue of escape, and execution seemed a very undignified way to die. As if the fear of being killed by the Germans was not enough to contend with, my June appointment with Mr Brittain proved even more terrifying. Looking at my right foot, which was now beginning to turn outwards, he said he would have to operate. He explained to my father that he would cut and tie the ligament to strengthen the foot. Cold panic gripped me. This nasty man was proposing to cut my foot open! While I waited in dread for my operation there was a dramatic change in events. Because of the anticipated invasion the authorities decided to evacuate the town. In June 1940 my brother and sister, who had both won scholarships to the grammar school and high school went with their schools to East Retford in Nottinghamshire. My brother wrote to say that the father of the lady he had been billeted with kept canaries and it was duly arranged that he would take all my birds. Shortly after that, my school left the town.

Early in the morning my parents put me on the train at Vauxhall Station with all the other children from our school. We each had a name tag tied to a buttonhole, our gas masks, in cardboard boxes, hung round our necks and we carried a few items of clothing in little cases or bags. It was just a few days holiday, we were assured. The other children may have believed that but I did not trust adults. So, aged not quite eight, I was being parted from my parents once again. It had been only just over a year since I left hospital.

The train chugged along steadily, taking us farther and farther from home. We finally reached a station where we were unloaded and taken to a large hall. There we were given a sandwich and a glass of milk. After a very brief medical examination, they loaded us onto motor coaches and we set off again, travelling for a long time. It was late afternoon before we reached the end of our journey and we were ushered into a school classroom. We just sat quietly at the desks. Soon people started to arrive. Usually it was a man and a woman or sometimes a woman on her own. They would look us over and then pick a child and take him or her away. Three quarters of the children had gone when an old woman with grey hair, hooked nose, pointed chin and spectacles, came in. She looked like a witch I thought. She looked round, pointed to me and then to Alfred Sherwood, saying 'I'll have him and him.'

Alfred and I went with her to a little cottage in a terrace of five, at the end of a short road. The cottage was clean but very small. The whole terrace was served by a block of dry closets at one end of the terrace. There were no lights and going to the lavatory at night was a frightening experience. At the other end of the terrace was a large pump, encased in wood with a long handle. Each morning she gave us two metal buckets. These we had to fill at the pump. To get the water we had to throw the pump handle in the air until we got suction and then pump up the water. One bucket she took inside. The other we had to stand just outside the kitchen door. After taking our shirts, she gave us a small piece of soap and a hand towel. Whatever the weather we had to stand stripped to the waist and wash in the icy cold water. Only when she was satisfied that we were clean would our shirts be returned to us and we were allowed inside for breakfast. However she was not unkind. Indeed we fared better than many boys who found themselves in more salubrious accommodation but were thrashed on a regular basis. The village we had ended up in was Keyworth, seven miles from Nottingham.

There was only one incident that distressed me. We had not been there long when one Sunday evening she said we were going for a walk. The walk went on and on. Eventually we reached a public house at Plumtree some two and a half to three miles away. By then I was physically exhausted. My legs were not equipped for this sort of walking. The return journey was little short of a nightmare. Every step was agonizing, it seemed impossible to proceed, but wearily I dragged myself home.

Apart from this episode, I enjoyed Keyworth. The village had a church, a chapel, two pubs, one or two small shops and a wooden hut off the village green that fried chips. There was no piped water or sanitation and the main street was always covered in cow dung. The village was totally surrounded by beautiful open country. Meadows full of flowers and butterflies, ponds full of frogs and newts, hedges and copses full of birds. To me it seemed like paradise. We helped on the nearby farm. I learned to milk cows and feed calves and poultry. Every week I wrote to my parents and always enclosed a letter for Aunt Nellie and Uncle Arthur.

Because there were too many of us for the village school, the Yarmouth children were taught in a large chapel. Here we sat on forms, grouped by ages and the teacher had three blackboards. She taught the first group, then moved on to the second group, leaving us to complete sums or writing from the board. There was no paper. We had slates and slate pencils.

After a week or so, Miss Thacker, the headmistress, came to say that I had to go to see the orthopaedic surgeon at the Cripples Guild in Nottingham. She took me on the bus. The Cripples Guild was a dreary building, softened only by the stuffed wallaby in the waiting area. Next to us was an elderly lady.

'Don't let them cut you about, duck' she told me.

When I saw the surgeon, a young man, I told him that I did not want the operation. He laughed, saying I did not need an operation but I would have to wear callipers to keep my legs straight. Waves of relief swept over me and when rejoining Miss Thacker I could have kissed her. In due course the callipers were fitted. These had rings round the top, at my thighs, and metal rods down each side of the leg, that slotted into a metal tube through the heels of my boots. Long bandages wound round my knee to pull the knee to the outside rod and straps round my ankles secured the bottom of the callipers. Walking had to be stiff-legged but it was not uncomfortable, once I had learnt the art of swinging my legs from the hips. They also fitted me up with a padded metal support to my back and a plaster front plate over my stomach, braced together with straps. The only real disadvantage was that I had to sleep in my callipers. But this was a small price to pay to save being cut up. Miss Thacker took me three times a

Eight years old and in callipers, but happy at Keyworth

week to the Cripples Guild for electrical treatment, the same as I had been having. We chatted on the bus and sometimes I made her laugh. She was not awesome any more. She was very kind and I became quite fond of her.

We had been at Keyworth only a few months before my parents came with my grandmother. They took rooms in a house in the village and of course I moved in with them. To be reunited with my family once again was wonderful. The accommodation was slightly cramped. We had just one room on the ground floor and two bedrooms. My grandmother occupied one bedroom and I slept on a narrow canvas camp bed in my parents' room. The camp bed was hard and cold and with my callipers on my circulation was impaired so that, in winter, I suffered terrible chilblains on the calves of my legs. My mother was in the last stage of pregnancy and another sister (Grace) was born in early November 1940. Living conditions in the one small room now became difficult and I preferred the freedom of the open fields. When Grace became a little older, I took her miles in a large, low-slung pram, armed with clean nappies and a feeding bottle of milk. The pram helped me to walk and, on the down slopes, I could stand on the metal bar of the frame, between the rear and front wheels, and use the pram as a scooter, holding the handle in my left hand and the forward side of the pram in my right hand. The judicious use of my body-weight guided the pram, which at times reached fast speeds on steep inclines. There was the occasional miscalculation, whereby we ended up in a ditch, but without injury. The pram had other advantages. On every trip I collected a large bag of dead sticks for kindling, which sold for two pennies in the village. In due season there were primroses, violets, blackberries and mushrooms to be picked and gathered, for which there was a ready market. All this money was hoarded.

There was one memorable day when my mother came with me to Bluebell Woods. We picked huge bunches of violets. Some of these we packed into a box, with damp moss, and sent them to Aunt Nellie.

But life was not totally idyllic in Keyworth. One of my friends lived in a large detached house near the chapel, with extensive gardens where we played. When I first went to the village I met his father, just once, a tall, kind, handsome man dressed smartly in his officer's uniform. A little later they said he had been captured by the Japanese. So my friend lived alone with his mother. She was in her thirties, a big, strong woman. To say that she was fat would imply a degree of softness; rather she was a shapeless mass of solid flesh. One afternoon she invited me to come for tea. This was served in a room looking out onto the front garden. My friend and I sat opposite each other, and she sat at the end of the table. The tea consisted of bread and jam. We had no sooner sat down when I saw that she was holding a thick leather strap, some eighteen inches long.

'Sit up straight!' she said to her son, striking him a sharp blow across his back with the strap. He winced, fear darting in his eyes. 'You have not washed your hands properly!' she said, striking him a harder blow with the strap.

'I have, I have!' he said fearfully.

'Don't lie!' she hit harder. He writhed with pain and started to cry. 'Cry baby,' she taunted and struck him again and again. 'Why can't you be like him?' meaning me, she said, giving him another vicious blow. He was now in great distress and seemed terrified. Each time she hit him her face became animated with pleasure. It seemed that she really enjoyed watching him suffer the pain and terror she was inflicting. By making me watch, she was making me suffer also.

'I have to go home now,' I said shakily and, getting to my feet, left the house as quickly as possible. She said nothing and did not move from her chair. As I hurried down the path to the gate, the terrifying screams from the home told me that the thrashing was continuing. I felt sick with disgust. How could any woman flog her own son? The answer was beyond my understanding.

After the love and kindness showered on me by my mother and Aunt Nellie, it was difficult to accept the fact that, by and large, women were cold, cruel and callous. At least, many of them that I had encountered seemed to be so, and it was a short step to the conclusion that, of the two sexes, men were much kinder. This preference for male company probably explained why I often sat with the old men of the village on the seats at the back of the village green. They congregated there every evening when the weather was fine, sheltered by tall, thick elderberry bushes. Sitting quietly, I listened to their talk. They talked of farm work, horses, dogs, rat-catching, their school days, pranks, drinking, pubs, football and cricket and much besides. All the time they smoked their pipes. The spiralling blue smoke from their pipes smelled exotic. I thought I would smoke a pipe when I grew up.

My wariness about women was to serve me well a short while later, when the school was immunised against diphtheria. A very beautiful nurse with blonde hair and a middle-aged doctor took up positions at two small tables loaded with phials and syringes. We were told to remove our jackets and jumpers, roll up the sleeve of our left arm and form two queues. Everyone fought to be in the nurse's queue. I made a beeline for the man. I felt hardly the slightest prick as he gently inserted the needle. From the other queue came sharp cries of pain as the nurse jabbed in the needle ruthlessly. Three or four of her patients fainted.

Another kind man was Jack Warden, who lived opposite to where we were lodging. He and his sons operated a greengrocery and wet fish business. Apart from the shop, they had a small lorry and a horse-drawn dray, with which they toured the surrounding villages, selling door to door. We would have had a worse time than we did, had it not been for the vegetables and occasional piece of fish that Jack Warden gave to my father. Almost every day, when he came home with the lorry, Mr Warden would beckon me over and putting his hand into his overall pocket, would pull out a big handful of cigarette ends for me. He apparently had a habit of lighting a cigarette and, as he went to serve a customer, he would nip it out and put it in his pocket. He never relit them and as a consequence he ended up with a pocketful of nearly whole cigarettes. I shared these cigarettes out with the other boys and we used to sit and smoke in some old buildings, formerly pig sties, in the field behind the church.

One day Mr Warden called me across the road and told me the pony was sick with a cold and asked if I would take it a feed. The pony was more horse than pony and was renowned for its bad temperament. Usually his son looked after the pony and I knew Mr Warden was frightened of it. Anyway, when he offered me a florin to do it, I put my apprehension behind me and agreed. He then produced a bucket of warm mash into which he tipped half a bottle of whisky. The pony was stabled in a building in the centre of the village. As I walked there with the bucket an old man asked me what it was. When I explained my mission he looked doubtful.

'You mind she don't kick, lad. Keep away from her rear. Here, take this stick,' he said, breaking a thick stick out of the hedge and sharpening one end with his knife. 'Keep the blunt end against the wall as you walk alongside her, with the pointed end towards her side, so she can't squash you against the wall.' He came with me to the stable. She was tethered to the stall with her rear to the door. The old man watched and instructed me from the doorway. Edging down the side of the wall, I spoke to her gently, holding the bucket in one hand and the stick in the other. She seemed massive. Halfway along the stable she suddenly lurched sideways. 'Keep the stick steady,' shouted the old man. Once she felt the sharp point of the stick she moved away and I proceeded quickly to the manger. She eyed me suspiciously but made no move as I emptied the bucket into her feeding bowl. Intent on her tea I was able to withdraw with no problem. The old man laughed with glee. 'Good job I told thee about the stick lad.' I thanked him and took the bucket back to Mr Warden, who was waiting at his front gate. He looked relieved.

'Alright?' he asked.

'Yes. I put it in her bowl and she is eating it,' I told him. I did not mention the old man or the stick.

But I did not always get away lightly. With some dread we learned that the dentist had arrived. He took over the front sitting room of a small house near the school as his surgery, and after a cursory examination, we received instructions to visit him. He was a lean old man with grey hair and spectacles. Although I had never had toothache or, as far as I was aware, anything wrong with my teeth, he proceeded to drill and fill every one of my molar teeth. He used a ramshackle foot-pedalled drill. At best the pain was considerable and made me cry. Occasionally the drill slipped and gashed my gums. He snarled and bullied me to sit still. It was a painful and bloody business. I vowed to keep away from dentists in future.

When the weather was really bad, so that it was not possible to go out, I played draughts with my father. I became so good at the game that my father always lost. He must have said something about it at the pub, for one day, two men called at the house and my father said that they would like to play draughts with me. We played many games. At first they played confidently but soon became very serious and considered each move carefully. But it was no use. I won every game.

'There you are,' my father said triumphantly, 'I told you, he is unbeatable!'

They looked much put out as they left and I heard one say to the other, 'He's abnormal.' I did not like that. I wanted to be normal.

But what is normal? If being normal was being like many people in the village, then normal was to be as stupid as they were. There were two incidents that confirmed that view. Although we had no air raids near the village, we had seen the distant skyline aglow as fire bombs rained down on the distant cities and occasionally fighter planes flew over. On a sunny afternoon somebody spotted a man descending on a parachute. By the time he touched down in a meadow off Selby Lane, he was surrounded by a small group of people armed with sticks and pitchforks. Although he was dressed in British uniform and spoke perfect English, nobody would believe that he was not a German and he was forced into the village at the end of a pitchfork. When the village police constable took charge of him, there were a lot of mumbled excuses about how he might well have been a German.

There was another occasion when a woman, about thirty years old, set up a little easel in the main street and started to make a water-colour painting of the village church. When we went to look over her shoulder to watch her paint, she irritably told us to go away.

'I bet she is a spy,' a boy said.

'Yeah, she's a spy,' everyone said, although we all knew she was just a woman painting a picture.

This childish talk soon reached the ears of an adult and within minutes, spread through the village. Two or three women gathered to discuss it. They were quickly joined by others. In no time at all an excited, angry mob of about twenty had gathered. They moved in on the artist and proceeded to give her verbal abuse. The policeman arrived on his bicycle. The artist, clearly upset and annoyed, told him that what was happening was unbelievable, as she was just painting a picture. He agreed she was doing nothing wrong but insisted that in her own interests she should leave. With tears of anger in her eyes she packed her things and mounted her bicycle. 'What stupid, ignorant people!' she told the policeman. I felt sorry for her. But I supposed that was because I was abnormal.

Another of my abnormalities was the desire to find out all about God and Jesus. Most children went to Sunday School in the chapel on Sunday afternoons, but I also went alone to church, morning and evening. At Sunday School we were told the bible stories and sang all the popular hymns. The singing was led by a tall, old man with silvery hair and a big walrus moustache. He had one googlie eye that watered and a deep but trembly voice. But he did not seem to know much about God or where heaven was. The vicar talked about God the Father, God the Son and God the Holy Ghost. People explained to me that God was the creator of the world and the universe and his son was Jesus Christ, whom he had sent down from heaven to earth to teach men to be good. That seemed logical, even if a bit vague, but who was the Holy Ghost? Sometimes I was told it was also God, some said God was also a ghost, some said it was also God's spirit. Then I asked, if the Holy Ghost is God's spirit, does it mean he also has a body like man? Everyone talked of God and Heaven but it seemed that they did not know what they were talking about. As people left church after the service, the Vicar would stand at the door and speak to everyone as they went out. But he never spoke to me. He just looked over my head, as if I were not there. Perhaps I was like the Holy Ghost, I thought. Although I am here, people like the Vicar cannot see me. But I was determined to get an answer. Seeing the Vicar walk towards me on the footpath one day, I stopped him and asked about the Holy Ghost. He did not want to talk. 'You will understand when you grow up,' he said as he went briskly on his way. I smiled to myself, confident in the knowledge that the Vicar probably knew no more about the Holy Ghost, than anyone else.

Selby Lane was one of the main roads out of the village and about half a mile from the built-up area was a large isolated house, cloaked in large dark trees. The house was occupied by three elderly sisters, one of whom, it was said, had been knocked down by a bus and sustained head injuries that had left her mentally deranged. Sometimes she was let out and wandered about the lanes and even the village. She had an educated voice but if she stopped to speak, she rambled on about all sorts of things that made no sense. Once she told a group of us that Hitler had injured her head and she was going to appoint each of us respectively as a general and an admiral, so that we could go and kill him. Coming home on the bus from Nottingham one day we had to stop because she was standing in the middle of the road. When she saw the bus, she bent down and lifted her dress to reveal her bare bottom. The conductor had to lead her gently to the verge so that we could proceed. She never showed any sign of violence, but if I were alone and saw her coming along the lane, I avoided meeting her. I was sorry for her but could not face the ordeal of an encounter. This made me feel guilty and I wondered whether some people avoided me for the same reason.

When harvest time arrived, three army lorries came to the village with men to help. They were tall, bronzed and very happy, laughing and singing all day. We could not understand what they said but they were friendly and played games with us during the lunch break. A man who worked on the farm said they were Italian prisoners of war. It was difficult to see these happy, friendly, young men as the hated enemies that the government said were not human. The years of hate propaganda were dissipated after a few minutes with these men in the sunny harvest field. What made us laugh was their guard, a short, bespectacled, little chap with a very old rifle. He carried it with him but it lay on the ground as he sat reading or sleeping under the shade of the hedge. By evening some of the Italians were working several fields away.

Gradually the number of children from Great Yarmouth dwindled as parents took their children home or located them elsewhere. This made no difference to me as I was friendly with most of the local boys. However, it enabled the rest of us to integrate into the village school.

We had a lovely teacher. She was very keen on poetry and it was at this time I learned many of the poems that would stay with me through life.

As the months passed, my walking improved and I mastered the knack of walking with callipers. My arms became very strong. In the field behind the church stood several very large trees. One of these was a massive horse-chestnut. Obviously it had been a favourite tree for generations of boys, for large nails had been hammered into its trunk to provide a means of climbing to the lower branches. Enviously I watched boys climb this tree and wished to do likewise. One sunny morning I found myself alone at the tree. Reaching up and grasping a nail I lifted myself up to reach the second nail with my other hand. Without any thought of danger I found myself in the branches and climbed higher and higher, using just my arms, my legs dangled helplessly below me. Soon I was in the topmost branches and was amazed by the view, for it was winter and the branches were bare.

It was then I saw my mother walking along the road, some fifty to sixty yards away. I shouted to her in glee and, as she looked up, I let go with one hand to wave to her. The look of shock and horror on her face was never to be forgotten. She rushed through the gate and ran to the tree, telling me in a choking voice, to come down as carefully as possible. I could not understand why she was upset. Hand by hand I made my descent. On reaching the ground she hugged me, crying and sobbing with relief. Only when she pointed out what could have happened if a branch had snapped, did the realisation of danger dawn. She made me promise never to climb a tree again. Who wanted to climb a tree anyway? It was easy, I had done it.

A strange incident occurred one afternoon when several of us decided to pick up some windfall apples we could see through a field hedge that bordered a small orchard. Now, whether the farmer knew we were there and decided to cut off our retreat back across the field or whether it was just a coincidence, is not certain. But we heard shouting and saw that a large bull had been let loose from the far end of the field. It eyed us wildly. The gate by which we had entered the small field was some hundred and fifty yards away. Everyone started to make a run for the gate. In wild panic I joined in and found myself passing my companions. First at the gate, I grabbed the top rail and literally threw myself over it. Lying face down in the grass, my lungs bursting and gasping for air, I was joined a split second later by one of my companions. He turned his face to look at me. 'I (gasp) thought (gasp) you said (gasp) you couldn't (gasp) run!' There was no answer to that. I do not know how I achieved it. The capability of the body to respond to sudden crisis by a short, unbelievable surge of power, seems to be an inherent part of our survival mechanism.

If I was enjoying Keyworth my poor mother was definitely not finding life there tolerable. Trying to cope in one room with an aged mother-in-law, disabled husband, a son and a baby, without proper facilities, obviously became too much to bear. Usually a very quiet, patient and tolerant woman, my mother never made any demand. So it came as a surprise to see her crying and upset one day.

'I have had enough!' she told my father 'I want to go home!'

He was clearly shaken by her outburst and soothingly said 'Yes dear, we will have to start saving for the train fare'. That had the impact of a cup of cold water thrown into a pan of boiling fat.

'I'm not waiting, I want to go now,' my mother screamed. With the hangdog look of a defeated man, my father started rummaging through his pockets. He placed a few coins on the table, a few copper coins and fewer silver pieces.

'Have you any money Mother?' he anxiously asked my grand-mother. She managed to find a ten-shilling note and a small amount of coins. My mother started to cry bitterly.

I started to say 'I have some...'

'Be quiet,' my father cut me short agitatedly, 'can't you see your mother is upset!' I knew it was no use arguing, so I simply went to my hide-away for my tin. There were several pounds. How many bags of sticks, baskets of blackberries and mushrooms and bunches of flowers it represented, I have no idea, but it stopped my mother crying.

The next day we were on the train heading home to Great Yarmouth. It was just before Christmas 1942.

CHAPTER 4

Bombed and Machine-gunned

We arrived at Yarmouth Vauxhall Station late in the afternoon and made our way wearily along North Quay to our house, with all our belongings in two battered suitcases. In the fading light we inspected the house. It was cold, damp and dirty. The kitchen door stood wide open. Looters had taken anything of use. The three Fox sisters who lived on the opposite side of the road came across and seeing the situation, kindly offered to accommodate us until we could sort the place out. These women had all lost their husbands in the First World War.

My mother got word to Aunt Nellie and she arrived within the hour to take me to hers. It was a long, dark walk, through empty streets. After more than two years I was once again in a comfortable bed.

The next morning it was just as it had always been. Getting up, having a good wash, my hair combed and sitting down to breakfast in a very orderly way. During the morning I chatted to Aunt Nellie as she worked in the kitchen, telling her about Keyworth.

A thunderous bang shook the house. Instantaneously the air raid sirens wailed. Aunt Nellie rushed me into the back room and into the Morrison shelter. This was like a large, heavy, metal table with thick wire mesh sides. We lay on the blanket on the floor. I had never before seen Aunt Nellie looking frightened. By now there was a continual banging as all the anti-aircraft guns fired and several very large explosions. The ground seemed to jump up under me and punch me in the stomach. Then it all ceased. Total silence reigned. Aunt Nellie held me close. She was trembling. Then the all clear signal sounded and we climbed out of the shelter. I was worried about my parents but when a lady called shortly afterwards and told us the bombs had landed in St Nicholas Road, Aunt Nellie said she was sure they would be alright.

A few days later she took me home. Walking through the streets it seemed strange that there were so few people about. Some houses had the doors and windows boarded up, many were just empty. Here and there was an empty space where a house had once stood. The front and back paths would be visible but the remainder was bare earth, with broken bricks and concrete. Some of the sites were covered in grass and weeds. On one large site was a barrage balloon. Crossing the Haven Bridge, Aunt Nellie pointed out the tall steel platform with a gun on top, to shoot at the planes. Near the centre of the town there were vast open spaces, which I remembered as roads full of shops and houses. My mother had worked hard on the house and it was now all clean but seemed rather bare; however, my mother seemed happier than she had been for a long time. I went round the house and garden delighted to see again half-forgotten things. The children I had played with were gone. The roads and passages were deserted. I do not remember that Christmas. We had enough to do to cope with daily life.

In the new year, 1943, my father enrolled me at the Priory School. My old school, the Northgate, at the end of our road, was now empty, except for a part used as a first aid post. I was put in Miss Lawrence's class. She was a wiry woman about forty years old. She was never still, constantly walking up and down the aisles between the desks and talking continuously.

'Do not take your eyes off my face,' she instructed us constantly. She carried a thin, pliable cane and as she talked she bent it until both ends met. As she walked and talked, she would, without any break in her flow of words, slash the cane across the shoulders of anyone not paying attention. One day she hit a girl called Pamela. Pamela was a big girl, with a long blonde plait. She jumped to her feet defiantly, saying ,

'Don't you dare hit me!'

Without a word, Miss Lawrence grabbed her by the scruff of the neck, threw her across the desk and gave her several hard strokes of the cane across her bottom, before thrusting her back on her seat. Miss Lawrence then carried on as if nothing had happened. She kept reminding us that we would soon have to sit for the scholarship examination for the grammar and high schools. She said that her pupils always secured at least five of the ten grammar school places available and that this year was going to be no different. We had to work and not let her down. We certainly worked. Her little cane saw to that. Our only relief from the drudgery of the classroom was a trip on most Friday afternoons to the garden, which had been developed on an open area of wasteland adjoining the north side of the old Town Wall. Here we grew vegetables as part of the war effort. It was a pleasant walk out of the rear door of the Old Priory Hall, past the ruins of the church, which had been fire-bombed, and through the old cemetery, one of the few places with trees in Yarmouth. Our efforts in the garden seemed unlikely to contribute much to its success and we were regimented as if doing forced labour. The best afternoon was when I found myself with a pretty little girl called June, hidden deep in the potato rows. We did more kissing than weeding. But these were fleeting moments of normality in a far from normal existence.

We were just about to have breakfast one morning when the machine gun and cannon fire started. My mother, sister and myself ran for the Morrison shelter in the front room. My grandmother was no longer with us, having gone to live with my aunt in Norwich and my father could not use the shelter because, he said, he could not get on the floor with his artificial leg. We were hardly in the shelter when massive explosions erupted. The curtains and venetian blinds were lifted to the ceiling as the windows came in. The whole house shook under the dreadful noise. The air was full of dust. Planes screamed overhead with a continuous chatter of machine-gun fire and the thump, thump, thump of anti-aircraft guns firing. I thought that at any minute we were going to be hit. The moment I accepted that death was imminent, there was a strange experience of peace and calm. It was all over in a matter of minutes and then there was that weird stillness and silence that always follows an attack. As the all-clear sounded, urgent voices on the road brought us all outside. The Northgate School at the top of the road, some eighty yards away, was no more. Smoke and dust rose from the huge heap of rubble that had once been a large school catering for boys and girls as infants, juniors and seniors. Alderson Road, as far as one could see, looked a sorry mess. Without exception, every house had lost its roof and windows. Our front door had, by some trick of the blast, been wrenched off its hinges and blown right through the house, where it landed at the far end of the kitchen. My father seemed unconcerned about his narrow escape and much more worried about the loss of the roof. My mother made some tea and cooked porridge.

After breakfast I went to school. My route to school took me past the Northgate School site. The rescue teams were digging in the rubble and I watched them bring out the bodies of some of the nurses; they were all dead.

By the time I returned home from school, the repair gangs had cleared all the broken tiles, nailed rubberoid over the windows and placed tarpaulin over the roofs. But gathered on the road outside our next door neighbour's house, and about forty feet from our front door, were several people inspecting a large dent in the road. It had a diameter of about four feet and a depth of about nine inches at its centre.

'There is another one on North Quay' one man said and they all went to look, so I followed. Sure enough in the centre of the roadway was a similar dent but not so wide or deep. The men discussed this and came to the conclusion that a bomb had dropped, failed to explode, bounced over the terrace of houses, the railway line and properties facing the Quay, landed on the Quay without exploding and bounced again into the river. When I told my father he just laughed.

'A miss by an inch is as good as a miss by a mile,' is all he would say on the subject.

There was only one serious air attack while I was actually at school. The headmaster had told me that if there were an air raid I was to stay at my desk until the other children had left the room, in case I fell down and blocked the way. So when the siren went and the guns started to fire, I waited until the class had gone before setting off for the shelter. From our classroom there was a long corridor, then a long flight of stone stairs to the entrance way. This led out to a small playground. I made my way across the playground and alongside the school new building to the large playground. At the corner of the building I stopped. The shelters were against the old Town Wall at the far side of the playground. To reach the shelter doorway I would have to cross a good fifty yards of open ground. The guns were hammering continuously now and large pieces of shrapnel were striking the tarmac. A young male teacher appeared in the shelter doorway, under the entrance cover, and beckoned frantically for me to come across the playground to the shelter. I weighed up the situation. At my speed and the frequency of the shrapnel hits on the ground, I reckoned that I would be hit before getting a quarter of the way across. I made my way back, hugging the walls, until I reached the comparative safety of the entrance porch to the old priory. Nobody mentioned my absence from the shelter when class resumed. My father listened quietly when I recounted the event.

'Well, you have learned a valuable lesson,' he told me, 'never expect help. If it is given, accept it gratefully, but remember that the only person you can rely on in this world is yourself. Don't attempt to go to that shelter. Stay in the building and shelter under the stairs.'

The next time the sirens went and the school evacuated the building, I did just that. The question of where I was during the raid was never asked.

The only time that I was in real danger was one morning on the way to school. Walking along Northgate Street I was joined by another boy. We walked along together, turning the corner where there was a public house called the Turk's Head, and proceeded past the houses and shops on the north side of Church Plain. We had just reached the high metal railings adjacent to the church entrance when there were several loud explosions. Looking northwards through the railings we could see a column of black smoke rising into the air.

'That is about where I live,' the boy said in anguish and ran back the way we had come into Northgate Street. There was a rattle of machine-gun fire and a single plane passed low overhead going south. I had started back following the boy but realised the impossibility of catching up with him and stopped near the shop that sold herbal remedies. Within seconds the plane reappeared just clearing the buildings at the southern end of the Market Place and coming straight towards me. It was not more than forty to fifty feet from the ground. For a brief moment the pilot and I looked each other in the face. There was a dart of flame, the zing and thud of bullets hitting the wall and then he had passed overhead and away. Brick dust settled over me. He had missed. The bullets hit the wall about six feet above my head. All around lay the bullets. They were red hot and I had to use my handkerchief to pick them up. They were silver coloured, as thick as a pencil and about one and a half inches long, with many shallow grooves running from end to end. Hurrying to school I proudly displayed my trophies to my classmates, who were very impressed. Miss Lawrence told me to put them away and get on with my sums. During playtime I managed to swap one of the bullets for a large bag of marbles. My father looked very grave about it and said I was not meant to die yet. Mother hugged me and cried, asking whether I had been very frightened.

'No,' I told her, 'it was quite exciting. I have seen a German and actually looked him in the face!' To my mind it had been a game like 'Cowboys and Indians'. He had shot and missed, so I had won. Aunt Nellie also cried when she came and said that there was an angel protecting me. This seemed unlikely to me. I thought the German was just a rotten shot.

The full realisation of the seriousness of the event did not dawn until a few days later when I heard that the boy with me, who had run back round the corner, had been cut to pieces by machine-gun bullets. One of the bombs had been a direct hit on his house and had killed his mother. It occurred to me that, had I been able to run, I would certainly have been with him and probably shared his fate. At school his death was not mentioned. As children we seldom spoke of war or the air raids. At the time they happened they were frightening but quickly forgotten. They had become a normal part of life. A thunderstorm or heavy fall of snow was much more noteworthy.

If I were becoming acclimatised to air attacks, my father was even more relaxed about them. Perhaps he had experienced so much shelling in the First World War that he had become immune to fear. There was one night when he had gone out to the White Swan public house on North Quay, when an air raid took place late in the evening. There must have been several planes involved for the guns put up a sustained barrage of fire. We were fearful for his safety and the sound of the rear gate closing was a great relief. I rushed to the back door. Unhurriedly he came up the garden path whistling, as if nothing was happening. He seemed oblivious of the shells bursting overhead. He entered the house, removed his coat and hat and hung them carefully on the hook on the back of the kitchen door. I was distressed at his disregard for safety, by walking home through what must have been a storm of shrapnel from the bursting shells. He just smiled.

'If one has your name on it you will get it wherever you are and if it hasn't, you won't,' he said.

Apart from the air raids life went on as usual. At least I no longer went for treatment and could concentrate on my school work. In late May we had the scholarship examinations. Apart from arithmetic, writing a composition and papers showing misspelt words and unpunctuated sentences that we had to correct, there were two intelligence test papers. The latter were worrying. How could you know that you had chosen the right answers?

'I have failed,' I told my father. He just grunted and said something about not jumping fences until you come to them. At the end of July the school closed for the summer holiday. A week or two later a large brown envelope arrived to say that I had passed the examination and had been awarded a place at the Grammar School. A form of acceptance had to be returned.

'You would have to go away again, to Retford,' my father explained. I did not want to leave home but there was never any question about it. I was going to follow in my brother's footsteps and go to Grammar School. My brother had left school the previous year and was working in Norwich, training to become a telephone engineer, but I would not be alone this time, as my sister was still at the High School at Retford.

Our next door neighbour had a daughter, Patricia, a year younger than myself. We had played together as small children. They had moved temporarily to a riverside holiday bungalow at Potter Heigham, about eight miles from Yarmouth, to escape the bombing. She invited me for a few days' holiday before going off to school.The bungalow was a small, wooden structure, with a small lawn to the river's edge.

'Do you like fishing?' Pat asked, leading me across the lawn.

From under a bush she produced a thick stick, about four feet long, with a piece of string tied to the end. At the end of the string was a small hook. Taking a small piece of bread she squeezed it into a little ball and pressed it on the hook. I watched in amusement at this childish attempt at fishing as she lowered it into the water. There had been some surprises in my life but none as great as when, a second or two later, she lifted a large roach onto the grass. She expertly took the fish off the hook and placed it in a large bath of water. I could not wait to get my hands on that primitive little fishing rod. It was incredible. As soon as the bait sank, a fish would bite. They were mainly roach but also large bream. It was so easy that after a time it became boring. But the fascination was undiminished and we fished for a time every day.

My sister Ivy had come home for the summer holidays. On the 10th of September 1943, I was dressed in my new school uniform (it seems incredible that my parents found the money for it) of dark blue blazer with the Great Yarmouth coat of arms embroidered on the breast pocket, short grey trousers, grey knitted pullover and dark blue cap, again with the coat of arms in colour. My mother had knitted grey woollen bands to cover the bandages on my callipers.

CHAPTER 5

Grammar School

Once again my parents waved me off at Vauxhall Station. This time they knew where I was going. The train was a 'special', put on to take us back to school. Although children had to make their own way to Yarmouth, in the mind of the Government, taking us back was part of the evacuation scheme and the travel was organised free of charge.

The children had segregated themselves by some unconscious arrangement. One carriage was occupied by senior boys and girls, others seemed to be exclusively boys or girls and graded in general by classes. I went with my sister into the seniors' coach. Their conversation was very boring and as my sister seemed to be embarrassed having me tagging along with her I decided to explore the rest of the train. In one part there were boys of my age, all in brand new uniforms, sitting quiet and apprehensive about what lay ahead. Farther down the train were several compartments full of boys about twelve or thirteen. They were laughing, shouting out of the windows, pushing, jostling, eating and drinking from bottles of lemonade. There was litter everywhere. They looked a scruffy, dishevelled bunch. Elsewhere along the train, older boys were talking or playing cards and most of them were smoking. Several compartments had both boys and girls and they seemed to be having a good time. I stopped to look in one compartment where older boys were playing cards.

'Clear off you little twerp,' one shouted.

In the late afternoon the train slowed and everyone crowded to look out of the windows. 'We're here. Here's the dump,' somebody shouted. The hubbub was terrific. As we alighted from the train, two girls came forward to meet us. One was olive-skinned, with long black hair, a big round, smiling face and large dark eyes. This was going to be my foster sister, Mary Bean. Her companion, Gwen, had a broad, chubby face, light brown hair and giggled nervously.

My new home was in a large, rambling house behind the butcher's shop in Bridgegate, just off the Market Square. Mrs Bean was a heavily built lady with raven black hair. She had something wrong with her hip and walked with a pronounced limp. Mr Bean was a small, quiet man. He worked in the wire works. He always seemed to be at work and I saw little of him. The only other occupant was their son, Tom, who was eighteen. Like his father, he was also quiet, hardly ever speaking. But he was pleasant and friendly. I had a bed in his room, which was quite large, on the first floor. Ivy shared Mary's room on the second floor. There was also a rough-coated mongrel terrier, called Vicky. I was quite happy there, but my sister was always complaining that she had been forced to leave her marvellous digs, next to the High School, to look after me. She made it clear that I was an unwelcome liability. 'Go back to your old digs,' I told her 'I have been on my own before and can manage perfectly well on my own.' But she remained at Bridgegate. The day after our arrival I went to school, the King Edward the Sixth Grammar School, which was on the other side of the Town and quite a distance to walk. We shared the building with the Retford Grammar School. They occupied it during the middle of the day, while we used it 8.00 – 10.10 a.m. and 3.20 – 5.00 p.m.

As I walked through the gates a prefect stopped me. In one deft movement he pushed my cap to the side and back of my head.

'That is how you wear your cap,' he said, 'wearing it straight makes you look stupid.'

Everyone assembled in the school hall by classes, the juniors in the front row and the higher classes progressively behind. The sixth-formers seemed more like men than boys. Prefects were sorting everyone out. The head boy stood on the platform. There was no talking. Then the masters (two were women), dressed in black gowns, arrived. They took up positions down the side of the hall, next to their respective classes. After a moment the Headmaster, in black gown and mortar board, strode onto the platform. He was tall, thin, wore black rimmed spectacles and had a grim-looking face, with his skin stretched taut over his cheekbones. His lips were so thin that it looked as if he had hardly any lips at all. We said prayers, sang a hymn and then the Headmaster made one or two comments about the need for better behaviour, more industry and certain events that were pending. Then he said,

'Finally, you will all notice that we have a new boy who is different from the rest of you. He is an unfortunate who does not need your ridicule, rather he needs your help and support.' Poor devil, I thought, I will certainly help him if I can. The Headmaster continued, 'The fact that he has to wear callipers on his legs and cannot walk properly, will not be a matter for jest.'

With horror I realised he was talking about me. After all my efforts to be normal, just like any other boy, here was the Headmaster telling the whole school that I was not normal but different. My cheeks burned in embarrassment and shame. It was with a heavy heart that I made my way to our classroom in a corrugated annex next to the main school building. That first morning we were issued with masses of books. Among them was the infamous Prep Book. Our form master, Miss Roche, whom we had to call 'Sir', explained the rules. The Prep Book was basically to record items set for homework each day but at the end of the book pages were reserved for conduct and work signatures. The system was that all the masters and prefects could impose punishment for misconduct by inserting the date and signing the book to record the offence, this was a 'signature'. They could be given as single, double or treble signatures. If three signatures were recorded in a seven-day period they were bracketed together by the donor of the final one and the monthly half-day holiday was forfeited. If two sets of bracketed signatures were delivered within the month, the recipient would automatically receive six strokes of the cane from the Headmaster. Where exceptional bad behaviour occurred, a boy could be sent straight away to the Headmaster for caning. The same rules applied to poor work, where masters could award 'work signatures'. It looked grim. To be well behaved and escape punish-ment might be possible, but punishment for poor work looked unavoidable. Conduct signatures could be given for anything, such as talking, answering back, i.e. denying that you had committed an offence, not wearing the school cap, failing to call a master 'Sir', eating in the street, running in the school, disobeying any order and so forth. And if that was not enough to contend with, the head boy could also cane you if he thought you deserved it. They said that he caned more viciously than the Headmaster. In addition to these penalties, there was an evening curfew. For our class it was 7.30 p.m. Caning was no trivial matter. Boys who had suffered it would have angry, raised, red weals, over an inch wide, across their buttocks. The agony of their injuries allowed them to take only short steps and they were excused sitting down at their desks for a couple of days until the bruising subsided.

The school was run virtually as a 'Public School'. More than two thirds were private pupils, the rest were scholarship places. Whether other pupils from the Priory School had won a scholarship and had not taken up the opportunity, because of having to leave home, is not known, but I appeared to be the only one from Miss Lawrence's class that year at either the Grammar School or at the High School.

At 10.10 a.m. the class was dismissed and as the door was opened for us to leave, the Retford boys piled in. The doorway became a frantic mêlée of pushing and shoving, as the tide of boys pushed out or pushed in – something akin to a rugby scrum. It happened every day.

There seemed to be nothing much to do in the middle of the morning so I volunteered to do shopping for Mrs Bean, which I did on a regular basis. When I asked if I could take the dog for a walk, she said he would pull me down. Eventually she agreed. As soon as the gate was open the dog shot through it like a cannon ball. I just managed to hold on to the gate handle to prevent myself being hurled into the road. By gradually shortening the lead, he became manageable. We went out every day, round the shops, along the river bank or along the canal towpath. Gradually he learned not to pull and trotted along happily beside me on a slack lead.

Mary's friend, Gwen, lived in a big house on the opposite side of Bridgegate. The two of them were always together, whispering and giggling about boys. Mary went to dancing classes and one of the boys, Kenneth Macmillan, who was in the fourth form of the Grammar School, also attended. Mary and Gwen were always out with him and his friends. I think they both had a 'crush' on him. The very mention of his name used to make Mary go all starry-eyed. Gwen worked in a photographer's studio and art shop. She used to buy me water-colour paints and brushes, but she was very possessive and always wanted me to go with her to places like her father's garden near the river. It was a lovely garden full of fruit trees. She also took me to the pictures but there was a catch; I had to kiss her goodnight. I was uncomfortable about this because she was so old and it did not seem right or proper for me, as a young boy, to be going out with a woman out at work. One night she took me to see the film 'Bambi'. When we left the cinema there was a heavy frost and the ground was very slippery. 'Hold my arm' she commanded. I refused and promptly slipped down. I had to walk home arm in arm with her and of course kiss her goodnight. I liked her as a friend and could not understand why she wanted to act as if we were a courting couple.

At weekends gangs of Grammar School boys and High School girls gathered in the park. It really was a wonderful place with carefully tended lawns, flower beds, goldfish ponds and a large summer house. It was here that I met Molly Blockley. She was probably about thirteen, with long, dark, curly hair but she must have been at least six feet tall. What she saw in me is difficult to say but I thought she was beautiful. We saw quite a lot of each other for a while. The only problem was that I had to stand on a park bench to kiss her properly, otherwise she had to kiss me, like a child.

In the dark evenings, the gathering location switched to the Market Square. Groups of half a dozen or so boys and girls occupied every shop doorway. In such a group one evening, I made a joking remark to a little High School girl who, in turn, gave me a playful push. It sent me flat on my back. When they helped me to my feet she said she was sorry and we started talking. Her name was Kay Tooke. After that we were inseparable. It was my first big romance. She was small, dark and a year older than myself.

We were walking along the road one afternoon when a middle-aged lady stopped us. She asked how I was and said I was walking nicely. Her face seemed vaguely familiar, she said she was pleased I was well, gave me a big smile and hurried on. Only after she had gone did I realise that she was the masseuse who had looked after me in the Jenny Lind hospital and taught me to walk again. Without her white uniform I had not recognised her. I felt upset that I missed the opportunity to thank her for what she had done for me.

Going out with Kay meant that I had to break the wretched curfew every night. Most boys did not observe it as, in the darkness of the blackout, you would have to be stopped to be recognised. But I suppose my distinctive gait was a giveaway. One morning Miss Roche said from the front of the class that she had seen me out with a High

School girl in breach of the curfew. What did I have to say for myself? My legs might be slow but my wits were quick. Although from behind me somebody whispered in amusement

'Kay Tooke', I said 'Do you mean my sister, Sir? She is in the sixth form at the High School.'

Miss Roche hesitated, unsure, no doubt, whether such a small girl could have been a sixth-former. 'Well just remember all of you, the curfew must be strictly observed.'

A general murmur of 'Yes, Sir' seemed to reassure her and the matter was dropped. I took care to avoid the major roads at night after that.

Miss Roche taught us English, arithmetic and nature study. She was about fifty, short and plump with a very sensual mouth. She was quite strict and severe but not unpleasant. We had to go to the laboratory for chemistry with a Mr Hare. He was young and it was a mystery why he had not been called up for military service. Once we had to shake some crystals in a test tube to make a solution. As I shook mine the bottom of the tube shattered. He gave me another one but the same thing happened. He became very angry shouting

'You stupid, clumsy oaf, I'll tip this over your silly head!' He was brandishing a bottle of concentrated sulphuric acid. I backed away fearfully and he chased me round the benches. When visiting Gwen's home one day, I opened the door to the kitchen and there was Mr Hare kissing Gwen's elder sister. I don't think he liked me.

Mrs Pereira taught us French. We did not deal with written French but had to learn a phonetic version. I could not make head or tail of it. The best lessons were Art with Sammy Sayer in the woodwork room. He could really draw and paint and I held him in high esteem. Also he was a very pleasant man with a fine sense of humour.

School work was very difficult. Concentrate as I might, most of what the masters said went over my head. It seemed like a thick fog in which there were no landmarks. This, coupled with the rigid discipline, made school life a dreary business. There was one occasion when the school was assembled. We were waiting for the masters to enter when the head boy, coming down the three steps from the stage to the floor of the hall, slipped on a step and fell spread-eagled on his back. The whole school roared with laughter. In a trice he was back on his feet, flushed with annoyance. The laughter ceased as abruptly as if it had been mechanically switched off. 'I will thrash the first boy who blinks,' he announced. Two hundred and fifty boys, aged from eleven to seventeen, stood silent and motionless at rigid attention. It was uncanny, like being in an empty room. If a feather had dropped it would have impacted like a thunder clap. We were all relieved when the masters entered and the assembly began. This was a demonstration of power and discipline never to be forgotten. What made it even more remarkable was the fact that, not only had the head boy never caned anyone, nobody, including senior boys, could ever recall being caned by any head boy. It seems that the threat of force, where it is positive that it will be used, is as effective as its actual use.

Christmas 1943 arrived and we went home for the holiday. Kay came to my house and I visited her house at the far south of the town. That was the beginning of the problem. If Kay was a little beauty, her mother was a knockout. I became totally bewitched by her. She was the most exotic person I had ever met. But my relationship with Kay continued the next term and until after Easter. By then I was having problems with the work at school and finding it difficult to devote so much time to going out with Kay. In any event, my infatuation with her mother had blunted my feelings for her. When I told her that I thought we should stop seeing each other, she took it very badly.

'I hope no other girl will ever love you,' she said tearfully.

Perhaps that was the second time in my life I had been cursed. I soon regretted my thoughtless decision but I was never able to win her back.

In July 1944 at the end of the summer term the school left Retford. My end of year report was not good. Several B minus results and some Cs. The remarks on my French and Chemistry indicated that I had failed to grasp the basic principles. My father was disappointed.

CHAPTER 6

Home Again

The food situation was very bad now. Like most people, we kept a few chickens and rabbits in the garden shed but this did little to alleviate the dreadful shortage of meat. Uncle Arthur and Aunt Nellie had managed to get an allotment on marshland near their house and I spent much of my time there.

In Alderson Road many more children about my age, both boys and girls, had appeared. There was quite a gang of us. We talked, played on the bombsites and amused ourselves with games. It seems strange that when away from home I felt older, more grown up than my years and conducted myself accordingly. But now, back home and playing with a horde of children, I quickly reverted to the behaviour and aspirations of a twelve-year-old.

On a very hot Sunday afternoon I went into the garden. As I passed my brother he, unthinkingly, put out his foot to trip me up. I fell heavily, smashing the glass bottle of water I was carrying in my right hand. Seeing blood, I rushed into the kitchen and put my hand under the tap. Immediately the sink filled with blood. Frightened, I turned from the sink. Blood was now spurting freely everywhere. As I collapsed onto the kitchen floor, I drifted away on a soft cushion of darkness. The next thing I was aware of was my father sitting next to me, gripping my arm. We were both covered in blood. How he managed to get on the floor with his artificial leg, I do not know but it must have been difficult. Ambulance men arrived and applied a tourniquet. Soon I found myself on a couch in a dismal room at the General Hospital. An irritable, middle-aged doctor came in and was soon joined by six or seven nurses. I watched in fear as he took a short, thick, curved needle and threaded it with thick catgut. On his signal all of the nurses held me down. The pain of that needle being pushed into the palm of my hand was excruciating. It was more than I could bear. Screaming in agony I kept heaving the nurses from me. But they struggled back and held me down as the torture continued. When eventually it was over, I lay there totally exhausted. There had been no anaesthetic, no painkiller, no blood transfusion. The ambulance men took me home to my bed. It was three weeks before I had gained sufficient strength to get onto my feet. There was a one and a half inch gash across my palm with the flesh held together by three ugly rough knotted pieces of catgut. The necessary visit to hospital to have the stitches removed filled me with dread. A nursing sister sat me in a chair. Of course, my legs stuck out in my callipers. 'Pull your feet in!' she snapped, kicking my boots. I explained why I was sitting with my legs out. With a sour face she ripped the stitches out without further ceremony. The wound took a long time to heal. The mental anguish never got better.

After the summer holidays Ivy, having passed her Higher School Certificate examination, went away to Goldsmith's Teacher Training College in London. So there was now only Grace and myself at home.

In late September we returned to our own school near the seafront. It was larger, more modern and better equipped than the Retford Grammar School. But there were other major changes. The 1944 Education Act had brought about a drastic revision to the composition of the school. Where our age group had been two classes, A and B, there was now created an additional class C of new entrants brought in from the elementary schools. Private pupils were no longer taken and there was a ninety-pupil intake of eleven-year-olds by scholarship. So our numbers rose from two hundred and fifty to nearly four hundred. There was nothing official, but the new head boy lost his power to cane. The whole atmosphere changed, and standards of discipline and behaviour started to decline.

For the first time I experienced problems of mobility at school. The buildings were vast and we now moved from room to room for different lessons. Often this would mean negotiating a long corridor, coming down two flights of stairs, another corridor, crossing the main hall, climbing two flights of stairs and then passing along another corridor. My callipers made the climbing of stairs slow and difficult. My classmates quickly appreciated my situation and some of the bigger boys soon came to my rescue. They instructed me to bend my arms, then a boy on each side would place a hand under my elbow, lift me off my feet and bear me away. There was no patronising, no comment. They just provided the necessary support when I needed it. They were all wonderful boys, the best classmates one could wish for. Without their assistance life would have been very tough indeed.

Although air raids had ceased, an enemy plane came over occasionally. The Headmaster announced that it would be necessary to have air raid precaution exercises. Each class would proceed to an allotted brick shelter, a row of which had been erected on the school field immediately at the rear of the school buildings. He announced that he would personally direct any evacuation of the premises, and if danger threatened he would blow a whistle, on which signal we were to prostrate ourselves on the ground.

Mid-morning the next day the school bells rang their coded message for evacuation. We filed outside. It had been raining heavily, and the ground around the shelters was a virtual mud bath full of small puddles. Soon we heard the shrill, urgent, blowing of a whistle. It was with incredulity and amazement that we watched the agitated approach of a tall figure clad in black, shiny, oil-skin leggings and coat, wellington boots, military style gas mask strapped to his chest and to top it all a black steel helmet.

'Down, down,' he screamed, pointing to the ground. We looked at the muddy puddles and carried on walking to the shelter. One or two timid little boys were making a token gesture to obey by leaning forward, with hands on the ground. The Headmaster forced one poor unfortunate into a prostrate position and then seemed satisfied.

I wondered whether the Headmaster had actually experienced an air raid. It seemed doubtful, or he would have known that a prostrate figure provided a larger target for machine gunning or falling shrapnel. Perhaps it was fortunate for all concerned that the school had been at Retford during the air attacks of previous years. Happily the air raid practice was not repeated.

The school work seemed to become a little easier. The phonetic French nonsense was abandoned and when we were introduced to the written language, it made more sense. Not that I ever liked the subject or ever surmounted the frustration of dealing with the ludicrous business of everything being either masculine or feminine. The haphazard allocation of gender was at variance with my logical approach to matters.

Chemistry also took a turn for the better with the departure of Mr Hare and the arrival of Dr Sachs. Dr Sachs was an elderly, podgy, little man. He had been a professor at some German University but, being Jewish, had to flee from Nazi Germany. His command of English was extremely limited, but at last we did experiments. His slow delivery as he searched for words to explain what was happening, suited me fine. At last the subject started to make sense. He proved to be one of the best teachers I ever had. But school work was no picnic and I had to apply myself assiduously to keep abreast of it. The pace was formidable, but life had settled into a routine. School, homework, playing with the local children, looking after the rabbits and chickens and occasionally visiting Aunt Nellie.

Early in 1945 there came a summons to see the orthopaedic surgeon. He said that I no longer needed to wear my callipers but my right leg was not growing properly and the boot on that leg would have to have the sole further raised. The big boot was now becoming pronounced. But without the callipers, getting on buses and climbing stairs became easier.

It was about this time that I saw a canary in a fancy cage, in the window of a newsagent's shop in Northgate Street. Every afternoon, after school, I went to stand and look at it. The shop owner, Mr Annis, must have noticed my visits. One day he came to the door and asked me what I was doing. Once he knew of my interest he invited me in to see his other canaries in the shop. I spent hours talking to him and pestering him for birds. In the end he loaned me a pair. With them installed at one end of my bedroom I was back in the canary fancy. They produced some good young birds and, after joining the Great Yarmouth and Gorleston Cage Bird Society, I exhibited them at the first bird show after the war, in October, with considerable success.

If I was pleased with my birds, I was dismayed by what was happening with my playmates in the area. Gradually they all acquired bicycles. More and more often they cycled off to places to which I could not go and I found myself alone. Ivy's old bicycle was in the shed.

'I have got to learn to ride a bicycle,' I told my father.

'I don't think you can manage that, son,' he said sadly.

I pestered my brother to teach me to ride. Eventually he got the bicycle out into the passage, lifted me onto the saddle and walked alongside holding the back of the seat.

'Go on, pedal' he said. I was very nervous and the pedals seemed so stiff that my right leg could not push the pedal down. He turned the machine around and returned the twenty yards to the gate. 'There you are,' he said shortly, lifting me off, 'you can't ride a bike – your legs are not strong enough.' With that he went indoors.

Disappointed, I stood looking at the bicycle. At least I can sit on it, I thought. By holding onto the gate handle I managed to climb onto the saddle. Adjusting the pedals so that my stronger left leg could get a full thrust down, I pushed off hard with my right hand, pressing the pedal down as forcefully as possible, grabbed the wobbling handlebars, leaned sideways to put maximum weight on my right leg, managed to get the pedal down, and so I wobbled unsteadily down the passage. Coming to the lamp post at the passage's junction, I made a desperate grab for the post. Although ending in a tangled heap with the bicycle, I was unhurt. Looking back down the passage, I noted with grim satisfaction that I had come on the bicycle all the way along the passage. The ride was repeated again and again. Each time, I became more confident and managed the steering better. Eventually I learned to stop gently, with the brakes, and put my left foot on the floor so that I could dismount safely. The next day I found it was even easier on the road, where I could push myself off from the pavement with my left leg and stop near the kerb, where it was easy to put my foot on the pavement to balance the machine.

Within a week I could ride a bicycle as well as the other children. It was the most thrilling experience of my life. After many years of limping slowly along with a restricted walking distance, I was now free. Gliding swiftly and smoothly along with minimum effort seemed miraculous. The difficulty of walking had been overcome. I was now as good as the other boys. My new-found freedom opened up the world again. I cycled to see Aunt Nellie; she was surprised and delighted. I cycled along the seafront, explored every part of the town, went along the riverbank and cycled to school. I was elated. There was no doubt in my mind, the bicycle was the most beneficial machine ever invented.

But, in this time of euphoria, death stalked me again. Among the crowd of children in our area was a girl called Rita. She was the archetypal 'tomboy'. Tough, wiry and strong, she ran with the boys and fought with the boys. She and I were alone together one day in one of our favourite playgrounds, the derelict Yacht Station off North Quay. A slip-way to pull up boats had been constructed in the river bank and the sides of the slip-way had a post and rail fence. The years of neglect during the war must have allowed the wood to rot for, as I leaned on the fence looking down into the oozy grey-brown mud, it collapsed. I virtually dived head first into the soft, watery mud, with only my legs and bottom protruding. In that cloying, sucking, morass I could not move. I was drowning in the mud. With great presence of mind and using her considerable strength, Rita grabbed me by the seat of my pants and hauled me out. There is no doubt, she saved my life. She helped me home in great distress. My mother said I was like a cat with nine lives. Aunt Nellie later said it was my guardian angel looking after me. I asked her if it was my guardian angel saving me, who was it trying to kill me all the time?

As far as I was concerned my guardian angel on this occasion was Rita. Rita's family owned a milk retailing business and several of her uncles, who worked in the business, lived in the immediate area, so nearly half the children in the locality belonged to this family. It had one big advantage in that the large building on Alderson Road, where they garaged the milk vans and carts, was empty all day and we were free to play in it.

It was one of those days when we were in the garage, out of the rain and bored with nothing to do, that the idea occurred to me that the garage would be an ideal place to hold a 'concert'. My suggestion was taken up with great enthusiasm. The 'concert' was to take place the following afternoon and this intelligence was soon broadcast via the children's information network. The attendance price was fixed at one penny.

On the afternoon of the 'concert' children came from far and near. Seating was arranged with planks and upturned milk crates and the garage was soon packed with an audience some fifty or more strong. Our programme was varied. Three of the girls would sing popular songs, there would be recitation, a comedian telling jokes, and Sheila would do a 'Salome Dance'.

The preliminary performances were not brilliant but the audience seemed satisfied and clapped each turn. Then came Sheila's dance. Sheila was a well built, podgy girl, with a snub nose, freckles and feline eyes. She knew the boys all found her attractive. As she stepped from behind the rough screen of sacking, the audience fell silent in wonder. There was Sheila, draped in chiffon scarves of varying hues. Whether she was totally naked I am not sure but there seemed to be a lot of flesh showing. As she weaved and swirled in front of the boggle-eyed youngsters, she started throwing away the scarves, revealing more and more of her body. The atmosphere was electric. The young audience were held spellbound by the spectacle and fascinated by the anticipation of its finale.

At that moment a milk van returned to the garage and of course it just had to be Sheila's father. For a second he stared in disbelief as he watched his half-naked daughter gyrating in front of a horde of hungry-eyed children, then with a bellow of rage he rushed into the garage. As he came in, I left hurriedly and soon children were running for their lives.

Sheila's brother told me the next day that they would not be allowed to play with us any more, because I was a bad influence and the ring-leader. I felt hurt about this because all I had suggested was a concert. Tempers soon cooled and Sheila was back with us again after a couple of days.

Air raids, as such, had now ceased and the V1 flying bombs (doodlebugs) that escaped our fighter planes over the North Sea, all passed over us to fall inland. On their approach the air raid sirens wailed their warning but, with the knowledge that we were not their target, we became somewhat blasé about their danger and were reluctant to leave warm beds to take shelter. However, one night, several must have penetrated the fighters' defences and the anti-aircraft guns were putting up a sustained barrage in attempts to shoot them down. The noise of the guns was horrendous and my mother became so frantic in her appeals for us to take shelter that, with great reluctance, I went down to the Morrison shelter. When the all-clear was sounded a quarter of an hour later I returned to my bed. In the indentation in the pillow where my head had rested, was a torn gash through which the feathers protruded and this was matched under the pillow by a hole ripped in the sheet and mattress. Under the bed, sticking upright in the floor, was a large jagged piece of shrapnel some four inches long, and one and a half inches in diameter, tapering to sharp points at each end. A large hole in one of the top window-panes marked the point of entry. Had I not obeyed my mother's pleading to take shelter, there seems little doubt that this missile would have gone straight through my head.

On a sunny mid-morning the largest explosion we had ever witnessed shook the town. The very earth seemed to convulse. A V2 rocket had landed some miles away.

As the Allied Armies moved into Europe, for us the worst was over. By now everyone was war weary. We had been bombed, machine-gunned and half starved. It was time to take stock of the damage. The beautiful parish church was a burnt-out shell, large parts of the town centre were wastelands of grass and weeds, there was hardly a road in the town that was not pockmarked by gaping holes in the façades where a house or groups of buildings had been demolished, the beaches were a tangle of barbed-wire and mined and everywhere looked tatty and neglected. Nearly every family had lost somebody. My father's cousin and her teenage son, a brilliant young violinist, had been killed on Frederick Road. Ivy's best friend had died in a direct hit on her house in Northgate Street. At school the roll of honour for ex-pupils, killed on active service, grew steadily. It was all very depressing. Mrs Holmes, who lived farther along Alderson Road from us, expressed her feelings forcibly.

'When this war is over I am going to dance naked in the street' she told everyone. It became her favourite saying.

Then came the announcement of V.E. Day. The war in Europe was over. Nobody seemed sure what should be done. To me it seemed just like any other day. In Alderson Road a large crowd of children started to gather. There were not only the local children but many from the large housing area of Newtown, from the nearby Maygrove estate and even some from Runham Vauxhall on the other side of the river. The children's grapevine had spread the news far and wide of the startling event that was to happen – Mrs Holmes was going to dance naked in the street. Alderson Road was like a vast school ground at playtime. The noise was unbelievable, as excited boys and girls jostled for the best positions to witness the promised spectacle.

'She won't do it,' I told my friends.

Eventually the front door opened. There was a hushed silence. Mrs Holmes, in her skirt, jumper and apron, stepped outside. For a moment she stared in amazement at the crowd of expectant faces.

'What are all you kids doing?' she demanded. There was a slight pause. Then an excited little voice said,

'We have come to see you dance naked in the street.' A look of shock and total disbelief registered on Mrs Holmes' face as she realised the crowd's purpose.

'Clear off. Go on, go home,' she shouted angrily, going into the house and shutting the door firmly behind her. Disappointed the children drifted away, except for a small band who sat disconcertedly on the garden walls, hoping she might change her mind. The rest of us spent the day building a huge bonfire on a large bombsite in Northgate Street, which before the war had accommodated some thirty homes, shops and stables.

With the end of hostilities the riverside was opened up again and a few fishing boats arrived for the herring season. My father had obtained a small nine-foot fishing rod for me. The top length had been broken but, when glued and bound with twine, proved serviceable. We caught the bus to the fish wharf. My father instructed me how to cast the line into the river and with a little practice I managed to get it several feet from the quay. My only problem was having to stand well back from the edge in case my legs suddenly gave way, as they often did, but there were plenty of fish and we soon had a large bag of dabs and whiting.

As soon as they opened the piers I fished there, as I could balance myself against the rails to cast and there was no danger of falling into the sea.

Fishing had to be restricted to the weekends because the amount of homework had now increased. For the first time I was having problems with mathematics. The main stumbling block was algebra. To follow the rules was one thing, to know what it was all about was another. It was like being a blind man in a maze. During the lunch period boys often played chess in the school library. I learned to play but never attained more than average skill. There was, however, a young new boy, who happened to be the son of my doctor, who was a brilliant player. Everyone lined up to play him, but he was never beaten.

It was during this period that the game of 'Knights' was re-established. On coming to the school just before the war, the Headmaster had banned it, considering it to be rough and uncouth. It was still banned and if played would involve serious punishment. The masters turned a blind eye to it, and it was only the Headmaster's 'bête noire', but when he was at lunch or otherwise engaged the opportunity to play was taken. The game was simple. A large strong boy would be the horse, a small lightweight boy on his back would be the knight. Horses could charge and push in an attempt to push each other down, but could not use their arms, with which they supported their knight. The knight's role would be to unseat the opposing knight, either by pushing or pulling him from the horse, but punching or kicking was not allowed and a knight must not touch an opposing horse. One of my friends was a massive chap called Roll. I weighed only about six stones but had powerful arms and shoulders. We proved a perfect team. The game was fast, rough and physical. Sooner or later you would be brought down and ground into the turf by other falling bodies, but it was a case of just remounting and making another attack. At the height of play it was like a giant rugby scrum and a lot of boys said they preferred 'Knights' to football.

Another of my friends was Bernard, who lived on the next road. I used to call on him in the mornings and we cycled to school together. He was very good at fretwork. I bought a fretsaw and we spent many happy hours in his kitchen doing fretwork at the kitchen table. I managed to make a letter rack but woodwork was not my forte. Sammy Sayer, who gave us woodwork lessons at school, described me as a 'penknife and chopper carpenter'. To the amusement of the class he said 'you might manage a field gate, or even a barn door, but you will never make a living as a cabinet-maker'.

Bernard's other interest was chemistry. In his shed he had a large number of chemicals. We made gunpowder and created one or two small explosions on a nearby bombsite. One of his party tricks was to light some sulphur on an old spoon. It burned with a low blue flame. The fumes affected the larynx and made you speak with a squeaky voice. He thought this was hilarious and was always doing it. When we cycled home one Friday evening, he was laughing and joking as usual but when I called for him on Monday morning, his mother opened the door, her eyes were red with crying. 'Bernie is dead,' she sobbed. 'Why couldn't it have been you?' Naturally, I was shocked and very sad about Bernard's death. He had been a lively, interesting friend but I was also upset by what his mother had said. Clearly she was in a state of great shock and grief, but those words 'Why couldn't it have been you?' betrayed a deep-seated assessment of me as second rate, of not much value, a cripple who was expendable. She may always have had that opinion in her sub-conscious, but when it came to the crunch of a choice, it surfaced in an unmistakable manner. How many other people saw me in that light? Perhaps it was everyone. They said that Bernard had died of bronchitis. I often wondered whether he had inhaled too many sulphur fumes.

By the spring of 1946 I had several pairs of canaries nesting and my birds occupied most of my spare time. Next door, Pat and her mother had returned from Potter Heigham. Pat was not allowed to play in the street with the rest of the children, as her mother thought they were common. She had school friends and I saw her only for the occasional chat over the garden wall or when I went to her house to help her with her homework.

On an evening in late June, she told me over the wall that her mother had some lodgers coming the next day. There was nothing unusual about that as nearly everyone let rooms to summer visitors. 'They have a girl about your age and as we haven't enough room, she is staying at yours,' she said laughing, thinking it was a bit of a joke. To me it just meant a disruption in the routine of the house.

Arriving home from school the next afternoon, there was Pat, all giggles, over the wall.

'This is Rosalie,' she said. There stood a girl of about my age and size, with short, wavy, brown hair; in general she appeared non-descript. She did not appeal to me at all, so I just said 'Hello,' and went to see my birds.

After going out in the evening I returned home and heard voices and laughter coming from upstairs. My mother said it was Pat and the girl unpacking. Later I went up to bed. The door to the front bedroom was wide open and there was Pat laughing and talking. She said something casual, about had I had a nice time out. The girl looked at me with a confident, amused smile.

'I've just come to kiss you goodnight,' I joked. The girl's smile broadened. It was almost challenging. I will soon have you running and squealing in panic, I thought, advancing into the room. She never moved and the smile did not falter. I put my arms around her and kissed her on the lips. It was a very strange experience. A feeling of deep, utter peace engulfed me. All fears, anxieties, tensions, stresses and strains of life vanished. A feeling of great relief surged within me.

It was the relief, at last, of finding something very precious that has been lost a long time and for which there has been a continuous search. I stood there completely bewildered. This was not the real world. It was some sort of dream. Her smile was now very gentle as she pulled me towards her and kissed me. I really did not know what was happening to me as, in a trance-like state, I left the room. Sleep came immediately, as to a weary traveller who has at last found a resting place.

As I was getting my bike out of the shed the next morning, Rosalie came running down the garden, all smiles. We exchanged several kisses.

'I will meet you out of school,' she said. Sure enough, there she was at the school gate and after that we spent every available minute together. When she had to leave at the end of the holiday, it was as if something in me was being torn apart. For me this was no holiday romance, but a total commitment. The only thing that mattered was to be with her. We wrote letters to each other every day.

My school report at the end of term in July was an improvement on the previous year but my father said I had to do better. Without the pressure of school to occupy my mind, I fretted for Rosalie. She was like a magnet drawing me to her. Eventually the power became irresistible and one morning I simply got on my bike and headed for Wells-next-the-sea, on the other side of Norfolk, where she lived. It was a ride of nearly sixty miles. Bearing in mind it was a rusty old bike with no gears, and the weakness of my legs, it was quite a feat. Very tired, I reached Wells late in the afternoon. Just to hold her in my arms was more than worth every gruelling mile.

Rosalie's father was a quiet, good-natured man who managed a grocery business. Behind the shop was large rambling accommodation, which was only partly used. Her mother was a plump, typical country woman, who was very talkative and jolly. She bred springer spaniels, which were kennelled in a small barn at the rear of the house. I shared a bed with Rosalie's younger brother, Roger, who was a very likeable, easy-going, boy. First thing every morning, Rosalie's mother released the dogs, which galloped excitedly upstairs. A dozen lively springer spaniels bouncing on the bed was guaranteed to get anyone up.

In those glorious hot days of that week we spent many hours at Rosalie's beach hut, fronting the dunes, looking out onto the golden smooth sand that, when the tide was out, stretched as far as the horizon. Behind the dunes was a wide belt of mature pine trees, where we walked hand in hand through their cool fragrance to Abraham's Bosom lake. When the tide was in, covering the saltmarshes, we took the family boat and rowed out in search of samphire or just to drift among the bouncing waves. Always she was in my arms. Occasionally we went to the nearby Holkham Park, the seat of the Earl of Leicester, which was open to local residents, and spent happy hours in the woods and beside the lake. For me, Wells seemed like the garden of paradise and Rosalie was a beautiful, perfect goddess, with whom I was passionately in love.

I think Rosalie's parents were amused that a mere slip of a boy should be so besotted with their young daughter. Anyway they were very kind and allowed me to stay a week. When the time was up, I held my darling girl in my arms, savouring every second of our close embrace, as we said our emotional goodbyes.

It was a long heart-breaking ride back to Yarmouth, for I was aware that every turn of the pedals took me farther and farther away from where I wanted to be. Our daily letter-writing was now the closest we could get.

By now my bedroom was full of canaries. What was obviously needed was a proper bird room. The shed at the bottom of the garden had been cleared of chickens and rabbits but was in poor condition. My father suggested that some good timber might be found in his old bird room at my grandmother's house, so I made a visit. On a piece of land at the rear of the house there still stood my grandfather's workroom, just as he had left it when he died in 1913. There was the bench where he, my father and uncles, had sat, plying their trade as tailors. The exception was Uncle Fred, who had won one of the two yearly scholarships available for the Grammar School and had gone on to a successful career in the Foreign Office. Beyond the workshop were two other derelict sheds, where my grandfather and Uncle Stephen had housed their canaries and finally my father's bird shed. After thirty years of neglect it was a wreck. I salvaged some good planks and also found his old thermometer and cage scraper. The dereliction was a grim reminder of the havoc caused simply by the passage of time. With the planks I repaired our shed and I bought a roll of roofing felt. My father watched apprehensively as I climbed a rickety step ladder and heaved myself onto the roof to do the job of re-roofing. He had arranged for a man to come and concrete the floor but he made such a hash of it that I had to finish the job. My father asked how I knew what to do. 'By watching other people do it,' I told him.

The birds were moved into the shed but we were short of cages. Hearing that a lady in Newtown had some old breeding cages for disposal, I went to see her. They turned out to be a block of four cages, measuring six foot six by three foot one, built of solid wood with wire fronts and were awkward to handle and very heavy. I managed to heave them on to my bicycle and push them home. My father looked at them in amazement.

'Are you telling me you balanced those on your bicycle and walked back all the way from Garfield Road?' he asked incredulously. 'It is not possible!'

As I struggled to get the cages into the shed, it seemed to me also to be an impossibility but I had done it. It was shortly after this that I sold some of the Borders and bought two pairs of exhibition Norwich Canaries.

My monthly attendance of the Cage Bird Society meetings gave me great satisfaction, for here were men and women of all ages and from every conceivable walk of life, joined together by a common interest. It did not matter whether you were old, young, a bank manager, a doctor, a shop assistant or a dustman, physically fit or disabled, everyone was equal and accepted. The only unwritten rule was that you abandoned your personal identity at the door. Everyone was just a bird-fancier.

Apart from organising an annual show, the Society arranged lectures on bird-keeping. At one meeting Mr Annis asked if I would give a talk on breeding, as I had been so successful at it. It seemed ridiculous as I was only a fourteen year old boy with limited experience, but I had to agree when other members added their voices to the request. I spoke for about an hour, explaining the breeding system handed down from my grandfather, to my father and then to me. The applause for my talk was embarrassing. That was the first of many lectures I was to give to many different bird clubs.

Later in the year, my brother returned home from his compulsory Army Service. My grandmother was now living with us again and when he said he wanted a new pipe, she instructed him to go to her house where there were a number of pipes that had belonged to our grandfather. He returned with several pipes, one of which was very small, carved in the form of a hand supporting a narrow bowl, with an amber mouthpiece. The bowl was made from a strange, reddish wood that exuded a strong, exotic aroma, that was the same whatever tobacco was smoked in it. My brother let me have it and so my addiction to pipe-smoking had begun. My father simply said,

'Don't make yourself sick.'

At school, lessons were becoming more interesting. There had been constant switching between A and B streams each year for which there appeared no pattern. This year I found myself in 4A and adding biology to my list of subjects. In both that year's issues of the school magazine I had articles published, one on bird-watching and the other on moth-collecting. The collecting of butterflies and moths was all the rage in school at that time and boys ranged far and wide, over heath, marsh and woodland in search of the various species. But the greatest prize eluded them. On a bright sunny day a Camberwell Beauty butterfly flew along the road past the school gates. After recovering from their astonishment, several dozen boys set off in pursuit, but it flew away strongly. I was pleased, for it was truly a magnificent creature.

The school had introduced a scheme where, apart from the annual school play, every year-group performed a short play. Some boys were very keen to act and were soon allocated roles. I was not interested in theatricals and paid scant attention to the proposed play for our class when the matter was raised during an English lesson. There was one part of an old man and everyone in the class, in turn, had to read his principal speech. When my turn came I read it in a deadpan voice, void of any expression.

'Excellent, excellent,' said the master, 'you will be Carriagilo.'

'I can't act,' I gasped in horror.

'Nonsense, of course you can. You will have to be Carriagilo.'

There was no escape. Unwillingly I turned up to rehearsals and on the big night went on stage dressed in some ridiculous attire, which consisted of women's stockings, a fleecy padded female blue dressing gown, and a fancy felt hat with a large feather stuck in the brim. Thankfully I got through my few brief lines without mishap and heaved a sigh of the greatest relief when it was over. On my next school report it said, 'Shows great interest and aptitude in the performing arts,' which I noted with some amusement. At the end of the year my exam results were very good and I won the form prize, but this was not achieved without difficulties. At the end of each term, all marks were added up to produce a final result out of seven. In the autumn term I obtained a six, followed by two sevens in the spring and summer terms. At the end of the year the form master announced that the form prize had been won by Powell. When the class was dismissed I said to Powell,

'So you got three sevens then?'

'No,' he said 'two sixes and a seven.'

After the class had left the room I spoke to the form master and asked him how Powell had won the form prize if he had a total of nineteen marks and I had a total of twenty marks. He opened his ledger.

'So you have,' he said grimly.

'Does that mean I have won the form prize, sir?' I asked.

'Yes,' he said grudgingly. He looked sour and displeased. I know that he spoke to Powell, but he made no announcement to the class. Rightly or wrongly, I gained the impression that he knew perfectly well what the class positions were but had deliberately attempted to deny me the award.

On prize day, when my name was called to receive the form prize, what should have been a moment of pride and pleasure for me was marred by a feeling of bitterness and embarrassment as I limped across the stage to receive my book prize from the Chairman of the School Governors, for I had come to the conclusion that the Headmaster probably was not pleased to parade a cripple as an example of the school's standard of excellence and that was why the attempt had been made to pass me over. I was mindful that on many occasions when I had passed the Headmaster in the corridors he, like the Vicar at Keyworth, never once saw me, his gaze always being diverted well over the top of my head. It seemed that if little boys should be seen and not heard, cripples should be neither heard nor seen.

My father said he was pleased but I had to keep at it if I was to obtain my school certificate in the coming year.

That summer was wonderful. Rosalie came and stayed for a fortnight at mine and a little later I went and stayed a fortnight at hers.

There was no doubt about it, she was the most wonderful person in the world. I was head over heels in love with her and deliriously happy.

Just after my fifteenth birthday it was back to school. We were studying full blast now and with three hours homework each night there was little time to spare. I did, however, join a small group to study astronomy with the science master, one evening a week. The school had a small telescope through which we had a good view of the moon and planets on fine clear evenings. Otherwise we spent the evening indoors learning about measuring star distances, galaxies, the planetary system and so forth.

'Do you think we will ever reach the moon, sir?' a boy asked.

The master laughed, 'What is the speed of our fastest fighter plane?'

'Four to five hundred m.p.h. sir,' somebody volunteered.

'Exactly! Well, it is calculated that it would need a speed of eighteen thousand m.p.h. to break free of the Earth's gravitational field. At that speed nobody knows what would happen to the human body but it is fairly certain that the craft would burn up by the friction with the atmosphere and, if you did survive that, you would be in zero gravity and float about weightlessly. In addition, unless the craft were totally pressurised, your blood would boil and your body would explode.'

'But sir,' a boy interjected 'is it not possible that advancement in science will find solutions to these problems?'

The master laughed, 'You have been reading too much science fiction.'

The astronomy lessons were basic but they introduced me to a new dimension to life, and contemplation of the universe put the activity on Earth into a different perspective.

My class this year contained some of the heavyweights among my peers. There was Frosdick, who sailed through French, as if it were his native tongue, quickly mastered Latin and went on to Greek. And there was Cullingford who was a total enigma. He seemed never to do homework, was out every night chasing girls and yet seemed to be brimming with knowledge. He spent most lessons openly reading baby comics, like *Chicks Own*, where the words were broken up to help five-year-olds to read them. Obviously he found them amusing, chuckling every now and then. The masters ignored this idiosyncrasy for, when calling upon him to continue a French translation, he would lay aside his comic, give a fast and perfect performance, before resuming his reading. He seemed to know what was happening in class and be reading at the same time. It was just the same in maths. He would suddenly look up when the master was in the middle of a complex calculation on the blackboard and say, 'Excuse me, sir, should the fourth line down be 3x-y, not 2x-y?' Of course he would be right, he was always right. On one occasion he corrected the Headmaster, who was giving us a special maths lesson. The Headmaster stood his ground.

'No. It is in the book.'

'The book is wrong, sir,' said Cullingford. We all cringed in our seats. The text book in question had been written by the Headmaster. Undaunted, Cullingford then proceeded to take us through the whole calculation and clearly demonstrated the mistake. The Head was flustered, but had to admit the fact and thanked Cullingford for drawing his attention to what had obviously been a printer's error. In science Cullingford was even more knowledgeable. Looking up from his *Dandy* or *Beano* comic, he would challenge information, quoting verbatim the up-to-date views of the scientists as published in recent scientific papers. Nobody could compete with a brain like his, Cullingford was in a class of his own, but his presence was a great stimulus for all of us. What intrigued me most was how he managed to find the time to read all this literature, bearing in mind the amount of homework and the fact that he was always out enjoying himself.

All through the spring and early summer of 1948 I swotted hard for School Certificate examinations. About a fortnight before they were due I was in trouble at school for the first time. We had art lessons every Friday and at the end of the lesson Sammy Sayer looked over the top of his glasses at me.

'Dix. Where is your homework? You have not submitted a picture for a month.' Each week we were required to produce a set picture. They were large pictures on paper about eighteen by twenty-four inches. I had been so intent on swotting up on other subjects that the work had not been done.

'I did them, but the dog chewed them up, sir,' I lied desperately.

'A likely story!' Sammy said sarcastically. 'Your brother offered the same excuse years ago. Unless I get the pictures in first thing Monday morning you can go to the Headmaster.'

Sammy was a strange character and could well have meant what he said, so I painted furiously the whole of that weekend and took in the five completed pictures on Monday morning. Sammy studied them thoughtfully. 'Who painted these? Your brother?'

'No, sir, I did,' I replied hotly, resenting the suggestion that my brother was the better artist although it was truly the case.

'Well explain,' he continued 'how it is that you paint far better pictures at home than you do at school?'

Still smarting from his previous comment, I said boldly, 'At home I can smoke my pipe while painting, sir.'

He gave me a long, searching look. 'If you smoked during the examination, would you be able to paint as well as this?' he pointed to my pictures. 'Yes, sir,' I said.

He looked thoughtful. 'There is nothing in the examination rules to say a pupil should not smoke. We have very large drawing boards and if you sat up the far corner with the window open, I would not be aware that you were smoking. Do you understand what I am saying, Dix?'

'Yes, sir' I replied in amazement at the idea.

The examination week duly arrived. All the questions seemed fiendishly difficult, particularly the French paper. In addition to the written work we were to have an oral examination. This I feared most of all. Somebody had the bright idea that if you prepared a few set pieces, it would be easier to talk a lot, rather than face numerous questions that might not be understood. I was well aware of the problem, for my older cousin had married a Frenchman, spending the war in occupied France, and I was unable to understand anything she said. My father, who had been in France during the First World War, seemed to understand her sort of French. He had asked me what 'selby' meant. I had no idea. When he asked my cousin she replied immediately 'dirty beast!' I thought if 'sal bête' is pronounced 'selby' and other words are similarly distorted, I am going to understand nothing. When I found myself alone with the examiner my nerves were just a jangle. I understood roughly what he said, to which I made one or two standard replies and then managed to get some of my set pieces across before the interview was over. 'I have failed the oral examination,' I told my friends miserably.

The art examination involved three pictures to be executed on three separate days, each session lasting three hours. The first part was in the morning. On entering the art room, Sammy indicated my seat in the far corner of the room near the window. The window was open and my position had a huge drawing board on the easel. The significance was not lost on me. The task was a pencil drawing of an open umbrella, a pair of wellington boots, one upright and one on its side and a draped raincoat. I lit my pipe and set to work. The next day we had a large display of flowers to paint. There was a choice, blue and purple lupins or an array of bright multi-coloured flowers, with lots of honeysuckle. I chose the latter although most boys went for the lupins. The final picture was a composition. A week earlier we had been given five titles to suggest a picture. I went for 'Harvest Festival'. With my memory of this event at Keyworth Church etched into my mind, I reproduced the altar piled with vegetables, fruits and sheaves of corn, with a foreground of worshippers' backs and the whole scene tinted with colour from the sunlight streaming through a stained glass window. Despite my strongly critical opinion of my own efforts, I knew this was the best work I had ever produced. Throughout the whole nine hours, Sammy never came anywhere near me and true to his prediction, never noticed the smoke that gently curled above my head and out of the window. I never mentioned it to my classmates and strangely maybe they never mentioned it to me. Perhaps they never noticed. Had they done so they would have thought I had taken leave of my senses or was taking a hell of a risk.

By early July it was all over. We were all mentally fatigued. The Masters said we need not attend classes, provided we amused ourselves quietly. Under a hot blue sky, some played cricket, some sat around talking or reading. Much of this time was spent with a friend, Brian, who lived near to me. 'When the school breaks up, do you fancy a camping holiday?' he asked. It seemed a good idea.

So as soon as the school closed, we set off on our bicycles armed with the smallest of tents, a groundsheet, two army blankets each and rucksacks with sundry provisions.

We took it slowly, enjoying the countryside on the coast road, and in the afternoon reached Cromer, where we pitched camp on a clifftop camping site. That night the wind rose and driving rain battered our worn little tent, which was about seven feet by four feet and three and a half feet to the ridge.

The next day, after drying out, we continued along the coast road and reached Wells just after lunch. As the familiar landmarks appeared my excitement became unbearable. We camped amid the pine trees at the rear of the sandhills. I told Brian about Rosalie and he, good chap that he was, said he did not mind me going to see her. Our meeting was emotional. She came back to the campsite for the evening and then I saw her home. She was working in Fakenham, but I arranged to see her in the morning, before she went to work.

Early the next morning, I set off down the long beach road towards the town. She, with the same idea, had set out towards me. We met halfway along the road and went into an adjoining meadow, where in the long grass, damp with morning dew, we lay locked in a passionate embrace. We were so hungry for each other. We spoke of our great love and the agony of our long separations. We discussed our predicament sadly. We were caught in circumstances beyond our control. The only prospect of resolving the situation was for me to get a job.

Rosalie's father had said we could borrow the boat and Brian and I spent the rest of the morning rowing out to the East Hills. Brian was a superb oarsman and he taught me the finer points of rowing. We went to Holkham Park in the afternoon. Brian had arranged to contact a friend who would let him know if the exam results were through. When we telephoned, Brian's face lit up with great excitement. We learned that not only had we passed, but that we had both matriculated. We had to report to school for the details, and boys who were leaving would have to have a school medical examination.

I met Rosalie again in the evening when she came home but, to be fair to Brian, I had to limit our meeting. That night there was a violent thunderstorm and torrential rain. We were literally washed out of our tent and we sheltered under a nearby caravan for the rest of the night. We did our best to dry out but the fine weather was breaking and, as it became clear that Brian's little tent was inadequate to protect us from the elements, we decided that we had better head for home.

Brian agreed to delay our departure from Wells until teatime, so that I could see Rosalie before we left. It was a sad parting. Then we were on the road for Cromer and eventually back home.

CHAPTER 7

The World of Work

A letter awaited me confirming what we had been told on the telephone. I now had to make up my mind about the future. Earlier I had been interviewed by the Careers Officer, who said I was not suitable to be a teacher but he would find me a good job with the Victoria and Albert Museum. He never contacted me and so I had nothing in view. To go on to the sixth form and spend another two years at school seemed pointless if teaching were no longer a possibility, and the chance of gaining a State Scholarship to University was remote. The financial situation at home was desperate, with my mother selling furniture, her clothes and anything that would bring in a few shillings for food. There was only one option and that was for me to leave school and get a job.

When I duly reported at school the results were much better than I had expected. The marking categories in the School Certificate were distinction, credit, pass and failure. I had obtained a distinction in Art and credits in English Language, English Literature, Mathematics, French, Geography, Science One and Science Two, which embraced Chemistry, Physics and Biology. Of the ninety boys sitting the examinations from our school, I had come eleventh.

Still glowing with pride and excitement at my achievement I went into the school dining room for the medical. There was a middle-aged man and woman in white coats. After a basic examination, the man said, thoughtfully, 'You have a problem.' Then turning to the woman he asked whether she thought they might be able to help. She agreed. He addressed me again.

'We may be able to get you into a home. With a little training you should be able to do basketwork.'

I could not have been more surprised and stunned if he had punched me in the face.

'Basketwork!' I exploded. 'I have just obtained a good School Certificate.'

Unperturbed the man said 'Yes, but who is going to employ you?' I was now furious. Without answering and hot with rage, I dressed and left.

With no communication from the Careers Officer, every day I went to the Youth Employment Agency but they said there were no vacancies. It did not escape my notice that some of my classmates, with school certificate results inferior to my own, were getting jobs in banks, insurance offices and the Town Hall. As the days passed my self-esteem fell lower and lower. Those words, 'Who is going to employ you?' haunted me. A friend who had secured a position in Norwich with a major assurance company, told me they had vacancies, so I submitted an application and had an immediate call for an interview. I could not go in my school uniform, which was well worn, but somebody had given my mother a chocolate and white, hound's tooth chequered sports jacket. It was in good condition but much too large for me. Under my father's guidance, my mother cut up a pair of his old grey trousers and made a pair of trousers to fit me. Attired in this unusual garb I presented myself for the interview. The cold look of the fat little man, behind his big desk in a wood-panelled office, signalled my rejection as I limped through the door.

If I thought the world was against me, I had seen nothing yet. A couple of weeks later came a summons to see the orthopaedic surgeon for my annual examination.

This time it was Mr Brittain. 'You have a severe curvature of the spine,' he said. I knew that it was getting bad and that my body was not growing evenly. 'I will have to operate,' he announced.

'What sort of operation?' I queried.

'We will open up a leg, take a slice of bone, then stretch your back straight and fuse the bone to your spine,' he said. Horrified, I told him I would not have it done. Mr Brittain became very angry.

'Don't be a fool,' he roared 'if you don't have it done your spine will collapse within ten years!'

'I'll take the ten years,' I told him.

'Right, I won't waste any more of my time on you,' he snarled and walked out of the room.

It was a death sentence. I was just sixteen and by twenty-six life would be over. There was nothing to be done except carry on as normal until the fateful day arrived. But I felt sick in my heart and wished that death had come all those years ago when polio had struck.

By mid-September there was still no prospect of work. In desperation I went to Norwich to see Uncle William, in the hope that he might be able to give me some advice. While he had lunch I told him the situation. At teatime he announced that he had arranged a meeting with the Youth Employment Officer at the City Hall. The following day, Uncle William loaned me one of his navy blue suits, which fitted me fairly well, and came with me to the interview. The man we saw was very jovial. After hearing my story he phoned his opposite number in Yarmouth. He referred to my good school results and asked,

'What the hell are you playing at in not fixing him up with a job?' There was a muffled gabble from the other end. 'No excuse, no excuse,' he said, 'don't bother. I will see to him.' He opened a file. 'Would you take a job in the advertising department of Coleman and Co.?' he asked.

I said 'Yes'. The next day I went for an interview with the Advertising Manager, who said he could offer me the job at £1.10s. 0d a week. I accepted, and started work the next morning. The man in the white coat was wrong. There was somebody who would employ me. The work was interesting and I quickly learned much about the commercial world and advertising. My sister Ivy loaned me £7 to buy a brown suit from the Co-op, which I paid her back at five shillings per week. Aunt Maud and Uncle William kindly agreed that I could lodge with them, but it meant that once again I was forced to leave home.

I left the house at about 7.45 a.m., had lunch at a café in the city and returned just after 6.00 p.m. The evenings were long and boring. But coming in to tea one day Uncle William announced that the Civil Service chess team were a man short for a chess match that evening, and that he had said I would play for them.

'But I am not up to that standard,' I protested.

'Oh that's alright. Nobody will expect you to win' he said airily, 'they are playing against the crack Norwich Union A team.'

A man called for me with his car at 7.00 p.m. We went into a large carpeted room with subdued lighting. Six tables, each illuminated with a spotlight, were set out with chessboards ready for play. Everyone looked about sixty years old, dark-suited, grey and balding. They ignored me, chatting away among themselves for a while. Then we were each allocated a partner and we sat down. My opponent was tubby, affluent-looking, nearly bald with dark-rimmed spectacles. He just gave an insincere, frosty sort of polite smile. I had the first move. Now, whether he was over confident of his superiority to a callow youth or whether he was thrown by my unorthodox play, I am not sure, but he made a mistake. No man could have looked more flabbergasted than he when I moved my queen down the board to checkmate him after only a few moves. The whole game had lasted not more than about three minutes. As the adjudicator moved forward to confirm the result, the other players came from their tables to look at the board. They all laughed and ribbed him in a strange, polite sort of way. He just raised his hands in disbelief. 'What can I say?' he shrugged.

The other five members of the Civil Service team lost their games. My uncle chortled with glee when we arrived home and the man who gave me the lift related what had occurred. Clearly my aunt and uncle were very proud of me that evening. In a way I felt sorry for the man I had beaten. No doubt he was the better player, but then chess is about concentration, guile and, as always, luck. Luckily for me he had misread the intention of my moves. What did give me satisfaction was the fact that I had got the better of a senior man from the organisation that, a few weeks earlier, had decided I was unsuitable to work for them.

My job at Colemans had settled into an easy routine. Our main products were Wincarnis tonic wine, Odol toothpaste and Vitacup. Each day, my job was to look through all the newspapers and mark up our advertisements and those of our competitors, ready for the manager when he arrived at the office. There were records and charts that had to be kept updated and errands run for the manager. The man I worked under, Leonard, was very quiet and hardworking. He did not say much but was quite friendly and let me ride his racing bicycle to deliver things in the city when the need arose. Being able to ride a bicycle was a great asset for me. One of my other small tasks was to sort out the various shop display advertisement boards required by the sales representatives, which I had to take to the despatch department to be packed into their sample boxes. The despatch department was at the other end of the building and to reach it meant passing through the factory area where women were attending machines that automatically filled tubes of toothpaste. Some thirty women worked in the factory.

About a week before Christmas Leonard asked which way I went to the packing department. I told him it was the direct route across the factory floor. He frowned and said it would be better if I went outside and along the side of the building. This would mean going down a rough unmade way, very muddy and full of pot-holes. I could not see what objection there could be to going through the factory. After trying the outside path and finding it difficult and hazardous, with big lorries bumping along the narrow way, not to mention getting mud splashed and wet in the rain, I reverted to the indoor route. Leonard never mentioned the matter again. A couple of days later, I was halfway across the factory floor when there was a shout. The women all left their machines and rushed towards me. Before I knew what was happening they had bundled me onto a large table and were ripping open my shirt and trousers. The world turned into a whirling mass of white overalls. Strong arms pinned me to the table and eagerly clutching hands groped every part of my anatomy. It reminded me of the time when my hand was being stitched, except now it was not my hand that was being assaulted and the screams were the women's screams of delight and laughter. Then, still laughing, they returned to their machines. Sore, scratched and bruised I climbed off the table and made my way to the toilet. My face and body were coloured red, pink and purple. Some of it was lipstick, some of it was marker pen ink. My private parts had been painted bright blue. With great difficulty I managed to clean most of it from my face. On returning to the office, Leonard looked up. 'So they got you then? They do it to the junior every year,' he said.

'You might have warned me' I complained.

'I did advise you not to go through the factory,' he said.

'Yes, but you didn't say why!' He smiled slightly and resumed his work.

It was about this time that Uncle William drew my attention to an advertisement in the local paper relating to a vacancy in the County Architect's Department. He helped me to write an application. Just after Christmas I had an interview. Uncle William came with me. The man was quietly spoken and seemed very sincere. He explained that, as the job would lead to being a trainee and required the person to carry heavy equipment over rough ground, he thought that it would be unsuitable for me. However, he felt sure that a more suitable post would arise and he would put my name forward. I knew he was right, but doubted that he would take any further action.

It came as a great surprise therefore, when at the beginning of February a letter arrived asking me to attend an interview for the post of junior clerk in the Clerk of the Councils Department of Norfolk County Council. Uncle William came with me. The interview was with the Chief Clerk, Mr Way. He asked me only one or two basic questions and spoke more to my uncle, who assured him that I was most industrious, honest and well-behaved. There seemed to be an understanding between them that I could not fathom. Mr Way told me that the annual salary for my age was £135 and if I handed in my notice to Coleman and Co. the next day I could start work a week later, on the fourteenth of February 1949.

There were three office boys in the Clerk's Department, John who was the senior, then Michael and myself. We sorted and delivered post, did filing, kept records, fetched and carried, collated and despatched committee and Council papers. Avidly I read as many letters, papers and documents as possible as they passed through my hands. When showing me around the vast office buildings, Michael told me to watch out for the senior solicitor who was a bit fierce. The senior solicitor was a very tall man called Stephen Rhodes. I had only been there a couple of days when called upon to take him a file. Advancing nervously to his desk to hand it to him, I stood on a short piece of carpet which skidded under my foot on the polished floor and shot me under his desk. Roaring with laughter he hauled me to my feet. Ever after he grinned when he saw me and always spoke to me in a friendly way.

The man in charge of the office boys, Mr Cutting, had started off as a male typist and was not really an administrator. Although he was constantly bustling about as if he were busy, everything was done on the run; he had no idea of systems or order and he was a chaos of agitated muddle. He belonged to the Plymouth Brethren sect and was always trying to convert us. 'Believe in the Lord Jesus Christ and you will be saved,' he told us, all day, every day. Yet this man who purported to be such a devout Christian was a real torment to me. To be charitable, it was perhaps because he did not understand the result of his actions, yet within a couple of weeks he had run me ragged.

The County Council staff members were accommodated on a large site overlooking the railway station yard at the rear and Thorpe Road at the front. It comprised three very large office blocks of three storeys and basements and numerous large houses, both on the site and in the neighbouring area, the County Land Agents being half a mile away in one direction and the County Planning Department about the same distance in the opposite direction. After the morning post had been opened, sorted, and delivered around the office, there really only remained the task of collecting, filing and finding files. The busy time was late afternoon and evening when post had to be packed and committee papers printed, collated and dispatched. During the middle of the day there was insufficient work to keep three boys busy. We could have been usefully employed revising and updating creaking filing and record systems but that was not the way Mr Cutting worked. Instead he kept back unimportant papers, such as routine internal memoranda or government circulars. He would then hand out one paper saying, take this to the Weights and Measures department. When you returned he would give out another paper saying, take this to the Education department. And so it went on most of the day. Often it required visiting the same department half a dozen times within an hour, each time delivering one item. The Treasurer's department general office was on the second floor of their office block, so a delivery there required the climbing of two flights of stone stairs. In one morning I had to climb those stairs ten times. I was whacked. When I suggested it might be more efficient to collect the papers and make one delivery, he went berserk. Red in the face he shouted and raved that it could not be done.

When Uncle William asked about the job, I told him that I did not think it possible to carry on because of all the unnecessary running about. He looked thoughtful and asked which was the most difficult journey. I explained about the stairs in the Treasurer's department.

'Right,' he said, 'the next time he sends you there, go into the lavatory and stay there for half an hour. When you go back to the office tell the other boys, in a loud voice so that he can hear, about the fantastic girl in the Treasurer's office. Do the same every time he sends

88

you on that journey but do the other errands as usual.' Always an apt pupil, I followed my uncle's instructions to the letter. After three trips to the Treasurer's, Mr Cutting was about to send me again, changed his mind and sent Michael. Whenever the Treasurer's was mentioned I volunteered eagerly, but I was never allowed to go there again.

Mr Cutting's other trick was to write on a scrap of paper his postage stamp requirements, such as, 'three at two and a half pence, two at one pence and five at a half pence.' He would scrabble in his petty cash box, hand over a few coins and send you off to the post office, which was at the other side of the busy Thorpe Road. This would be repeated many times in a day. I solved this problem by simply arming myself with a supply of low denomination stamps so that his requirements could be met without me having to leave the building. I spent quite a bit of time having a smoke in the lavatory, but it kept him happy and gave my legs a rest.

My real salvation came in three ways. The man who did the Local Land Charge Searches was moaning about the time it took him to get the plans printed. He leapt at my suggestion that I could organise that for him. Then there was the checking of the Electoral Registers when they were returned by the printers. Most people hated sitting there checking names. I became a willing helper when required. But it was after I managed, in the jungle of the basement files, to find information that a senior officer required, that my reputation for research was established and I was soon in demand. Searching through the old records I was in my element. Not only was it interesting and enjoyable but gradually I acquired a great knowledge about the overall work of the Council. Provided I was occupied and busy, Mr Cutting seemed content and the errand running was reduced to a reasonable level.

With my now increased salary I was able to save and buy a railway season ticket, which was four pounds a quarter, and in April I returned to live at home, just in time for the beginning of the canary-breeding season. However, it did mean catching the 7.00 a.m. train in the morning and not getting home until 6.30 p.m. or later. But I was back with my parents again and in my beloved Yarmouth. The train proved to be a reunion of old boys as I met up again with many of my former classmates, who were working in insurance, banking, engineering and commerce. There was always enough of us to fill at least one compartment to play cards or talk. The trains were frequent at peak times, as hundreds of people travelled to and from Norwich to work.

CHAPTER 8

The End of Happiness

At the back end of August I managed to get a week's leave. Rosalie came to stay and we had a fantastic time. Just being with her seemed to make the world a bright, happy place. Ivy was engaged to a school teacher called Roy and they joined us on some outings, so that we were a happy foursome. Alas, all too soon it was over. Again we said our sad farewells and it was back to the office.

With my seventeenth birthday there was an automatic pay rise but it was only a few extra pounds a year.

Ivy and Roy got married and when I had a few more days' leave in November, they invited me to visit them at their flat in Kennington Lane in London. Ivy thought London was marvellous but I was not impressed. The elevators on the tube were too tricky for me to use them alone. Getting on was alright. It was the getting off that posed the problem. So I went nearly everywhere by tram. I took in all the usual tourist attractions, while Ivy and Roy were at school teaching. I spent hours in the Natural History and Science Museums. Roy took me to the House of Commons. They were debating Home Rule for Scotland. I was appalled. The House was almost empty, with members lounging in their seats. Some appeared to be asleep and very few seemed to be listening to the debate.

My biggest shock was to see the underground at 4.00 p.m. A sea of black-coated, pin-stripe-trousered, black-hatted men, like ants, swarmed everywhere, a seething crowd, hurrying, scurrying. Their faces were expressionless and they spoke to no one. They appeared to be human automatons. What a life, I thought, if this is London it is my great good fortune that the promised job in the Victoria and Albert Museum never materialized.

Ivy had told me that their landlady, who lived in the bottom flat, was a disagreeable old bat. On the third day of my visit I met her at the bottom of the stairs and she invited me into her flat for a cup of tea.

Suddenly the whole room began to shake violently. Ornaments on the mantelpiece rattled as they vibrated up and down. The woman smiled at the sight of my alarm.

'It's alright dear. It's the underground. It passes right under the house.'

How anyone could live with that racket was beyond me. She asked if I had been to the Tower of London, and when I said I had not, offered to take me. That afternoon we went to the Tower and saw all its treasures, then she took me for tea in a big restaurant near the Elephant and Castle and finally we went to see a film at the Trocadero. She was kind, intelligent, knowledgeable and full of fun and good humour. Despite Ivy's opinion I thought she was a lovely, kind lady. It is strange how people react to different people. Perhaps it is a question of interpretation. For example, if you smile at three different people, one will regard you as a grinning idiot, one may think you are friendly and the third may suspiciously be wondering what you are after.

The Chief Clerk had told me that to advance my career I should try to get some qualifications. The only available course locally was the Chartered Institute of Secretaries and although this was primarily a commercial qualification, it was recognised in local government. So on four evenings each week I went to the College of Further Education to study English, Company Law, Economics and Accountancy. It appeared that none of the lecturers was a professional teacher; they were doing teaching part-time to supplement their earnings. They may have known their subjects but they were not particularly adept in conveying their knowledge to us.

This now meant that I was leaving home at 7.00 a.m., working all day in the office, going straight from work to college, and studying until 9.00 p.m. If the bus was on time it would get me to the station to catch the 9.20 p.m. train. More often than not the bus was two or three minutes late, leaving me a long wait for the 10.10 p.m. This train went the long route, stopping at all stations and arriving in Yarmouth at 11.00 p.m. I then had to go home and have a meal. In essence I was working a sixteen-hour day with about six hours sleep. The reading list was a long one and of course there was the homework.

Autumn passed into winter and winter passed into spring. On the treadmill of work, one day seemed like another, so one was hardly conscious of the passage of time. I wrote to Rosalie less frequently now and sometimes two or three weeks would pass before she replied.

In May 1950, I was promoted to a clerical post in the Administration Section which dealt with town planning, highways, coast protection, land charge searches and ancillary services.

At first I was assisting Mr Snell, who serviced the County Planning Committee but later was given responsibility for the footpaths survey. The head of the section, Jimmy Withers, just shouted to me

'Catch!' throwing a large Act of Parliament entitled National Parks and Access to the Countryside Act 1949. 'Part IV is the relevant section, it's all yours,' he said.

I went with Mr Snell to all the Planning Committee and Sub-Committee meetings. The second time we went to the Control of Advertisements Sub-Committee meeting he asked me to do the 'minutes', recording what was discussed and the decisions made. He said this was excellent and in future I should do the Sub-Committee on my own. Then he said the Broads Joint Advisory Planning Committee was mine and later the Development Sub-Committee. I also did the minutes of the main Committee, which he corrected where necessary. After about five months he left to take up another job. Mr Withers asked me if I could manage the Planning Committee on my own for a bit. And so it was that I became a Committee Clerk at the age of eighteen. Although I did the work, the Chief Clerk, now a Mr Lacey (Mr Way having retired), explained that because I was inexperienced I could not be paid the higher grade at this time. To me this seemed unfair. It was during that period that the pressures overcame me. As a means of escape I had bought a two man gun-punt and a houseboat on Breydon. The latter was a hulk moored on the mud adjacent to the north wall of the estuary, some two and a half miles from the town. On the top of the tide I could row over the mudflats to my houseboat. With the ebb came total isolation in a panorama of shining mud, miles of open marshland and an infinity of sky. At night I could light my stove with driftwood, cook a meal and lie on the wooden bunk with my dog, Rusty, a smooth-coated, sandy-coloured mongrel terrier, listening to the calls of waders and duck. It was perfect peace.

I had bought a long-barrelled 410 shotgun. I fired it a few times, but killing for sport was not in my nature. Carrying it was part of a strange make-believe world I had entered, where I was a cross between an ancient wildfowler and Robinson Crusoe. So much time was spent in solitary state up Breydon, with books and my pipe, and of course my dog that went with me everywhere, that Ivy said she feared for my sanity and that I was turning into a recluse.

My gun came in useful one day, however. On a sunny afternoon at the houseboat, Rusty growled ominously. Looking out of the door, I saw a man standing on the bank at the top of the gang plank leading to the shore. He was about thirty years old, dressed in an immaculate light grey suit and wore rimless spectacles. His pale blue eyes were expressionless. We looked at each other for a few moments. Then he stepped forward onto the gang plank. I reached inside for my gun. It was loaded. Pointing it at him I said, 'Stay where you are or you're a dead man.' I had every intention of pulling the trigger. He looked at me and must have realised that I was not bluffing. He stood still, just staring at me for several seconds, then turned and returned to the bank.

'Keep walking' I told him 'or I'll drill a hole in your bloody back!'

He took the advice and, from the bank, I watched him until he was out of sight. I would have killed him without compunction if he had advanced. But what bothered me was the thought of what might have happened if I had not had the gun.

The pressure of work and the fatigue of long hours of study were having their effect. It was becoming clear that the tuition on the Chartered Institute of Secretaries course was not satisfactory and I was not making much progress. With reluctance, I gave it up.

By now I was unwell, weighing just seven stone. My father told me to see the doctor. After the third visit he said there seemed nothing wrong, but asked whether I was drinking enough.

'Drink as much as you can' he advised.

Jokingly I said 'What? Beer?'

'That would do very well,' he said.

When I returned home and my father asked what the doctor had said, I told him he had said I was to drink as much beer as possible. My father nodded in accepting this was good advice and said,

'You can come out with me tonight.'

So I went to the pub. I liked the pub atmosphere and talking to the men but the beer tasted vile. However, within a short time, I acquired a liking for beer and soon was visiting town centre pubs. Here I met up with four boys. Three were called Roy and the fourth was Ken. They introduced me to the Liberal Club, where there were four snooker tables. We drank pints of black and tan (mild beer and Guinness) and played snooker every evening.

With a general election looming, we were coerced into helping the Liberal campaign. A Young Liberal group was formed and I was elected Chairman. We attended party election rallies, had our own social life and attended the Liberal Association dinner. It was there that Cardew Robinson ('Cardew the Cad') and Beryl Read asked if they could join us for the evening. Their contribution to the enjoyment of the evening was memorable. They were lovely people.

On my eighteenth birthday the boys took me out on a drinking binge. The aim was to have a pint in every pub along the seafront. We did not get to the end of the promenade as we were all too drunk.

These boys were all big tough lads who could look after themselves, although they never caused trouble. We frequented some of the roughest pubs in town, one of which was the Star and Garter. Here one evening we were sitting on the settle opposite the bar when a rough-looking man, who was obviously drunk, said something to us. His speech was so slurred that I could not make out what he was saying. The next moment he grabbed a pint beer bottle, smashed it on the bar counter and turned towards us with the jagged bottle in his hand. The boys slipped cut-throat razors out of their top pockets and folded the blades over their knuckles. The man turned pale and putting the broken bottle on the counter, walked out.

On another occasion the pub was packed with Scots fishermen. For no apparent reason there seemed to be a spontaneous explosion of violence. Within a second the peaceful, convivial crowd turned into a raging, fighting mob. As the chairs and beer mugs started to fly, the boys said, 'On the floor!' In double quick time we were on the floor and rolling under the settle. For no more than a minute there was shouting, swearing and the crash of breaking glass and then it was over. There was the sound of running feet as the conflict moved outside. When we emerged from our shelter, the bar looked as if a bomb had exploded. I have never ceased to be surprised by the speed and ugliness of violence. When it occurs you can almost smell the stench of evil in the air.

Being eighteen I was required to register for Military Service at the Labour Exchange. The man at the counter took one look at me and said, 'We do not need you.'

'But I want to go into the Navy,' I said in devilment.

'You can't go into the Navy,' he said in exasperation.

'Alright' I said in a resigned voice, 'I'll go into the Army.' By now he was annoyed and sent me packing with a few well-chosen words.

Ken was not so lucky. Within days he was called up into the Army. After six weeks training he was sent to Malaya and within a week was shot dead. His death hit us badly. What a senseless waste of a handsome, happy, kind, young man. I was angry. Not with the people who shot him, but with the idiot establishment whose actions resulted in him going to a conflict that was not even a threat to Britain. What were we fighting for, ideology, financial interests?

On the train journey home from work, one of my companions drew attention to a letter from a woman in the evening newspaper, saying that, with the war now well behind us, was it not time for the American service men to return home. She expressed the view that, with their stock pile of atomic bombs, America was using Britain as a giant aircraft-carrier ready to launch an attack on Russia and, as a consequence, we were all likely to become a prime target for any Russian counter strike. This led to a lively debate and everyone agreed she had a point. The next evening the newspaper carried three letters on the subject, all castigating the woman for daring to criticise our gallant American allies.

As a bit of fun I wrote to the paper supporting the woman and my letter duly appeared. It was customary in those days for the paper to print the address of the correspondent but I was unprepared for the response. Within a couple of days I received over a hundred letters. Some said I was a communist swine and ought to be hanged. Several contained death threats. Many said I was a true patriot and ought to be knighted. My letter seemed to have touched a few nerves but what a strange mix of public opinion. My father was annoyed and frightened and said I should keep my mouth shut if I wanted to keep out of trouble. In a quayside pub an old man ambled over and asked whether I had written the letter myself. When I said 'yes,' he said simply, 'it was a good letter,' and returned to the bar. A week later my brother was summoned to attend before a disciplinary committee of the post office (he worked as a telephone engineer) and questioned about his contact with me and his and my political activities. He was not best pleased with me.

A month or two later I realised I was under surveillance. With all their skill and cunning MI5 or whoever they were made a big mistake. They sent their man everywhere, including the bird shows. What they failed to understand was that the cage bird world is like a huge family. I knew by sight every bird-breeder in East Anglia. So when a stranger appeared he was as conspicuous as if he were painted bright red. I noticed the stranger at the Dereham Show, then he was at King's Lynn, then Ipswich and again at Norwich. Nobody knew who he was.

Strangely enough, he started using my favourite pub in Yarmouth. Once I had spotted him I did the biggest pub crawl of my life, ranging right across town, from the smallest backstreet pub to the most fashionable cocktail bars. He followed like a faithful dog and must have been well tanked up by the end of the evening. I soon discovered that he had an accomplice and I found myself always followed by one or the other. Eventually I thought it was time to bring matters to a head. One night he followed me into the Great Eastern in Howard Street, a real back street dive. The bar of the Eastern had two doors, one leading out into a row (alleyway), which gave access to the 'gents' at the rear of the premises and the other leading into the narrow road. As he took the first sip of his drink I went out of the side door, walked round the corner and re-entered by the front door. He had gone but reappeared several seconds later looking flustered. Seeing me in the bar again he relaxed. Pushing through the crowd I stood beside him.

'What sort of birds do you breed?' I asked. He tried to ignore me. 'Come on,' I said 'don't tell me you are not a bird fancier. You were at Dereham, King's Lynn, Norwich, Ipswich, Lowestoft and Cambridge bird shows, you must be a breeder.' He muttered something about just liking shows. 'You are following me,' I said. 'Why?' He looked uncomfortable. 'You are wasting your time' I told him. 'I go to work, breed birds and drink in pubs, by the way, what will you have to drink?' He said he had to be going, drank up and left.

Whether they were replaced I did not know or care, but I never saw him or his companion again. It seemed ludicrous to me that the

Establishment had money to waste on such a petty matter. So much for freedom of speech! However, what surprised me most was how inept they were at the job. Had I really been a dangerous subversive, there were numerous occasions when I could have ambushed them and taken them out, in the many dark alleys through which they followed me. Certainly I could easily have evaded them, if I had wanted to, by the simple expedient of rowing up Breydon estuary in the dark and landing at some remote spot on either side of the converging rivers Yare and Waveney in the wilderness of the marshes. Had they followed over the treacherous mudflats, that I knew like the back of my hand, they would have been sitting targets. I came to the conclusion that the Establishment were not only devious and oppressive but daft as well.

It was also on my eighteenth birthday that my usual birthday card came from Gwen in Retford. She had sent me a card every birthday and Christmas since my return to Yarmouth. This time it was accompanied by a letter saying how boring Retford had become after the Grammar School had left and life was pretty drab. My father asked me about the letter and I told him its contents. 'That girl was kind to you in Retford,' he said, 'why don't you invite her down so she can have a little holiday.'

This was done and Gwen spent a week with us in late September. I managed to get two or three days' leave and we went on a coach trip to Sandringham, a river cruise to Wroxham, spent a day in Norwich, went rowing at Eel's Foot Broad and attended the Midnight Matinée at the Wellington Pier, where the best acts of all the summer shows were staged for charity.

By the end of the week it seemed that Gwen was getting romantic ideas. I told her very gently that we were good friends but were not suited to each other. I already had a girl and was sure she would one day meet a nice man. When I saw her off at the station I gave her a quick kiss on the cheek.

In January 1951 the Cage Bird Society elected me as their secretary and treasurer. Stan Annis was Chairman. Most Saturday afternoons were now spent in Stan's shop talking about birds and how we might advance the interests of the Society.

My grandmother died in March. She was ninety-five. I had known her only as an old lady. Born into a large family in Norwich, they had come to Yarmouth by stage coach when she was a child. She told me in graphic detail how, as a little girl, her father had taken her to see a public hanging and had sat her on his shoulders so that she could get a good view.

'Was it terrible?' I asked her.

'No,' she said 'as the man kicked about at the end of the rope everyone laughed and cheered.'

At the age of eight she had been sent out as a servant to an old lady in her eighties. This meant that the old lady would have been born before 1784 and would have remembered the Battle of Trafalgar. She might even have seen Lord Nelson when he came to Yarmouth. I never ceased to be amazed that my grandmother formed the link between someone alive in the 1700s and myself. Although Grandmother had apparently dominated her family, including my grandfather, she always spoke of him with great love and affection. In her time she must have been an indomitable lady. She was sixty-one, when she received news that my father, her youngest son, was lying wounded in France. She simply packed a bag, locked the house and set off for the Continent. Crossing the Channel on a troop ship, and either walking or getting lifts in army trucks, she made her way to the front line, where my father lay in a field hospital. There she nursed him and looked after him until he was brought back to a hospital in England. She told me how she went to the French farms for eggs, cream, fruit and wine for him. The French were dirty people, she told me, and expressed her disgust about the way men urinated in the street, even when walking along with a girl on their arm. I asked her if she had seen any fighting. She told me about the shelling and wounded men being blown up as they lay dying. Had she been frightened I had asked.

'What is the use of being frightened, that wouldn't help you,' had been her stoic reply.

As a small boy she had spoken to me often about her younger days and the poverty and hardship of that time. 'Today people are soft, they don't know they are born' she would say. Although she could not read or write she was good at handling money and had an astute eye for antiques. 'If you don't speculate, you can't expect to accumulate,' was one of her maxims. But I remember her best for the little song she often sang –

'Put a little bit away for a rainy day,
For the sun won't always shine.
You will never be as well as you are today,
So mind what I say.
Your best, best friend is your pocket in the end,
So always put a little bit away.'

She was lucid to the end but often sank into a reverie of her own little world, where she could live again in her past.

A photograph of her on her wedding day in 1877 portrays a very beautiful young woman. Time, I concluded, was a cruel monster, if in no more than sixty years it could transform a beautiful, vibrant young girl into a decrepit old woman.

After the Liberal Club closed I teamed up with Harry and we became bosom pals. Harry, who had been in the form above me at Grammar School, was small, about an inch shorter than myself, with curly, dark hair and a face always wreathed in smiles. Despite his size he was incredibly strong. At a dance one night a chap pushed past and I fell over backwards. When I was about forty-five degrees to the vertical, Harry's strong arm caught me and just swept me back onto my feet. He was a superb dancer and a delight to watch. We went everywhere together, rowing on the Broads, drinking, dancing and generally enjoying each other's company, for he was also a good conversationalist. But all good things come to an end and it was with sadness that he told me he was being transferred to London in the Board of Trade. However, we corresponded and the following Whitsun it was arranged that I and another old school mate, Alec, would spend a few days with him in London.

Harry had lodgings in a large house, ostentatiously called a 'club' in Earls Court. He had secured a room for us in the building, which turned out to be a large, sparsely-furnished room with two single beds. Alec, who was a sergeant in the Army, was also a small man, about Harry's height and it felt strange for me to be the tallest of the trio. Like Harry, Alec was also well built, strong, a physical fitness fanatic and a good dancer.

That first night, being a Saturday, we went down to Hammersmith Palais. It was the biggest dance hall I had seen. There was a revolving stage and after each number it turned so that as one band went off, another band came out playing. I told them to go and dance while I explored the balcony which had at least half a dozen separate bars. The place was full. I stood with a glass of beer in my hand when a waiter came forward with a chair for me, which he placed at a table that was empty, except for a woman in her late twenties. I just sat sipping my drink and taking in the scene. From nowhere a very large American Soldier appeared.

'That is my girl,' he said menacingly. Out of the corner of my eye I saw a row of half a dozen local lads getting to their feet. It was obvious that whatever happened I would get the first blow.

'I'm not interested in the girl, but this is my chair,' I said evenly and picked up the chair in one hand, my drink in the other moved to an adjacent table without a backward look. The row of local boys resumed their seats.

On going back to the dance floor, which was now packed solid, I found a sitting-out area equipped, surprisingly, with large sofas. Harry and Alec came along with two attractive girls and introduced them to me. We were talking when Alec and Harry excused themselves. After the next dance they came back with two more girls and so it went on. Eventually they had amassed more than a dozen gorgeous beauties and I was surrounded by them, which was their idea of a good joke.

We managed to catch the last tube train back to Earls Court. On entering our room we found two girls lying on our beds and drinking our booze.

'Hello boys,' they said, 'we've been waiting for you.'

With a few curt words, Alec had them out of the room in seconds. I was glad he was there, as they looked tough characters. The next morning we were heading for the West End and found ourselves in a broad but shabby street that was the incongruous mixture of warehouses, yards and large run-down houses that seem to characterise London. A thin, weasel-like, little man in a dirty raincoat accosted us with an offer of a good time with some girls. We said we were not interested and walked on but he persisted, if we did not want sex, would we like to watch? It seemed an incredible proposition. Alec said we preferred watching cricket and we just kept walking.

It was later in the day when again we found ourselves in a relatively empty street. Across the road were two young Indian ladies. They were obviously very rich, dressed in magnificent saris. Very tall, very elegant and very beautiful, they caught my eye and without thought I gave them a whistle of appreciation. They smiled in amusement. But walking behind were their escorts, two very tall young Indian men, dressed in very expensive Saville Row suits. Without hesitation they came across the road, their eyes blazing with fury. Harry and Alec intercepted them a few yards from me and explained that they should ignore the incident as I was a poor chap who was mentally retarded and not right in the head. With a lot of angry muttering and dark scowls at me, they seemed satisfied and returned to their ladies, who were now laughing, no doubt thinking it was very funny.

I wondered what would have happened if I had been alone. Was it just a clash of cultures, in which I had unwittingly committed a grave trespass, or was racial discrimination at the heart of the matter?

Because of the need to get to the station whatever the weather, I bought a mini-motor attachment for my bicycle. This was a great help, especially when strong winds made cycling difficult, if not impossible, for me.

At work there was a problem with a Parish Council about a footpath survey and Jimmy Withers suggested that I should go and see the Clerk of the Parish Council concerned. It was a warm afternoon when I cycled out to this very rural parish. On the way down a quiet, secluded country lane, I saw a car in the entrance to a field. The driver had his head back and was motionless. Fearing that he might have collapsed, I stopped to see if help were needed. It was the Careers Officer who had promised to find me a job with the Victoria and Albert Museum and from whom there had been no response. It was three o'clock in the afternoon and he was fast asleep. Not only was he lazy and inefficient but here he was asleep while he was being paid to work. It was virtually stealing public money. No doubt there were boys all over the country relying on this idle devil to find them employment. If they could see what I now saw, they would realise that they were pinning their hopes on a dead donkey. It certainly explained why nobody had heard from the Careers Officer after his officious and pompous visit to the school.

The mini-motor would make the journey to Wells much easier and when I broached the possibility of a visit at Whitsun, Rosalie invited me to stay. We would have only a few days together but, with the work situation as it was, there seemed no possibility of a long leave until the autumn.

I arrived in Wells, as usual, with my heart singing and every nerve in my body excited. During the days that followed, however, things did not go well. It seemed to me that there was some sort of friction between Rosalie and her mother. When I mentioned it, Rosalie said that her mother was just in one of her moods. But there was a sadness about her that I did not understand. The situation was not helped by her younger brother, Roger, who stuck to me like glue. If we went to the beach, her mother suggested we took Roger. If we went to Holkham Park, Roger came too. One morning Rosalie's mother said she needed Rosalie to help her. 'Take Derek and show him the old fort near Stiffkey,' she suggested to Roger. I did not want to see an old fort, I wanted to be with Rosalie. But she was so insistent and Rosalie seemed so subdued, that there appeared no option. Roger kept me occupied all morning. In the evening, Rosalie's father said he would like to take me to his club and play me at snooker. There was no way I could refuse. So some more precious hours were spent drinking beer and playing snooker. My heart was not in it and I played very badly.

In what seemed no time at all we were saying goodbye. I rode home with a troubled mind. On the surface everything had seemed normal and friendly, but a sixth sense nagged at me. In some subtle way there was something different about that visit. I could not put my finger on it but it seemed that Rosalie's mother was putting an invisible barrier around her.

I did not see Rosalie any more that year. We carried on writing to each other but the correspondence was intermittent. Sometimes I would reach a point of despair, then a letter came and my spirits would lift.

At about this time my sister Grace sat her Scholarship examination and passed for the High School. My parents were pleased. Their four children had all won Grammar and High School places. I knew she would pass. From an early age she had that awareness and comprehension that signalled an active mind. In fact I was quite envious of her abilities. When she was about nine she went for piano lessons. After lesson one she was playing with her right hand, after lesson two she was playing with her left hand and after lesson three she was playing simple tunes with both hands. Even then, when she was all long legs and pigtails, she knew that she was going to be a teacher.

On my nineteenth birthday my salary increased by another small increment but it was still a paltry sum. I worked hard, but there seemed no prospect for advancement. I volunteered for any job. Once they wanted someone to take notes at a special meeting that was being held between the armed forces, police, highway authority and similar bodies. I volunteered. It turned out to be a meeting to agree arrangements about the use of land for storage of atomic weapons. We all had to sign the Official Secrets Act declaration and it was all hush-hush. I took notes and produced a verbatim record of the meeting. The military representative wrote a letter to the Clerk, saying what an excellent resumé of the meeting it was. For four pounds a week the County Council were, I felt, getting their money's worth. I asked the Chief Clerk about a regrading. He said he could not regrade me without a qualification. He suggested that the Local Government Clerical Examination would be helpful. This time I went for a correspondence course. By using the time on the train, lunchtimes and weekends, it was possible to do most of the studying without encroaching on my free time. It was certainly less stressful than attending classes.

For most people the main task of the day is work, but for me it was actually getting to work. In heavy rain the slow drag up the hill from the railway station to the office would leave me soaked to the skin. But what caused me most difficulty and dread was ice and strong winds. Light snow was passable, but deep snow made walking impossible. The officer in charge of attendance was very understanding about my problems and on days when the weather made travelling hazardous agreed that I could be absent by taking holiday leave. Unfortunately, this meant that I had to reserve much of my annual leave entitlement to cover such eventualities. In consequence I had very little holiday time. I was also unable to take full advantage of lunch breaks. Whereas most people went home to lunch or went out around the city, this would be too arduous for me. So, after a quick lunch in the canteen, there was nowhere for me to go except back to my desk. Being always in the office I became 'reliable old Derek' who would always hold the fort if necessary.

I was now meeting many people. There were all the County Officers, professional people from other organisations and, of course, the Councillors. They were all interesting. Involuntarily one made judgements about people, but how was it possible to sort wheat from chaff? What criteria mattered? I had learned long ago that you cannot judge a man by his dress. Once, when I was an office boy, a tramp arrived at the public enquiry counter. He was tall, unshaven, unkempt and in a dirty raincoat. He was carrying a dirty, tatty, old polo stick.

'I want to see the Clerk,' he said. I asked if he had an appointment. He looked angry. 'Just tell him George is here to see him.'

He kept repeating it and was becoming more and more angry. There was nobody about at that moment to ask for advice. With some trepidation I went to the Clerk and started to explain. He cut me short.

'Oh, good. Show him in.' Very surprised, I ushered the man into the Clerk's Office. An hour later I had to take some urgent papers to the Clerk. There was George sprawled in a chair. They were talking about Council finances. I discovered that 'George' was the owner of a country mansion and a vast estate in West Norfolk. Most of the time he roamed the countryside as a tramp, although they said his intellect was as sharp as a razor.

Wealth was also a deceptive criterion. Some very rich Councillors were ill-mannered and boorish. On the other hand, the Norfolk gentry were modest, polite, charming and considerate. Despite their great wealth and power, they were the men who always took the trouble to chat to me while waiting for meetings to begin. They never talked about their wealth, even to each other. It was always mundane matters, such as a favourite Labrador bitch that had just had seven beautiful puppies, hearing the cuckoo, the increase of lapwing, the blowing over of an ancient tree or the abundance of berries on the hedges this year. They were always quietly spoken and friendly, usually addressing me as 'young man'. It was noticeable that women councillors never spoke to me. They always seemed to be in a state of alert, ready for attack.

If I had problems assessing people, so did others, like the little old lady, well over eighty, who toddled into the offices one day to complain about something the Council had done. An arrogant young solicitor gave her the brush off, whereupon she took the Council to court and won. The quiet little lady was Dr Mellor, who I believe was the first woman to get a Doctor of Science degree. For years she taught at the Notre Dame School. Now retired to a remote village in South Norfolk, she devoted her considerable scholastic abilities to fighting for public rights of way, rights of common and similar crusades. She was very thorough, examining each minute detail. To 'keep her happy' I was told to deal with her, no matter how much time was involved. She was fascinating. I learned from her many record research techniques. In fact we got on so well together that she invited me to tea. We had home-made bread, strawberry jam and cream. Then she took me to see a fourteenth century cottage that she had bought, pointing out the architectural and construction features that determined its age.

So on the one hand, I was meeting professional and business people, on the other there was Jap. Jap lived in a small house adjoining the river on North Quay. He had no job, was uneducated and spent most of his time sitting on the quayside or scrounging around Breydon. We met when I was painting my punt. Our common ground was Breydon and wildfowl. We soon became firm friends. There was the time when we were rowing up the main channel when a cargo ship came past. Its bow wave came rolling towards us, three to four feet high. In a punt with only six inches of freeboard, it threatened to swamp us if it hit beam on. From my position, sitting on the rear deck, with my feet in the well, I watched the advancing wave, waiting for Jap to turn the punt for the bow to take the wave. Jap watched me to see if my nerve would break. At the last moment he dipped an oar but instead of turning the bow, he turned the stern to the wave. It swept up my back and over my head, drenching me to the skin. As we proceeded we left the main river and went over the mud flats. The tide was ebbing and the water was getting shallow. 'I'll have to push it, Pirate,' he said. The flats were intersected with numerous drains three to four feet deep. I lay on the front deck with an oar to take soundings for locating the drains, as Jap pushed from the stern. We came to a drain. I said nothing. A second later Jap was in it right up to his armpits. I dragged him on board. He was now as wet as I. In such pranks we were bonded.

So where did Jap fit into the scene? Jap was a free independent spirit, full of quiet humour, with a home-spun philosophy developed from the endless days spent just watching the world go by. Above all he was constant. Through passing years he never changed.

To really get to know someone is difficult. At best we seem to get an impression of a person, either from what they pretend to be, the façade they present to the world, or an assessment we make from what we see or hear. For some time I had been in telephone contact with an engineer from the Gas Board about public rights of way. It meant looking up the records and giving him the details of paths that might affect the Board's pipelines. We spoke so frequently that a familiarity developed whereby the conversations became friendly. We often cracked a joke. One day he came into the office and I went to the enquiries counter.

'I have come to see Mr Dix,' he said.

'I am Mr Dix,' I told him, smiling.

'No, the Mr Dix who deals with footpaths,' he said.

'I am the Mr Dix who deals with footpaths,' I replied, still smiling. He looked confused. When at last he was convinced about my identity he made his inspection of the maps in silence. When he rang up in future he was always formal and the friendly relationship ceased. From my voice, he had apparently formed an impression. On seeing me he formed a different impression, presumably an unfavourable one. I was the same person, but seeing me he discovered I was young, small and disabled. I often wondered what it was he saw that he disliked.

Although on most matters my memory is clear, the timing of one event eludes me, although I think it must have been late in 1952. Just before lunchtime there was a telephone call from Rosalie, saying she had come to Norwich, and could we meet outside the railway station at 12.45. In a fluster and with a pounding heart, I made my way to the rendezvous. She stood there smiling broadly. She had on a black two-piece and was wearing make-up. I had never seen her with make-up before. It seemed to me that she had blossomed since our last meeting and had become much plumper. In fact she seemed altogether bigger than I remembered and in high-heeled shoes, she made me feel small by comparison. We went to an empty little park at the rear of Prince of Wales Road and sat on a seat in the sunshine. For the first time I felt shy and inadequate. Inside, violent emotions surged. Excitement, love and anxiety all became an intoxicating cocktail that made the fleeting moments unreal. Then time had moved forward and I had to return to the office. We returned to the station. Briefly we talked about my work and the immediate prospects. I told her how hard I was working and studying to get promotion, but it would take a little more time.

'Why don't you get yourself a proper job?' she asked, almost impatiently.

'I have a proper job,' I said desperately, 'it is just that promotion is slow.' She hesitated, but said no more. We kissed goodbye and she headed for the train.

After the Liberal Club closed and the three Roys had gone their separate ways, there had been friendship with Harry. But with him gone to London, I now teamed up with a new group. All of us were office workers and several were ex-Grammar School. We gradually evolved an ethos of our own. Certain standards were set, perhaps by example but certainly not by rule. It was clear that the group was not going to get drunk or engage in any activity of aggression or violence. Dress became uniform, a black suit, white shirt and a single colour silk tie. A long white scarf was almost mandatory. We drank in the best bars and went to the theatre and the pictures together. On Saturday night it was dancing, usually at the Britannia Pier, and after midnight we had a meal in a restaurant at the top of Regent Road. Here we sat until the early hours discussing politics, religion, philosophy and whatever seemed a suitably interesting subject.

The spring of 1953 found me studying hard for the coming examination in June. My whole being ached for success and that prized regrading. There was a despairing urgency about it. The correspondence with Rosalie had been spasmodic for some time but now although I wrote to her it seemed a long time since she had written to me. There was some fixed idea in my head that if only I could secure this regrading, I would be in a position to marry her and we would be together at last. That was my goal and I fixed my intent upon it. Part of me desperately wanted to go and see Rosalie. But what could I say, except 'the situation is the same as last time we met, goodbye, please write'. I fretted for time to pass.

The only salvation was the canaries. In the bird-room, nothing changed. Individual birds came and went but the stud was a constant. It was a little world of its own. This was one place where I was not in the cut and thrust of life, one place where the song of the birds acted as a balm to a distressed spirit.

The examinations were in June. By the beginning of August I had passed and a recommendation was going to the September meeting of the Establishment committee for my regrading. I was jubilant. But nothing is certain with committees and it seemed prudent to wait until the regrading was definite, before telling Rosalie.

In the middle of August, just a fortnight before my twenty-first birthday, Pat's mother called to me over the garden wall. She smiled as if about to say something pleasant. Then she said, 'Did you know Rosalie got married last week? Some chap from Birmingham'. For a moment I stared at her blankly, my brain not registering the information, not wanting to acknowledge what my ears had heard. Slowly, the words condensed into meaning and gradually permeated into my consciousness. 'Rosalie was married!'

I returned to the house. 'Whatever is wrong?' my mother asked. 'Rosalie has just got married,' I told her in a broken voice. Tears sprang to her eyes as she read the torment, anguish and suffering that must have been written on my face. After a moment, she said, 'God help any woman you meet in the future.'

In a trance-like state, I went to my bird shed and tried to come to terms with the situation. Had Rosalie just become tired of the waiting? Had she just fallen out of love with me? Had this man simply swept her off her feet? In the end, the reasons did not matter. The simple fact was that I had lost her. She was gone forever.

In utter grief and despair I realised that never again would her beautiful eyes smile me welcome, never again would her gentle hands touch my face, never again would her firm body press against mine in close embrace, never again would those soft lips kiss mine, speak my name or whisper her love for me and never again would her warm fragrance surround and comfort me.

As I thought of her it seemed as if a part of me was dying. All sense of purpose and all reason for living drained away. I knew that from now on I would always be alone, for there would never be another Rosalie.

I felt no sense of anger or betrayal. How could I? My love for her was total and unconditional. I just hoped that the man she had married loved her as much as I did and that Rosalie would be happy. I consoled myself with the thought that, for her sake, it was perhaps for the best. He would, no doubt, be able to give her a better life than I could offer, for, if Mr Brittain were right, I had no more than five years of life left. I could not wish such trouble on her and I told myself that it had been selfish of me to think otherwise. Such thoughts did not ease the pain, for although she had stopped loving me, I loved her as deeply as ever. One thing was sure, I would never again find true happiness.

In the months that followed, I went through life like a man sleepwalking. Nothing mattered any more. My family maintained a discreet silence and Rosalie was never mentioned again.

Four weeks after the news of Rosalie's marriage my regrading was confirmed and my salary rose considerably. As if the gods were mocking me, a few months after that I was promoted to an even higher grade. My salary was now substantially in excess of the average wage but it had come too late. All my efforts had been for us, Rosalie and me, but now that I was alone, money became irrelevant. Every night I went out and spent it in the pubs.

Rosalie

CHAPTER 9

Running Wild

In the months that followed the news of Rosalie's marriage I drifted like a rudderless ship. There was no direction to follow and no objective to attain. I met several girls and took them out a few times, but they were not Rosalie, and it all seemed pointless. But life went on.

At work, Jimmy Withers left to take up a new post, and Mick Buswell arrived to become our new section head. I liked him and I think he liked me. In fact it was his recommendation that secured my second regrading. Mick was a keen rugby player, and every Monday morning he limped into the office painfully, often with his face badly bruised and scratched. 'Why do you do it?' I asked him. On his invitation I went to see him play. As a fly-half he was very fast and very good. Having played Knights at school I could understand the excitement generated in the game, but the physical pain Mick suffered would, for me, have outweighed the pleasure.

That autumn my brother came back home having obtained a position in the Yarmouth telephone exchange. We spent most evenings fishing off the beach. My casting distance was no more than thirty-five yards, which extended just behind the breakers, but I caught fish. My brother, who was over six feet tall and strong, had a massive cast of more than a hundred yards, which took his line well out to sea, but his catch was less than mine. My suggestion that he might do better with a shorter cast was dismissed with the words, 'I am after the big one'. There seemed to be a moral in that somewhere. Was it better to go for all or nothing, or take what you could get?

The attraction of fishing was not just in the catch, but in the activity itself. There were warm October evenings when the sea was like a mill pond, gently lapping the shore, a large orange moon reflecting off the rippling water, and that magical tangy smell of the sea. But the sea was a changing creature, never twice the same. She could become a roaring, rolling, beast that hurled upon the shore with white teeth, threatening to take you off the beach. The foreshore is a dangerous place. One calm night I sat fishing alone. The waves were running gently up the beach to within ten feet of me. The light from my hurricane lamp illuminated the white tip of the rod, moving gently in the tide's pull. Lost in the peace of the night I watched that white blob, waiting for a bite. Suddenly, the lantern light went out. In horror, I found myself nearly up to the waist in the sea. Behind me the water was curling up the beach. Clutching the seat, and digging in my heels, I managed to resist that dreadful sucking power of the water as the wave receded. With the outrushing water went all my bait and equipment, except the rod, which remained firmly grasped in the spike set in the sand. I grabbed the rod and the seat and scrambled up the beach. It had been a freak wave, for the sea settled down again to its former gentle lapping of the original tide line. Just like life, it is the unforeseen, unexpected, one-off event that is the danger.

When not fishing, my association with my group of drinking friends continued. Christmas came and went. In the early part of the new year, 1954, the boys discussed the possibility of a holiday together. The main group members were John, Gordon, Freddie, Frank and myself. The final decision was that it would be a boating holiday on the Norfolk Broads. At the last moment John had to drop out, but the rest of us set off during the first week of May. We did the usual round trip, down the river Yare from Norwich to Great Yarmouth, and then up the river Bure to the Broads proper. We stopped off at all the entertainment centres, consumed gallons of beer, went to parties on larger boats with crowds of other young people, like ourselves, out on the spree. Gordon was a brilliant pianist. When he played in the pubs everyone bought him beer. Even with four of us drinking we found it difficult to keep up with the supply.

At Ranworth we had to moor in the centre of the Broad and go ashore in the dinghy. The big attraction was a dance at the village hall. It was there that we met two girls from London who had a yacht moored up not far from our cruiser. As they were alone, they accepted our invitation to come back with us for supper. Later, someone suggested a game of cards, which seemed to me inappropriate. However, the girls agreed. One of them took the pack and started to shuffle it. As her hands moved faster, the cards formed a perfect moving bridge covering the seven to eight inches between her hands. I had seen a lot of card-playing, but this was something new. When I asked her where she had learned to do it, she just laughed. I guessed it

On the Broads 1954, Gordon, Frank and myself

was in a gambling casino. If they were good at cards, they were no sailors. When we had brought them across in the dinghy to our boat, one of them had stepped on the edge of the dinghy to reach the deck. Under her weight the dinghy tipped and would have capsized had I not, fortunately, been holding tight to the cruiser. About 1.00 a.m. Gordon and Freddie set out with them back to their yacht. Frank and I watched their safe arrival, but then there was much splashing. Apparently the girl had repeated her trick in getting out of the dinghy, but this time had succeeded in turning it over, throwing them all into the water. Gordon and Freddie were both good swimmers, but they stressed how hard it had been even to keep afloat. Nobody was hurt, but I was glad not to have been involved as, not being able to swim, I would probably have drowned.

That whole week the weather was sunny and hot. The air, the food and drink, the relaxation and the comradeship, were just what was needed and I felt refreshed in mind and body. On the last night of our holiday we moored at a quayside opposite a quaint old pub and, after a meal, we went across for a drink. Sitting on a bench outside the pub were two local young ladies. Frank said they looked 'likely' girls. Gordon and Freddie were not interested, but Frank wanted the dark-haired girl and asked if I would take the ginger one, who was a big buxom country girl. Without any hesitation the girls accepted our offer to come on board. I had the fore cabin and Frank took the main cabin. There were no preliminaries, no exchange of details, and no kissing or cuddling. Before I knew what was happening I was confronted by a pair of huge breasts. She had big firm buttocks and strong thighs. She took me without emotion and as calmly as if she were shelling peas. It was not like I had always imagined it to be, but by the time the pub closed and Gordon and Freddie returned, there was a strange feeling of relaxation and satisfaction.

After the holiday I cycled out to the village to see this girl on a fairly regular basis. She was easy-going, spoke very little, and demurred only about going to certain places on the grounds that they were 'too posh'. It was only in bed that her self-confidence was evident. Once committed to the sex act I became hostage to her desires for, by doing no more than flex her muscles, she could bring me to a climax when and as often as she pleased. After one all-night session in a large hotel on Yarmouth seafront she left me so debilitated that I felt like a piece of tissue paper that might be blown away on the morning breeze.

'You're greedy,' she said.

'Hark at the kettle calling the pot black,' I replied. She grinned in acknowledgement. But our relationship was purely sexual. I cannot understand why copulation is called making love. For me sex had nothing to do with love. I was in love with Rosalie, but I was having sex with this eighteen-year-old girl, and the two things were poles apart. Love was a wondrous and beautiful thing, like the rare blossoming of desert flowers, whereas the sex act was more akin to having a good meal; enjoyable, but not something that touched the soul. It seemed to me that it would be possible to have enjoyable sex with any number of women, but real love, if it happened at all, occurred only once in a lifetime. As autumn approached I did not want to continue with the long journey to see this girl and the affair ended as casually as it had commenced. That was the difference between love and sex. You could walk away from sex without any sense of loss.

The 1954 bird show was the best we had ever staged, with over one thousand entries. We made more than £100 profit, which was used to buy some new tubular steel show staging, and I felt very pleased with my efforts.

One of our social group, John, was in a family syndicate that had a big win on the football pools. He never said how much, and we never asked, but from the proceeds he bought a car and now took us farther a-field. There was a big band due to visit Lowestoft Palais, 'Kenny Baker and his Dozen', and thinking that it would be a good night out, we all bought tickets at five shillings each, which was more than double the usual price. On the Saturday night when we entered the dance hall there was a line of trumpets blasting away for all they were worth, and the noise was horrendous. We retreated to the pubs to 'wait for things to get swinging', as Frank put it. But by ten o'clock the noise was still ear-splitting and the dance hall was half empty. We just looked at each other. There was no need for words and, as if of one mind, we returned to the pub.

Whether it was the big pools win, or whether it was woman trouble, or something else, we never discovered, but John dropped out of the group. Concerned about him, we deputed Frank, who lived near him, to make enquiries. Frank's subsequent report was disturbing. Our old friend, who was the liveliest and smartest of us all, one might almost say our mentor, had apparently given up his job and now spent his time in a small local pub playing cards with the old men. I visited the pub. There John sat, unshaven, dishevelled and scruffily dressed, playing cards.

'Long time no see, John. How are you?' I asked. He ignored me. I tried again, 'The boys have missed you, what have you been up to?'

He looked at me with cold eyes as if I were a complete stranger and said, 'Why don't you just piss off'. He then returned to his cards. This was not the laughing, debonair John that I knew, and clearly it was some sort of break down. We never saw him again, but soon the whole group had disintegrated with Freddie moving to Norwich, Frank going to work as a cartographer with the Admiralty in London, and Gordon starting to court strongly. I missed the company of the boys and, once again, I became a lone wolf, at least during the week.

At this time there was a loose association of young people about Town who might be described as the 'rich set'. Not very rich, but rich by small town standards. These were the sons and daughters of local business people. They appeared in the town centre pubs only on

114

Saturday evenings, when they thought it a bit of a lark to go slumming. They ended their spree every Saturday evening with a party. During the autumn, when the holiday season had ended, it was customary for local hoteliers to take their own holidays abroad, or attend to business elsewhere. Many left their empty hotels or guesthouses in the sole charge of offspring, and it was in these establishments that the parties took place. I knew none of these people and how I came to be on their guest list is something of a mystery. I was always well dressed and probably seemed to have plenty of money. Perhaps I was either mistaken to be one of their kind, or it may have been that one of them thought I might be worth fleecing at the card table. Anyway, I was invited to join them.

'Come to the party, number X Camperdown, and don't forget to bring a bottle,' a young man said. That was the entry fee, a bottle of spirits. When the pubs closed at 10.30 p.m., I jumped into a taxi, armed with a bottle of rum.

Arriving at Camperdown, a broad road off the seafront, lined with large guesthouses, the scene was astonishing. Taxis were arriving from all directions and disgorging their bands of merry revellers. A slim blonde girl took the bottle as I went through the door, and kissed me on the cheek. Inside, a noisy, laughing, crowd were rolling back a large carpet and putting French chalk on the floor for dancing. A record player was beating out dance rhythms above the constant high-pitched chatter. A young man, who was busily pouring out drinks, called me over to a large table laden with bottles, 'Just help yourself,' he said. In my time I had seen some heavy drinking, but nothing like this. Everyone was pouring spirits down their throats as if there would be no tomorrow. Some groups laughed and chatted, some danced, and there was a lot of smooching going on. There must have been at least sixty young people present. I found the card school in operation in an adjoining room. Some of them were good card players, but some had more money than skill. By 3.00 a.m. most people were very drunk. When play finished we went into the large room, which by then was nearly empty. One of the young men pulled a girl to her feet saying, 'Come on, Amanda, beddy-byes,' and carried her off. I realised that most of the party had paired up and were upstairs in the many vacant bedrooms. I flopped out in an armchair, like my companions, and was soon asleep. I was awakened by a very tall young woman shaking my shoulder. As I opened my eyes she thrust a plate of fried kippers, with a large dollop of jam, into my hand.

'Breakfast', she said with a smile.

By now the room was filling up as couples came downstairs. The atmosphere reeked of kippers as they all tucked into breakfast. The laughter and chatter began again, but soon people started to leave. The time was six-thirty. It was a long walk back to the town centre, and I did not arrive home until after seven. My father asked what I had been up to. I told him 'playing cards'.

The next Saturday I was given the message 'number X North Drive'. It was more or less a repeat of the previous week, except there were some people that I had not seen before. When we sat down to play cards, a ruddy-faced young man, with a mass of blond curly hair, said that he was not prepared to play for peanuts, and suggested that the stakes be raised from one pound to ten pounds. One or two seemed dubious about this, but finally agreed. I had just thirty pounds in my pocket, but said nothing. My fortunes were mixed, but I managed to keep in the game, whereas the young man who had suggested raising the stakes lost heavily. He obviously did not know that it is fatal to challenge Lady Luck. We had kippers and jam for breakfast again, and it was clear that this formed part of their ritual. Every Saturday night we repeated the same routine. If a woman singled me out, I obliged, but I never really knew any of them. Their conversation was always trivial, and they just larked about like overgrown school children. Their antics reminded me of the Grammar and High School pupils on the train going back to Retford after the holidays.

One evening the word went round, not for a party, but a card school on a Norwegian timber ship lying docked on the other side of the river. About eight of us went, and there was a similar number of seamen. A lot of hard liquor started to flow and we all got very drunk. As often happens, inebriation is not constant and for short periods the brain clears. During one such lucid period I looked around and saw that most of my companions were in a bad state, and some had passed out completely. Gazing down at the table I was amazed to see within the confines of my arm a vast pile of notes and coins. Who had been playing? My sub-conscious perhaps, for I certainly had no memory of the game. Knowing that I was now very drunk it seemed a good time to leave, but when my intention was announced there were voluble protests. My eyes met those of three Norwegians sitting at the table. There was no mistake in those looks. They would not let me go with all that money. It seemed harder to lose money than win it, but eventually the pile dwindled. When finally ashore, just before dawn, there was still £50 of winnings in my pocket. Whoever coined the saying 'lucky at cards, unlucky in love', certainly knew what he was talking about, I thought wryly.

This was not my only dangerous encounter. For a change of scene I decided to try the Norwich pubs, the most notorious of which at that time was the Buff Coat on Cattle Market Hill. It looked quiet and drab from the outside. I pushed open the door and was half way through it when a large knife flashed past my face to thud and stay quivering in the door only a foot from my head. The bar was crowded with black American Servicemen, who all jeered and shouted insults, the general drift of which was that white 'Limeys' were not welcome. It seemed inappropriate to talk to them about civil liberty and racial discrimination, so I left quickly.

One Saturday night the word was out that the party would be held on the *Golden Galleon*, a large pleasure cruise ship moored adjacent to the Haven Bridge in the centre of the town. This seemed doubtful, but sure enough by eleven o'clock the regular crowd had assembled, music blared from a small group playing below deck, and the whole ship was seething with happy party-goers. Drinks were being served in the small cabin, which was absolutely jam-packed. We were not usually entertained by live musicians. This thought had barely occurred to me when two beautiful girls, both in their early twenties, one a blonde and the other a brunette, stepped onto the small bar and started slow exotic dancing. Apart from their high-heeled shoes they were stark naked. The sound of the rapturous applause, shouts and whistles brought those up on deck down into the already packed cabin. The show lasted only a few minutes, but by then we were all gasping for air. When I left the ship in the early hours, everyone was very merry, and the noise was deafening. But, with no houses near the site, and presumably no complaints, the police turned a blind eye to our activities. One good thing about Yarmouth at that time was police tolerance. Provided that you did not annoy somebody, you could get drunk, sing, dance and generally enjoy yourself. There was little or no violence, apart from the Saturday night big fights. These fights were sporting rather than aggressive. It was all fists, no feet and certainly no weapons. Once a man was on the ground he was out of the game. When American Servicemen were in town it was them versus the British. When they were absent it was British servicemen against the local youths. And in the absence of any servicemen town boys fought country boys. Even so, I kept well clear of these skirmishes. The parties may have been wild, but there was never any violence, or even unpleasantness.

I became so caught up in the night life that I seldom arrived home until well into the early hours. My father was most upset by my behaviour.

'You're running wild,' he said, 'if you are not careful you are going to get yourself into a lot of trouble. I don't know why you have to visit the tripe houses. Anyone can bend down and pick up dirt'.

I never argued with him, but just went on my way. I had tried being a good boy and doing the right things the proper way, but that had not served me very well. Now, a perverse sort of madness seemed to have taken me over. If I had only a few more years of life I intended to enjoy them. From now on I would be game for a laugh, in fact game for anything that would provide a new experience or create excitement. But there was an incident when my resolve and my nerve failed me.

Again it was party time on a Saturday night. I had met a girl who said that she knew where there would be a good party. The venue turned out to be a large house near the town centre. When we arrived there were none of the usual crowd present, and it soon became evident that this was just a drinking binge. Just after midnight the room started to empty rapidly as couples all made their way upstairs. In the end there was only myself and the girl left in the lounge. She lay sprawled in an armchair, not paralytically drunk, but certainly not sober. I was shaking her in an attempt to bring her to her senses when a voice said, 'She will be no use to you. Come with me'.

Standing at the bottom of the stairs was a slim girl, about my age, with long blonde hair. I took her outstretched hand and followed her up the stairs into a large bedroom with a big double bed. It all happened so quickly, and my brain was so befuddled with drink, that I was not exactly sure what she intended, so I sat on the bed. Smiling, she started to unbutton her dress. At that moment the door opened and a woman in a large white flannelette nightgown entered the room. She was a big woman and looked about the same age as my mother. She wore no make-up and had coarse features. I must have looked startled, because the girl said reassuringly, 'It's alright, it's my mother'. I thought, I am in trouble now, she is going to make a scene about me being in her daughter's bedroom. But having advanced into the room, the woman said not a word. Calmly she commenced to remove her nightgown. All sorts of alarm bells started ringing in my head.

'You will have to excuse me', I said, in an even tone, 'but I have to go to the lavatory'.

Once out of the room, I hurried down the stairs, shook the sleeping girl I had come with into consciousness and, with her, left speedily by the front door. Thereafter I was plagued by speculation. What would have happened if I had not left that bedroom? There were several things that had put me to flight. Although I could cope with one woman at a time, two or more evoked frightening memories of my days in hospital. Then there was the occasion when a number of nurses held me down while I suffered the agony of having my hand stitched, not to mention the rough treatment I had received from the factory women at Coleman's. Another factor was the silence and size of the older woman; in hospital all women had seemed big, and their silence usually heralded something unpleasant about to happen. Yet I could not help wondering whether I had missed a wonderful experience. On the other hand I had probably escaped something very unpleasant.

By now I was leading a double life – the perfect Jekyll and Hyde syndrome. During the day I was the quiet, industrious, and respectable local government officer. At night I changed into a drunken, gambling, rake. They were two worlds apart, totally divorced by time and place and linked only by the railway line between Yarmouth and Norwich. Somewhere along the track, the door to one world closed and the door to the other opened. Each existence was inhabited by separate people. Only once was there a crossover, when a man from the business life crossed my path in the night life. He was a senior man in one of the public utility companies, whom I had met several times at public inquiries. He was about sixty, dapperly dressed in a black overcoat and homburg hat, and sported buff kid gloves. In one of the roughest pubs in Yarmouth, he stood at the bar, looking very serious, buying drinks for a woman we called 'Aggie'.

It is difficult to say how old Aggie might be. She could have been fifty or even sixty-five. She was small, extremely thin and, physically, the most unattractive person one could imagine. Her greasy, straggling, dark hair fringed a round wrinkled little face, with a large, shapeless, blob of a nose. She had no teeth and always wore a simpering idiotic smile. The poor woman appeared to be mentally defective. To cap it all, she was always dressed in a very thin, shabby, black dress that hung like a drape on her skeletal body, from beneath which protruded her two stick-like legs. I felt sorry for her, although she always seemed happy. She was certainly a favourite with the boys, who all bought her as much beer as she could drink in the hope that she would perform. They were seldom disappointed. When suitably inebriated, Aggie would do her party piece, which was to stand on a table and execute a sort of soft shoe shuffle little dance, and as a finale she would bend over and throw her skirts over her head to reveal her bare bottom. She always received rapturous applause, and basked happily in the glow of her admiring audience. Of all the women in the town, and there were plenty of them, this affluent gentleman had chosen Aggie. He spent half an hour filling her up with gin, and then they left together. During this time our eyes had met just once. If he recognised me he did not show it and, as a matter of courtesy, I returned a blank look of non-recognition. Perhaps it is a fortunate quirk of Nature that whatever you look like, and whoever you are, someone will see some attraction in you.

Aggie was not an isolated case. For some time a girl called Ann, pale, thin, scruffy and unattractive, haunted one of the low life pubs. Eventually she vanished from the scene. Months later, when I was passing the Star Hotel, one of the upper-class hostelries, a large black limousine glided to a halt. A tall, well-dressed, and quite handsome young man leapt out. I went round to open the passenger door. A pair of long, elegantly nylon-stockinged legs swung out, belonging to a stunning blonde in a chic black dress with a white fur wrap. It was Ann. Life, I thought, is full of surprises.

At this time the pubs were full of characters like Aggie and, when going out for the evening, there was no telling who you might meet or what they might get up to. One regular performer was Billy's

120

greyhound. Billy was a slight, small, man in his sixties who was always inebriated. Not one for conversation, he laughed a lot and dismissed everything with his oft repeated favourite saying, 'san faire rien' (ça ne fait rien) which he had picked up from his army days. His greyhound, that always accompanied him, was a quiet gentle creature with a brindled coat. We all knew it well, but American Servicemen, holiday visitors and other strangers fell for the challenge. 'I bet that my dog can drink a pint quicker than you can', Billy would say. Eventually a punter would take up the bet, pints of beer would be purchased and one mug placed in front of the hound. At the signal to start Billy let go of the dog who simply stuck its nose into the pot and sucked up the beer like a vacuum cleaner, emptying it in less than a couple of seconds. It never failed and I have seen it consume three pints in rapid succession. It seemed incredible that the dog should abandon the usual lapping way of drinking to suck it up, and to do it with such rapidity. It had to be seen to be believed, and was almost like watching a conjuring trick. Thanks to the dog, Billy always had a good supply of free beer and every night as he went home over the Haven Bridge it was difficult to determine who staggered most, Billy or the dog.

If we never worked out how the dog drank so quickly, we certainly never resolved the mystery of the card trick we witnessed one evening. A middle-aged man, who was a stranger to the Great Eastern, stood drinking quietly at the bar. As he finished his drink, he picked up a pack of well-worn playing cards from a nearby table, shuffled them and then fanning out the pack invited one of us to select a card without revealing to him the identity. The selected card was the ace of spades and, on the man's instruction, it was inserted back into the body of the pack. He shuffled the cards and then threw them in the air. As the pack hit the ceiling cards cascaded to the floor. Smiling, the man pointed to the ceiling, to which was stuck the ace of spades, then he just said goodnight and walked out. Someone was about to climb onto a table to retrieve the card when it fluttered down on its own accord. Eagerly we examined the card but, to our surprise, it was just an ordinary card that contained no sticky substance or any other abnormality that would account for its adhesion to the ceiling. The more we discussed it and speculated on how the trick had been worked, the more perplexed we became. The whole thing seemed impossible, yet we had all witnessed it.

I also witnessed a bizarre incident. Midweek during the winter months the town centre pubs were usually quiet and unless I encountered someone of interest I would wend my way back to the White Swan to join my father late in the evening. On entering the Swan one night I noticed a girl of about twenty standing at the far end of the bar. I say noticed, but you could hardly miss her; well built, with a mass of blonde hair, she stood out in her bright red plastic coat and white boots. Although her features were attractive in a coarse sort of way there was something sullen about her, or perhaps it was lack of interest, for she neither looked nor spoke to anyone. She was there again the next night, and the night after that. On the third night my father was playing cards. So I stood at the bar. Within a short time a man, who was a regular customer, came in and joined the girl, buying drinks for them both. They exchanged very few words, just drinking in silence. Then she said something, to which he shook his head. Drinking from the glass held in his left hand, his right palm rested down on the bar. The girl picked up a dart from a set lying on the bar and slowly and deliberately pushed the point into his hand. He watched her, apparently unconcerned, and took a swig from his glass. She applied pressure to the dart, but he never spoke or made any attempt to remove his hand. She pressed the dart in further. As if nothing was happening he took another swig of beer. Using some force, the girl pressed the dart deep into the flesh and then left it sticking upright in his hand. With no sign of pain or annoyance he pulled the dart out and laid it on the bar. Thick blood was now trickling out of the wound, which obliged him to wrap a handkerchief around his hand and put it in his pocket. Calmly he said something to her, whereupon they drank up and left together. I was intrigued by the fact that there had been no argument, no raised voices, and no emotion displayed by either of them. With cold deliberation the girl had callously wounded the man, who had allowed her to do it without flinching and without comment. The action by the girl and the reaction of the man seemed abnormal behaviour for which there was no explanation, except perhaps that they had a sado-masochistic relationship. I never saw the girl again.

I was now living at a cracking pace in a strenuous effort to make every minute count in the time remaining to me. Apart from the night life, there were the birds to be cared for, the Cage Bird Society business to be conducted, my job with the County Council, and continued study for the Diploma in Public Administration examination. Perhaps all this activity was also a vain attempt to block out unhappy memories.

Life at the Council was happy enough, but I was reminded how precarious one's position can be. The Council engaged a new typist called Janet. Not only was Janet totally blind, but she also suffered with some disabling disease, a form of rheumatism, that affected the bones in her hands and other joints. The head typist came to me and explained about Janet, asking if I would give her some work. She then brought her to my desk. Janet sat shyly next to me with a little braille machine which punched raised dots onto a reel of paper. I started to dictate a letter slowly and carefully. 'You can go faster', she said. Watching her operate the machine, I slowly increased the speed of dictation until getting into my normal rhythm. We were in a large office with many desks, tables and filing cabinets that would be difficult to negotiate. At the end of the dictation, I put out my arm and, with her hand resting gently upon it, walked her back to the typing room. Conscious of my own uneven gait, I said,

'Sorry I am a bit wobbly'. She gave a light laugh.

'You are a good guide', she assured me. Within an hour my letters were delivered. The layout, spelling and typing were perfect.

Janet did work for other people as well as myself, but I dictated much of my work to her. There were letters, reports to committees and minutes. She was always quick and the work was neat and accurate. Soon, her blindness became irrelevant. She was just a good typist whom I was pleased to have doing my work. But soon the grapevine was carrying news of rumblings of discontent in the typing pool. Some of the work was copy-typing, much of it documents. The girls did not like this because it was boring, and they shared such work out between them. Janet, of course, could not see to do copy-typing, and the girls in the pool were saying that it was unfair that she did not take her share of this work. Gradually the grumbling increased to open hostility. Janet left. Whether she was coerced into going by the management, or whether she left because she could not cope with the unpleasantness of her colleagues, was never clear. I was greatly upset by the affair, for I understood the effort and strain she must have endured even to get to the office, let alone do the work. As far as I was concerned, she was a better and more efficient typist than many of the other girls in the pool. Certainly she was a courageous and determined young lady, who deserved better treatment than she had received. I felt very sorry for her and very angry about the whole business.

Thinking back to the friendship, help and support that I had received from my schoolmates, the understanding shown, and allowances made for me now by my male colleagues, I concluded that the differences between men and women were not restricted to physical make-up but went much deeper. Men sacrificed their lives trying to save wounded comrades on the battlefield. Would women do likewise? In my mind there was some doubt. Women did not seem to have the spirit of comradeship, nor did they understand it in men. Boys, youths, middle-aged men and old men were not separated by age. They were all bound together by a bond of understanding that forged a common empathy. At least, that is how it appeared to me.

But 1954 was drawing to a close and for me ended in another close brush with death. It started innocently enough. Christmas had passed and everyone was looking forward to the big New Year's Eve dance at the Britannia Pier. A new group that I had linked up with had agreed to meet at our favourite rendez-vous, Alfredo's, a coffee bar on Regent Road, near the seafront, at 8.30 p.m. Arriving early, I bought a coffee and sat at a table opposite a blond-haired boy. He was a stranger to me, but he said,

'Would you like some rum in that?' He produced a full bottle of Lemon Hart rum and poured a liberal amount into my cup. We started talking. 'Would you like some more rum?'

'Thanks', I said. 'I'll get some coffee'.

'What do you want coffee for?' he grinned, dividing the bottle between us. Then we all proceeded to the pub across the road for several pints of beer, and eventually reached the dance, where more drinks were consumed in the bar. When the dance ended I was much more drunk than sober. On reaching home in this condition it seemed prudent to make a quiet entry, but I was surprised to hear laughter and revelry, and found a party in full swing. Pat from next door and her mother were there and the room seemed crowded. A big cheer went up as I entered.

'What will you have to drink?' my brother asked.

Without thought, I said 'Rum'. He handed me half a tumbler full. The stage had been reached where involuntary action had taken over, and I swigged it down, sitting on the sofa next to Pat.

'Refill', my brother insisted. Another half-tumblerful went down my throat before I realised it was gin. Shortly after that I passed out.

I remember my brother shouting, my mother coming into the bedroom, and hot coffee being poured down my throat. Vaguely the words, 'He is hardly breathing', and, 'he's as cold as ice', filtered through a vast empty space, like a far-away echo. Once there was a brief awareness of being on my feet, being dragged along, and the sensation of hands massaging my body. When I woke the next day they told me that they had worked on me most of the night, and my brother had wrapped his body around mine in bed to try and keep me warm. I should have been impressed and grateful, but the thought persisted that it would be a good way to go, and perhaps they should just have let Fate take its course.

CHAPTER 10

An Opportunity Lost

In the new year of 1955 there was the usual snow and ice that made walking conditions so difficult for me. Ordinary falls were bad enough, smashing my knees as they hit the ground, but falls on ice were always more violent and unpredictable. Such a fall in early January sprained my ankle, which seemed an unlucky omen for the year ahead. I hated winter, especially the time after Christmas, when not only did the world seem bleak but so did the people in it. The pubs were almost empty, as few people ventured out midweek.

I sat in the bar of the Mitre public house on a cold dreary evening in early February, feeling slightly bored with everything in general, when the door opened and a man and woman came in and stood at the bar. He was a big, macho type, over six feet tall, dressed in a red chequer cowboy shirt. She was just over five feet tall with curly dark brown hair and a plump figure. Perhaps she felt me looking at her, for she turned around. It sounds ridiculous, but something very strange happened. As our eyes met, something passed between us. It was like an electric charge – a violent spark. It was not love at first sight. It was more primitive than that – some sort of strong animal attraction had struck. Without any thought of the consequences I arose from my chair and went over to her.

'Hello. Would you like a drink?' I asked, looking her straight in the eyes. She said she would have a light ale. She had a throaty, rich Irish accent. The man fell back seeming not to know what the situation was, or if he did, not knowing what to do about it. We exchanged a few platitudes, such as 'have not seen you in here before', 'this place is alright, but I usually go to the Yare', and so forth. Eventually the man gathered his wits, drank his beer, and said they were going. She turned as she went out of the door, giving me a radiant smile. Bert, the landlord, said he did not know who she was, but an old chap standing nearby volunteered the information that she lodged at a house just down the row (passageway), and he described the house. On my way home I went past the house and noted its number.

The woman intrigued me. There was something dynamic about her. On impulse I wrote a letter to her, saying that we had met in the Mitre, and asking if she would like to join me for a drink in the front bar of the Duke's Head the next evening at 8.00 p.m. The letter was addressed to 'the girl with the Irish accent'.

To my surprise she walked into the Duke's Head the following evening with a big smile, saying, 'I thought it was you'. From then on we went out together every night. She was vivacious, alive, happy, laughing, party-mad, and even wilder than myself. But above all she was warm, demonstrative and sensual. Her eyes were dynamite. She had the ability to give a strange smouldering look that reached down to my loins and aroused me, just as surely as if she had made physical contact. Her kisses were something special. They fired me to a great passion.

If there were one thing that Julie did not like, it was a quiet life. If nothing were happening, then she made things happen, and the more outrageous they were the better she liked them. We would go into a quiet pub where there might be some old chaps of about seventy, sitting and minding their own business. In a matter of moments, and with incredible audacity, she would be sitting on an old chap's knee and ruffling up his hair. 'Let's dance', she would say. Within minutes all the old chaps would be fighting to dance with her, and everyone would get excited. She would be laughing and the landlord would protest that we would lose him his licence. She would call him a 'miserable owd divil' and we would both be thrown out of the pub. Within weeks we were barred from about a dozen pubs and half a dozen restaurants and cafés. Whatever she wanted to do, I was also game for a laugh. It was all great fun. Dozens of young men were after her all of the time, but she would just laugh them away. In exasperation, a young chap said to me one evening,

'What the hell does she see in you?' I just smiled. What she saw in me was somebody as wild as herself. I was not in love with her in the deep spiritual sense. You cannot love two people like that at the same time, and I was still in love with Rosalie, but a strong physical attraction bound me to her.

After a time I came to realise that she had a split personality. Once in a while, a quiet, educated, sincere, and caring Julie dominated her body. This was an entirely different person from the one who usually manifested as a carefree, bubbly, irresponsible personality. The switch from one to the other was instantaneous. The quiet Julie longed for stability, calm and respectability, whereas the other Julie wanted no restraint and indulged in impulsive gratification. At times her passion was uncontrollable. One night we were crossing the Vauxhall Bridge when she put her arms around me.

'Come on. Now!' she said.

'What – here on the bridge?' I asked incredulously. I managed to steer her to the embankment, under the trees, before, laughing, she pulled me to the ground. It was often like that. She would give me that strange, hungry look in all sorts of public places. We had sex on the back seat of an excursion coach when we parked at Wroxham, and even in a rowing boat in the middle of Ormesby Broad on a Sunday afternoon, when the Broad was crowded with rowers. Once, I nearly asked why she did not pick the middle of the Market Place on market day, but refrained from giving her such a bright idea. And so we frolicked, and drank, and sang through the early spring. I was physically besotted with her.

It must have been the quiet Julie who wanted to get married. We became engaged on the 2nd of April, and I bought her a diamond-studded engagement ring. She wanted to have a church wedding, and

With Julie, Irish eyes smiling as always

dragged me along to see the Roman Catholic priest at St Mary's. We then went to Norwich to arrange the purchase of a new bungalow being built at Drayton, on which I put down a deposit.

When everything seemed to be going so well, one day she said, 'I am frightened for us'.

'What do you mean frightened?' I asked.

'It is too good. It can't last', she said.

'Well of course it will last!' I assured her.

She shook her head miserably, 'You don't know me. I am my own worst enemy'.

'Look', I said, 'if you have wedding nerves, we can postpone it'.

'No, no', she said in a panic-stricken voice, 'I want to get married!' The problem was, which Julie was speaking?

Julie frequently came to my home, sometimes staying overnight, and everything had been pleasant enough, but I sensed that my parents were assessing her against Rosalie, and perhaps finding her lacking in some respect. They never said anything, although my father did ask what I knew about her background. That did bother me slightly, as she would never talk about her past. All I ever knew was that she came from near Dublin, felt strongly about Irish nationalism, had been reared by her aunt and had gone to a Roman Catholic school. My brother, who was never averse to making disparaging comments, seemed well disposed to her, and he and Barbara invited us to visit them for an evening meal.

Albert and Barbara had been married in the spring after a ten-year courtship. Barbara was small, dark and pretty, and all credit is due to her for her persistent patience. The wedding was at St John's Roman Catholic Church in Norwich, and I was 'best man'. I had never seen anyone more nervous than my brother on his wedding day, and so I took him into a large pub opposite the church for a few drinks to try and steady him before the ceremony.

'Am I doing the right thing?' he kept asking me.

'Good God man, you have had ten years to make up your mind', I told him.

As we waited in the front pew, Barbara's many relatives arrived. Each one said 'hello', as they genuflected in front of the altar. It seemed to me that this act of genuflection was an ingrained rite which they performed physically, without the need to engage mentally. Barbara looked radiant, and beautiful, in her white wedding gown as she came down the aisle on her father's arm. At last we stood before the priest. In one hand he held a small prayer book from which he gabbled in Latin, at such a pace that it would have been quite meaningless, even if one had understood the language. In his other hand he held what appeared to be a large whitewash brush, and after each exhortation he dipped the brush into a large brass urn of water and slashed the brush in vigorous strokes in our direction. Heavy sprays of water swept across us. When it ended, I was soaked and poor Barbara was drenched, her sodden wedding gown clinging to her body. She could not have been wetter if he had tipped a pail of water over her head. I could not help thinking that kippers and jam for breakfast was a much more civilised ritual.

I suppose, however well two people know each other, they present a façade, and what is going on in their hearts and minds is often kept hidden. It is, therefore, the seemingly unimportant little 'throw away' words that often provide the clue to their innermost thoughts. On a sunny Sunday afternoon, Julie and I had gone out into the countryside on bicycles and had stopped in a quiet lane to sit on a bank at the roadside. Julie lit a cigarette. We were sitting quietly, when she said, 'You're a mug'. I asked what she meant, but she would not explain.

Something had prompted the remark. Some inner thoughts about me had reached some conclusion and had been given voice. I remembered Rosalie's remark, 'why don't you get yourself a proper job?' That also betrayed a certain line of thought. Those three little words stuck in my mind.

One evening in late June, after seeing to my birds, I washed, changed my clothes and went to call for Julie at her lodgings.

'She isn't home yet', her landlord, a kindly old Jewish man with whom I had become quite friendly, told me. 'I expect she is having to work late'. It was already past 8.30 p.m.

Leaving her lodgings, I met two girls who worked with Julie, and I asked when her shift was likely to finish. They told me that it had finished at 6.00 p.m., and Julie should be home because Sam had given her a lift on his motor-bike. I called at her lodgings at 9.30 p.m. and again at 10.45 p.m., but she had not returned. Determined to see her, I waited all night, sitting on my bicycle, propped against a wall opposite the only door to the house. She did not appear and at 7.00 a.m. I went home to get ready to go to work. Now, perhaps I knew why I was a mug.

At work it seemed a long, endless day, but at last it was evening and with a sick feeling in the pit of my stomach I made my way to Julie's lodgings.

'Where were you last night?' I asked her.

'I had to work late' she replied.

'What time did you get home?' She became sullen.

'What has it to do with you? You don't own me!'

'No, but we are supposed to be engaged to get married', I reminded her.

'Well if you think that stops me doing what I like you had better have your ring back'. She tore the ring off her finger and threw it at my feet. As I picked it up, she said, 'If you must know I was out with Sam on his motor-bike'.

'What all night?' I retorted.

'If you must know, I slept with him!'

'Fine', I said, 'you have him'. I was hurt and disappointed, but it was not the hurt that I suffered when Rosalie got married. I sold the ring and retrieved my deposit on the bungalow.

In July I sat my intermediate examination for the Diploma in Public Administration, taking Principles of English Law, Economics and Civics. I passed.

It was on a Saturday night in August that Julie came into the Mitre with three other girls. She had been drinking. She made a beeline for me and started to use her considerable charms, but as far as I was concerned the special relationship that had existed between us had gone, and I saw her just as a very attractive woman to whom I had no emotional attachment. Neither of us mentioned the past or spoke of Sam. We were living the present, in which she appeared to be more comfortable. When the pub closed, a friend said he was going to a place for the night with a girl. We followed them to a large, dark, house in Howard Street. In a large room, divided into two by screens, we spent the night. We met once or twice during the next few weeks. It always ended in bed. On the last occasion, she said that she was fed up with Yarmouth and was going to Norwich, suggesting that we lived together. Why not? I thought, caring very little one way or the other. She told me that she had found a flat in Unthank Road, once a genteel area of the city, and on the 26th of September we moved in. It was simply the two bedrooms of a house. One room contained a double bed and a wardrobe, the other a table, two chairs, a sofa and an electric cooker. There was shared use of the toilet, and use of the bath by arrangement. It was sparse, characterless and depressing. We had to supply our own linen and necessities. Julie told the woman that we had just got married and, while the woman explained to Julie what was where, I spoke to her husband who was seated in a wheelchair. He was a big, friendly man who had lost both legs, and it was obvious that the rooms were being let to bring in some much needed money. He gave me a knowing look and said, 'You're a good judge of horse flesh'. I let the remark pass without comment. He was indicating that he knew we were not married.

I had taken some holiday leave from the office, and we spent all the time together. But apart from entertaining each other, what was there to do? We spent time in the city centre, but Norwich was large and sprawling, and lacked the vitality of Yarmouth. In Norwich, pubs were places where men drank beer and played darts, and were about as invigorating as a medical clinic. Day by day Julie became more and more restless. It was like watching an injured bird, taken into care and now recovering, straining to return to the wild. At the end of the week she said she did not like Norwich and wanted to return to Yarmouth. Moving to the isolation of Norwich had been a big mistake, and our living together in this dismal accommodation had not worked out. I was glad to get out of the place, and we paid our landlady and left. Julie asked what should be done with the domestic items we had purchased. I told her to keep them. I went home and she returned to her old lodgings. Two days later she told me that she was pregnant and asked whether I was going to marry her. When I asked who was the father of the child, she said, 'you should know'. The trouble was that I did not know. Until recently I had been with her only a few times, whereas she was still running around with Sam. Anyway, I knew that marriage to her would not work. Running wild in her world was alright, but it seemed doubtful whether she could settle down and live happily in my world. If all had gone well, we would have been married in midsummer, and then we might have had a chance of success, but that was an opportunity lost.

'I'll think about it', I said. She walked away. I let her go.

At the end of the week a mutual acquaintance asked me if I knew that Julie had married Sam by special licence. It did not seem to matter to me any more. Women were unreliable and their fickleness no longer surprised me, but I did have to acknowledge that I was developing a talent for losing women to other men.

Women might come and women might go, but there was always the birds. For me they were like a firm rock in the midst of tremendous quicksands. We had another successful show at Yarmouth and, as usual, I went with my father to other shows at Norwich, Lowestoft, Beccles and Dereham. It was at Dereham that we had one of our best days out. We arrived just before midday and after a brief look in the show hall, where judging was still in progress, we went for a drink in a small pub nearby called the Cock Inn.

'Two half pints of "two's", food for two weary travellers, and a drink for yourself', my father said to the landlady.

'I'm sorry, we don't do food,' she said, drawing the beer.

'You must supply food', my father said, good-humouredly and with a broad smile. 'All inns are required by law to supply food to

With our show-winning canaries

travellers, and you're an inn'. She laughed as she went through to the back room. A moment later she reappeared,

'Will cold beef, pickled onions and bread and butter be alright?'

My father said, 'You are a good and beautiful lady. It sounds just right'. She retired to the back. Turning to five or six elderly men peacefully seated nearby, my father said, 'I see that the Duke of Edinburgh has been up here and shot all your pheasants for you'.

It was like tossing a lighted match into a powder-keg. They all got excited, talking about the rights and wrongs of Royalty, the shooting of pheasants, and field sports in general. My father bought them all a drink, including the landlord who had now taken up position behind the bar. Great plates of meat and pickled onions with plenty of bread arrived, and the conversation became more animated. My father bought the whole bar another round, and even the landlord stood a round of drinks. What had been a silent little pub when we entered was now full of talk and laughter. The discussion got round to folk ballads. One old chap sang a little ditty about a ploughboy and his girl. Then my father started to sing. He had a wonderful, mellow, baritone voice, strong and vibrant. The whole pub joined in. People started to crowd into the pub, attracted by the jollifications. By now the beer was flowing freely. A man started to play on an old fiddle. The landlord must have sent for help, for he and his wife were joined by two barmen, and they were all kept busy as the demand for drinks increased. By closing time at 2.30 p.m. everyone was very merry. I felt

133

decidedly squiffy. The landlord asked whether he would see us again and, when my father explained that we were going to the bird show but might call in again for a drink before we left, he said that it was the best time they had had in the pub and, if we came back in the evening, the beer would be free.

I do not remember much about the bird show, spending most of my time trying to sober up. We left the show about 7.00 p.m. and returned to the pub. On entering we were met by a roar of greeting, as if we were long lost friends. The place was already full, and the fiddler had been joined by an accordionist. It was just as if there had been no afternoon interval. In a small town like Dereham, the news must have travelled fast, and there were more people trying to get in than the pub would hold. They were even standing outside the doorway, just to savour the atmosphere within. The last train out to make our connection at Norwich was at 10.00 p.m. With great difficulty, I persuaded my father to leave ten minutes before the train was due. We staggered out, accompanied by everyone in the pub who came to see us off, shouting their appreciation of my father's singing and their goodbyes. Somehow we managed to get on the last train for Yarmouth. When we arrived at Yarmouth we were in a pretty bad state. My brother was waiting for us at the barrier and helped us home, my father hanging on one of his arms and I on the other. All the way home he railed at us.

'What the hell do you think you are doing? There is one of you with only one leg, and the other with no good legs, and what do you do? You go and get yourselves bloody legless'. He went on and on. As I concentrated on walking, I could hear my father laughing.

The autumn brought the Scottish fishing fleet to Yarmouth for the herring fishing. The young Scotsmen were a rough, rowdy bunch, and we kept well clear of them. But a Scottish girl, Marion, turned up at the Mitre one evening in early November. She told me she was secretary to a large fish buyer. She was a big girl with dark wavy hair, a nice clean complexion, and brown dancing eyes. She dressed well, in quiet clothes, and was a happy, outgoing person. After a couple of encounters, it seemed that she had set her sights on me and, sitting with me, she started to get very friendly. The pub was full, and then I saw Julie pushing through the crowd. She grabbed Marion by the arm, dragging her to her feet, shouting,

'He is not yours – get out!' Poor Marion left in a hurry.

I said to Julie, 'What the devil do you think you are doing? I am not married to you. Anyway, where is Sam?' I then saw him coming in the door.

After about a quarter of an hour Julie said, 'We are going over the bridge. You come too, I've got you a "blind".' She pushed a big, plump girl towards me. This girl and I looked at each other with mutual distaste, but we both followed Julie and Sam out and over the bridge to another pub. We had a few more drinks. Sam was outstripping me three to one. Then Julie persuaded Sam to buy a crate of beer and, with that, we all piled into a taxi for their flat in Camperdown near the Wellington Pier.

Within half an hour the girl, who was supposed to be my new girlfriend, was asleep in an armchair and Sam, who had been pouring beer down his throat non-stop, was lying sprawled drunk on the kitchen floor.

'Come on', Julie said, leading me into the bedroom. An hour later the door opened and Sam came staggering into the bedroom towards the bed. I did not move but, as he reached the bed, I took hold of him, still lying on my back, and with my strong arms, heaved him right over the bed. I dressed quickly, went and shook the girl awake, and hurried her from the house. All the way across the ornamental gardens opposite the pier she kept saying,

'Don't hurt me. I'm a virgin'. Virgin be damned, I thought. Fortunately a taxi was stationed at the pier entrance. I paid the driver to drop me in the town centre and to take the girl home. She deserved that, at least, for the part she had played in Julie's daring escapade.

The next day, being Sunday, I went for a drink in the Mitre at lunchtime. Sam came in. I thought to myself, here we go for trouble. But he came to the bar with that idiot grin on his face.

'Hello Derek. What will you have?' he asked. I had a brown ale. He must have been very drunk the previous night. Had it been anyone else I might have felt sorry for them, but he had given no thought to me on the night he had taken Julie off on his motorbike. Perhaps it is true that 'all is fair in love and war'.

Christmas 1955 arrived with the usual family get together. When my father proposed the toast to 'absent friends and loved ones', it was still Rosalie that I was remembering.

CHAPTER 11

The Last Fling

If there had been any thought that a new year might herald a major change of events, this was soon dispelled. During the first week of January the phone on my desk at work rang in the late afternoon. It was Julie. She said that she was in Norwich for the day and could we meet and have a drink, just for old time's sake. When the office closed I met her outside the railway station. We went and had a meal and a few drinks. We did not talk about times past, the future, us or Sam. There was no point in me asking about him as I already knew what an idiot he was. Quite deliberately she played for time until we had missed the last train for Yarmouth. We took a taxi to a small hotel on Riverside Road and we spent the night together. This was her lifestyle. Do what you want today, you can always worry about it tomorrow. After breakfast at the hotel we walked to the station, where I kissed her goodbye before going to work. It was the only time I ever went to the office unshaven. Old Percy, who had a desk next to mine, said, 'You look as if you have been on the tiles all night'. I just smiled. He was nearer the truth than he imagined.

These continued encounters with Julie I knew were madness. She might find excitement in flouting convention with illicit sex, but I yearned for a stable relationship with a woman who loved me. Yet for me her attraction was irresistible. I was like an alcoholic who was occasionally being offered a bottle of whisky. A few days after seeing Julie I was approached by one of her friends.

'You are not being fair', she said, 'Julie will never settle down while you are available. Why can't you keep away and let the marriage have a chance. The baby is coming and will need a stable home'. She was right, of course.

I forsook the Mitre and other popular places, and used the rougher back street pubs where I knew Julie would never find me. Here I fell in with another group, headed by Jack, whom I knew from the Liberal Club days. They were a much harder bunch, and the drinking was now reaching dire proportions, particularly when out with them on Saturday nights. During the week I often drank alone, sadly contemplating the ruins of my life and haunted by the knowledge that my time was running out. Every night I drank myself into a stupor. Strangely enough my work did not suffer. If anything, it improved.

But times were changing. Imperceptibly at first, but gradually I realised that my generation had moved on. The Saturday night parties were no more; the dancing at the Britannia Pier had ended when fire destroyed the dance hall, and the groups of happy pleasure-seekers had dispersed. A more violent, rougher, and younger element was taking their place. Mid-week I found myself among the confirmed bachelor brigade. Aged between thirty and fifty, they were solitary drinkers, standing miserably at the bar like flotsam stranded by the tide of time. Their conversation was limited to last week's football results, who had won the 3.30 p.m. at Ascot races or, at best, the rising price of cigarettes. Wending their way among them were the ladies of pleasure. In general these were a hard-faced bunch of forty-year-olds, but there was one very attractive younger one, who looked pleasant and smartly dressed. I was tempted, but the terrible fear of venereal disease and the barbaric treatment for syphilis was enough to make anyone think twice. The night I saw this smart young lady in the company of a man who, I knew, associated with some of the roughest women in town, I was glad that I had ignored her smile.

In addition to the prostitutes, there were many other older women in town looking for casual sex. One evening in a crowded back-street pub several women, who were in about their mid-forties, sat at a table and one of them kept looking across to where I stood talking to an older man. I assumed that it was him that she was interested in. The route to the bar took me past her table and, on passing, she stopped me with her hand on my arm. She spoke quietly and, with all the noise going on, I thought she said that she fancied my companion and would like to have him in bed.

'I will tell him', I promised with a grin.

'No. Not him. I am talking about you!' Her eyes were penetrating and she sounded serious. She was a tall, raw-boned woman, who wore no make-up and was by no means pretty, but her whole being oozed sexual desire. I could not understand her interest in me but we left the pub together. She wanted to take me home, but I felt uneasy about this. Reason told me that a woman of this age must have a man about somewhere, such as a husband or a lover. Having sex was one thing, being beaten up and robbed was altogether something else, but she was unwilling for an open-air encounter and so I let her go home alone. My instinct had been right. Some weeks later I heard that a man she had taken home had been severely beaten up by her teenage son, thrown down the stairs and had suffered two broken legs. Perhaps I did have a guardian angel, as Aunt Nellie had said.

Although I drank mainly in the back-street pubs, often I took in the high-class places, sometimes switching from cocktail bar to quayside pub, and back again in a matter of minutes. The trick was the old raincoat, and it was like being a chameleon. Immaculately dressed in a black suit, it was possible to blend into the cocktail bar scene with my raincoat carefully folded over my arm. Moving to a rough pub, the raincoat hid my suit and turned me into an acceptably dressed nondescript. To witness the antics of both extremes of the social spectrum, was an entertaining experience. On the whole I preferred the unpretentious warmth of the back-street pub to the pseudo sophistication of the so-called high-class establishments.

My father had now become very concerned about my lifestyle. The drinking was excessive and the pursuit of the nightlife relentless. Once he said, 'Why do you chase after it? A plate of fish and chips would do you more good'.

As I had grown older I saw less of Aunt Nellie. We both realised that many years had passed and our relationship had changed. Uncle Arthur suffered from diabetes and often went into a coma. During the 1953 floods poor Nellie's immaculate home was inundated to a depth of eight feet, and they experienced severe hardship marooned in the upper rooms, with Arthur being without his insulin. In 1956, they sold up and moved to live with Arthur's nephew in Luton. That was another change in my life, for now Aunt Nellie had gone.

At work, life had settled into a steady routine. A woman, whom I will call Josephine to protect her interests, came to work for the Council, but in a different section to my own. Every lunch-time she came to my office for a chat. Josephine spoke with a well-educated accent and was always smartly dressed. Officially, she was thirty-four, although I suspected that her true age was around forty. She told me that she was married to a man well into his sixties, who was useless and a bore. I asked her why she had married a man so much older than herself, and she said that when you are young you do silly things that are later regretted. I could believe that! These lunchtime chats had been going on for a long time when, one day, she confided in me that the following weekend her husband was going away on a business trip, and she was going to take the opportunity to enjoy herself.

'In my situation I have to grab pleasure whenever I can', she said. Apparently, her pleasure was to entertain a boyfriend for the weekend, but she was not sure whether he would be able to make it, as he was married.

'Well, if he cannot make it, I am always free', I joked.

She looked doubtful, but by Friday it had been agreed that I should spend the weekend with her. She lived well out in the countryside and I travelled there on my bicycle with the aid of the mini-motor. Without waste of time we got into bed. She had a marvellous body – all solid flesh – but for me it was a disappointing experience.

If I had not particularly enjoyed it, she obviously had, for from then on we did not chat in the office at lunch-times, but went in her car to a secluded wooded area near the river, where we had sex on the back seat. I felt no emotional attachment to her and was not concerned about other men in her life, one of whom she had hinted was a senior officer in the Council.

Josephine was an astute woman, or gifted with feminine intuition. She once said,

'You have to go with women for sex, but really you don't like women, do you?'

She was right. I did not like women. I did not understand them, and considered them irresponsible, callous, selfish and greedy. Women might be sentimental about their children, but I doubted whether they knew what love was. They used the word, but to them it seemed to mean something different from a man's interpretation. Love, to a woman, appeared to be no more than a feeling of possession, in the same way that a man might love his car. As a car might be replaced with a new model, and immediately forgotten, a woman could exchange one man for another without a care for the former. It seemed a safe bet that by now Rosalie had forgotten that I ever existed.

Sometime in August, I met Julie on the seafront pushing a pram. The baby was a big healthy boy who, she said, had been born in June.

We chatted for a few minutes and I was pleased that she seemed happy.

It must have been about June that I received a letter from Gwen in Retford. In it she said that she now had a baby daughter – Rowena – who was just over a year old. The man concerned had abandoned her and had gone to Canada, and paid no maintenance for the child. She had a small job, but life was very hard. I answered the letter, saying how sorry I was to hear her news and after an exchange of several letters I suggested coming to see her as I needed a break from Yarmouth and had some holiday time due to me.

We held the annual bird show in the Assembly Room at the Town Hall at the end of October, and after dealing with all the paper-work for that event during the weekend, I went by train to Retford. As the train pulled slowly into Retford station late in the afternoon, Gwen came forward even before it had stopped. She wore a brown coat and a round, Russian style, fur hat. Looking down into her smooth face and large brown eyes it was like seeing her for the first time, and I realised how beautiful she was.

We took the bus to the town centre, and soon we were in Bridgegate and climbing the stairs in that big, dark, house. There was Rowena – pale, red-eyed with a streaming cold. She looked at me with the penetrating gaze that only the innocent can undertake without embarrassment. When everything had settled down, I could see that Gwen was not well. There seemed a sort of defeated air about her. Late at night, long after I was in bed, there came the sound of her mangling and washing – nappies no doubt. The next day we had a look around the town, where nothing had changed since I had left it as an eleven-year-old boy. Gwen seemed very nervous and edgy, and the next day became disagreeable. I really did not know what it was all about, and told her that I was going home. At this, she broke down into floods of tears and was full of apologies, saying that she could not help herself because she felt so ill and tense. It was while trying to comfort her and stem those tears that she fell into my arms like a sick child. Things then improved and she told me how she had always loved me, that I was the only man that she wanted, and how she had waited years praying that one day I might come to her. All she wanted was to be with me, love me and take care of me. I explained that now my time was very short and my spinal collapse was due to happen in less than two years, but she said that she still wanted to marry me so that she could enjoy whatever short time we might have together.

So, by the time I left on Sunday we had agreed to marry. I went home via Lincoln and a porter directed me to the Norwich train. It was packed with troops going out to the Suez crisis, and only when Ely appeared on a station signboard did I realise that I was on the wrong train. When I got off, a porter said,

'You were lucky. This was the last stop before Southampton'.

I kicked my heels for hours on the deserted station until the Norwich-bound train arrived. If being on the wrong train was a message from my guardian angel, I failed to recognise it.

In the weeks that followed, Gwen and I exchanged a stream of letters. When I told Josephine that I was getting married, she said urgently,

'Don't do it. You will regret it for the rest of your life'.

I did not tell her that the rest of my life would be no longer than two years.

The immediate problem was to find accommodation, and I thought that it might be best to live in Norwich to be near work. When I told the Cage Bird Society that they would have to find a new secretary in the coming year, one of the members, an estate agent, said that if I would carry on as secretary he would let me have a small house in Yarmouth at a rent of 7/6d per week. The house turned out to be in a small terrace at the far end of Cobholm, and was in a very bad state of decoration and very damp. The whole area had been inundated in the 1953 floods, and salt had permeated the brickwork. Gwen came to stay for a week and saw the house and, although she was not impressed, she agreed that it was the best we could do for the present. A painter and decorator was engaged to decorate the house throughout and, after I had given Gwen some money for urgent necessities for Rowena and herself, bought some basic furniture, such as an electric cooker, a table and chairs, two easy chairs, a bed, wardrobe and some cheap carpeting, I was broke.

Aunt Nellie sent me a canteen of spoons as a wedding present. In reply to the wedding invitation, Aunt Maud wrote to say that she supposed I had got the girl into trouble and was now forced to marry her, and in the circumstances it would not be appropriate for her to accept the invitation. Gwen's mother sent me a letter saying that she was opposed to the marriage, presumably because she was worried about the implications for Rowena. So it was that, on the 20th December 1956, I married Gwen in a short, austere ceremony at the Registrar's Office. It was a wet, cold and dreary day, and my father and brother were the only other persons present. There were no photographs and no confetti. We went back to my parents' house for a meal. No member of Gwen's family had attended and, after the meal, Gwen and I went to our house in Cobholm. One could not have devised a more low-key wedding, for nobody sang and nobody danced. It was less happy than a funeral. A week later, Gwen returned to Retford to collect Rowena and so, by the end of the year, I found myself with a wife and a child. My last fling had come to an end.

Gwen, friend from 1943, and wife from 1956

CHAPTER 12

Double Trouble

The novelty of marriage lasted no more than a couple of weeks. Gwen was not happy with the house, not happy with Yarmouth, and certainly not happy with me. Her outbursts made that abundantly clear. The only bright spot had been the Christmas Eve office pub session in the

Coach and Horses. Mick Buswell was leaving, and we gave him a memorable send off. By the time the pub closed I was blind drunk. I had always thought it was just an expression, and had not realised that there was a level of intoxication where sight was so impaired that one was literally blind. Having imbibed over fourteen pints, I now found myself in a shadow world. I recall a very tall young lady bending down, in what must have been a weird embrace, to give me a Christmas kiss. I remember walking down the hill towards the station, and being puzzled as to why the ground kept coming up to my feet before I actually put them down and, although I could not see him, I was aware of the porter at the barrier laughing and directing me to the open door of a carriage. And that is all I do remember. How I managed to get home is a miracle, as I had to ride an old bicycle through Yarmouth and negotiate some of the worst traffic junctions. It was perhaps fortunate that the mini-motor had been scrapped several weeks earlier. Perhaps it was not the sort of behaviour to inflict on a new bride although by then my finer feelings were blunted. But it was to give Gwen another reason for dissatisfaction and complaint. It was becoming increasingly difficult to placate her, and I sought sanctuary in my bird shed at Alderson Road whenever possible.

The marriage seemed to be a major disaster for both of us. We had been friends, not lovers, and we both had impediments to a happy relationship. My past impinged on the present, and her experience put prejudices in her mind. As I had rightly judged years ago, we were sexually incompatible. I was hot and passionate, she was cold and undemonstrative, believing that sex was only for the purpose of procreation and not for pleasure. By the end of February I was thinking that it was about time to end the marriage. I knew from watching the birds that there was always a period of disagreement when they were first paired for breeding and, although this quickly subsided in most instances, there were always pairs that never resolved their differences and had to be parted. But any thoughts I may have entertained of resuming a bachelor life were soon ended when, to my dismay, Gwen proved to be pregnant.

What money I had left after paying the basic bills went on the purchase of essential items for the home. Behind the house was a long strip of garden, covered in rough grass and weeds. I acquired a spade

143

and dug it over and planted it with vegetables. I was not the grandson of a farm labourer for nothing.

Gwen's mother came to stay when the baby was due, as it was to be born at home. By now she was happy with the close relationship that had developed between Rowena and myself, and noticeably warmed towards me. In the middle of the night Gwen started labour pains, and I sat with her. She cursed me continuously, telling me what a rotten, useless bastard I was. At 7.00 a.m. I fetched the midwife. Gwen's mother said that she could cope and asked me to take Rowena out of the way. We went to see the horses on the marshes. On our return, just after 11.30 a.m., groups of neighbours in the street (they were a very close-knit community who shared each other's every experience) told me that the baby had just been born. As I opened the door to the house, Gwen's mother told me happily that it was a big, 8 lbs, healthy girl. The word 'girl' made my heart sink. It was the fourth of October.

Gwen had said that as I had taken on another man's child she wanted to have one for me. I saw it as just a padlock on the marriage chains. Already I was fully engaged looking after Rowena and doing a lot of household chores. Now I had double trouble with dirty nappies to wash and a small baby to change, bath and feed. The Mitre seemed to be a million light years away on another planet. The Russians had just sent their satellite, called 'Sputnik', into orbit and I suggested that it would be a good name for the baby, but we finally settled for Annette. At the time I wondered what my old science master might be thinking about his assertion that man would never get anything into space.

When all the activity accompanying the arrival of the baby had subsided, I found myself alone with her. A feeling of great remorse swept over me. Sadness for the child and anger with myself for having brought her into such a terrible world where she would, I knew, suffer pain, frustration, disappointment and sorrow. If I could have undone the deed I would have done so. Gwen made it clear that she did not want to go through childbirth again. She need not have worried, for I never again wanted to be responsible for bringing a child into the world.

We went to my parents for Christmas. In the middle of the night Annette was ill with stomach trouble and so I cycled back to Cobholm for her medicine. I opened the door and put on the light. To a depth of three feet, dense white mist filled the ground floor, swirling and eddying in the draught from the door. It explained why newspapers left on a chair overnight were so damp that they would not burn the following morning. At night we could hear the rats in the loft as they ran across the ceiling. One night a rat came down the chimney into our bedroom. A well-aimed boot sent it clambering back up again, and further invasion was prevented by wiring down the chimney flap. I knew that I had to get the family out of this house, and wished that I might have a little more time.

The bad weather at the beginning of 1958 made cycling along the exposed North Quay to the railway station, against gale force winds and driving rain, difficult and exhausting. My father suggested that I should apply to the Department of Health for one of the little three-wheeled cars that they were issuing to the disabled. In response to my application I was summoned to have a medical examination in Norwich. As directed, I stripped naked and lay on the couch. A middle-aged doctor came in and gave me a thorough examination, then said that he would send in my helper. I told him I did not have a helper.

'But how did you get here?' he asked.

'On the bus', I told him. He now looked puzzled.

'Yes, but how did you get from the bus to here?'

'I walked', I said.

'Walked!' He almost shouted the word. 'You can walk?' I nodded. He looked at me as if I had said I could fly. 'Get off the couch' he said. I did so. 'Walk to the door'. I duly walked to the door and back to the couch. He became quite excited. 'Wait there', he ordered. He went away but was soon back accompanied by two other doctors. They both examined me thoroughly. 'Will he ever walk?' the first doctor asked the other two.

'I am afraid not', one said, and the other agreed. The first doctor said triumphantly,

'Walk to the door, Mr Dix'.

I obeyed. There were gasps of 'I don't believe it!' and 'Incredible'. Then they had me on the couch again, and walking again, feeling various parts of my legs as I walked.

'How does he do it?' the first doctor asked. They shook their heads.

One said, 'It is impossible. He doesn't have the muscles to stand, let alone walk'.

'But it *is* possible, because he *does* walk', said the first doctor. They all looked perplexed. As they left one said, 'Must be sheer bloody will-power'. He may have been right because, although I could walk, even when drunk, if something distracted my attention from walking my legs just collapsed under me.

I was allocated an 'invalid tricycle', but unfortunately it was a single-seat vehicle, which was not much help in taking the family out. On seeing the vehicle, one of my colleagues at work said testily that he felt it was unfair that I should have the car free. He could not afford a car and had to walk. He was quite upset about it and kept on and on saying to the assembled group how unfair it was. Usually I let remarks about my disabilities pass without comment, believing that they were made through ignorance, but this persistent tirade began to rile me. In the end I said,

'Look, Gus, let us do a swap. You have the tricycle and I will have your legs'.

I am not sure whether he got the message, but the others understood. When under attack, or being insulted, about my disabilities, I usually smiled, knowing that at any time it could happen to them and, if it did not, but they lived long enough, old age would inevitably bring them to my condition.

By now Grace was at a teachers' training college in London where she met an Iraqi student attending the London School of Economics. At Easter she did not come home for the vacation. Later we learned that they had gone to Gretna Green, where they were married. My parents were devastated, and my father spoke of her as if he were in mourning for a dead child. I could not share his concern. When we are faced with a set of circumstances, we make a decision for better or worse. It is no more than playing a card when the stakes are very high. Grace had played her card in the marriage game, and all I could do was wish her luck. Later she was to have a son and leave England with her husband to settle in Baghdad.

September 1958 arrived. The ten years since Mr Brittain had issued his prediction of my spinal collapse had expired. It could be any time now but, as I told Gwen, my body felt no different.

Later that month, Gwen arrived home from a walk accompanied by a lady she had met. She introduced herself as Cherry, and said that she had come down from London to see to her boat that was being repaired in a nearby boatyard. By profession she was a journalist and, although she could have stayed in a hotel she said that she preferred to stay with a family, which she found to be more interesting. Gwen had agreed to put her up for the night in the small bedroom at the back of the house. Cherry was small, and in her late fifties or early sixties. We sat up most of the night talking over a wide range of subjects. She propounded an interesting theory that there was no such thing as original thought. She explained that on several occasions she had written an article only to discover that, a couple of days before submitting it for publication, an almost identical article had just been published. This meant that two writers had, quite independently, produced the same piece. Such simultaneous knowledge was also true for inventions and scientific discovery. It was, she contended, evidence of a mass consciousness, a linking of minds by telepathy, so that two or more individuals either homed in to a basic conclusion of the group mind, or at least exchanged thoughts with each other. She stayed with us a couple of days.

We did not see Cherry again until just before Christmas, when she knocked on the front door.

'I have a taxi waiting', she said hurriedly to Gwen, 'you were so kind to me that I would like to take both of you out for a drink'. We explained about the children, but she must of course have realised that we could not leave them.

'Well, can I borrow your husband for an hour?' she laughed. Gwen said that she did not mind if I went for a drink, so I went with her in expectation of an interesting conversation. It came as a surprise when she stopped at the Blue House, at that time one of the rougher pubs in town. It was here that the three barmaids, all busty ladies, used to wear low-cut blouses to expose their impressive cleavages, and the boys used to flick sixpenny pieces into them from over the counter. If they believed that the weight of coinage would drag the garments lower, it must have come as something of a disappointment that it never happened. The barmaids encouraged the practice and no doubt made a fortune.

Cherry bought me a brown ale and, as we drank, said, 'After this we will go to the hotel. I have a whip in my bedroom'. My mind reeled at this startling turn of events and, as I searched urgently for words to explain to her that I was not into that sort of kinky sex, or any other form of sex with her, the door opened and an American Staff Sergeant came in with a female companion. They shouted an animated greeting to Cherry, who ran over to them. After a short, excited conversation she hurried back, threw a five pound note onto the counter and said, 'Must go – buy yourself a drink and take a taxi'. Without another word, or a glance back, she left with her friends. I put the money in my pocket, finished my drink and went home. I wondered what sort of life she had led to be running wild at her age. In a way it was quite sad, for it seemed that in a mad whirl to achieve gratification of base instincts, she was not finding deep and lasting satisfaction.

The train fare to Norwich was increasing rapidly, and many people were abandoning the rail service. It would be much cheaper to live in Norwich than to travel. The building societies were offering 90% mortgages on new properties, but this meant saving up for the other 10% plus legal and other costs. The problem was that house prices were rising faster than my savings. In the Norwich suburbs, developers were building hundreds of new bungalows at costs varying between £1350 and £1550. We went to have a look. They were no more than glorified dolls' houses. Just when we had given up hope of finding something better, somebody told me a semi-detached bungalow was for sale on Samson Road at Hellesdon. I went to see it on a beautiful spring day. The silver birch tree in the front garden was just beginning to break into its pale green foliage, and the rear garden was a mass of yellow forsythia and blue aubretia. A winding brick path led beyond the lawn and the flower beds, and away into a long grassy garden. It was in fact two plots, end to end. The bungalow had a small kitchen, but a large lounge with French windows facing south down the garden, a bathroom and toilet, and three large bedrooms. It was ideal. Unfortunately, the price was £1750, and I had just £165 in the bank. I knew it was possible to scrape together another £5 to get a mortgage on a £1700 property, but with the ancillary costs to meet I was stumped. The owner kindly helped me out. 'Pay £1700 for the bungalow and pay me £50 in a year's time', he suggested. The deal was done and we moved in June, 1959.

When Gwen was pregnant with Annette, I had spoken to her doctor about her general state of health and behaviour, which seemed to me to be in question. He had said that it was simply her temperament and he could not change that. But when we moved to Hellesdon I found an old scythe in the garden. A work colleague said that it would be useful to him and he came and collected it. In the office the next day, he asked me whether my wife was getting treatment for her thyroid condition. It seems odd that a doctor could not see what was wrong with my wife, but a non-medical man could make a correct diagnosis as soon as he saw her. Once on the appropriate tablets, Gwen was much better and life became considerably easier.

When we moved we had few possessions and no money. The woman next door asked,

'Did you win the football pools to move here?'

It did not seem a very friendly or kind comment. Unlike them, we had two small children and were living on one income. Once settled in, I decided to tackle the garden. There was about seven inches of top-soil on pure sand and, although the land was easy to work, the soil was very poor. Despite watering, the cabbages that I planted shrivelled in the blistering hot summer that marked our arrival, but at least the land was cleared and dug. An old metal shed in the garden was quickly converted into a chicken house, and a piece of garden enclosed with a high wire-netting fence to accommodate a dozen Light Sussex pullets. Slowly, but surely, I decorated the whole bungalow both inside and out, standing on an old chair to reach high and hang wallpaper. It was difficult and tiring, but I managed it.

Every two or three weeks I went to Yarmouth on a Saturday to see my parents, and usually had a drink with my father at the local pub before returning home. The birds were now in his care.

The old metal chicken shed soon became infested with rats, which I had to trap and kill, so during the winter I built a 12 feet by 8 feet wooden chicken house. Much of the timber was second-hand from a demolition contractor. The floor, made of old floorboards, was raised a foot off the ground on bricks, and the frame was 2 by 2 inches, on

Mum and Dad

was nailed weather boarding. South-facing windows ran the whole length, with one small window at floor level. A pop-hole at each end gave access to two fenced runs, each measuring 50 feet by 25 feet. A bench, two and a half feet deep and three feet off the floor, ran the whole length of the shed, so that the total floor area of the building was available to the birds without being fouled by night droppings. On the bench, three-inch timbers in a double row, and raised six inches, provided ample perching. Each week it simply meant lifting off the perches and shovelling the droppings into old feed bags for transit to the garden. The hardest part was climbing onto the roof to nail on the roofing felt. It was a purpose-built shed and functioned perfectly. I bought fifty day-old Rhode Island Red X Light Sussex chicks, and reared all of them in a home-made incubator kept warm with hot-water bottles. Not only did we have a liberal supply of large fresh eggs, but the chicken manure did wonders for the garden. Apart from potatoes, I grew all the vegetables we needed and there were plenty of greens for the chickens.

In March 1960 I built some canary cages and kept two pairs of my favourite birds – Cinnamon Canaries – in one of the bedrooms. But as numbers increased they were transferred to a small shed in the garden.

Outside of the office, my life was now devoted to the family, the home and the garden, and the night life of Yarmouth was almost forgotten. Apart from a drink with my father on alternate Saturdays I seldom went out. Norwich pubs seemed dismal places. When I asked the boys in the office about which was the liveliest pub, they all agreed that it was the Orford Arms in the centre of the city. On my visit, there were about half a dozen middle-aged men drinking at the bar, and three lads sitting at a table. These lads advised that the roughest pub was the Woolpack off Colegate, but said that I could not go there alone as it was where the heavy men hung out. In fact the Woolpack had a young couple playing darts and two elderly ladies quietly supping stout. Another night I tried the Spread Eagle Tavern, which at one time had been the headquarters of one of the Norwich cage bird societies, and where I had been with my father to several sale shows. Now, at 9.00 p.m., I entered the bar to find six old men sitting separately along the back wall, each with a pint in front of him. The landlady was reading the evening newspaper spread out on the bar. Eventually she looked up in a bored sort of way. I ordered a brown ale. She poured it, took the money without a word, and resumed reading. The men sat looking down, each absorbed in his own thoughts. In the silence, the only sound was the ticking of the clock. I drank my beer and said goodnight. The landlady roused herself to say goodnight as she stifled a yawn, but the men never moved a muscle. It was uncanny. I wondered if my arrival might have interrupted some important discussion. I went back and listened at the door, but the only sound was the ticking of the clock. I did not bother going out again. Norwich night life was about as exciting as a church crypt on a wet Thursday afternoon.

During the winter of 1960-61, I built another chicken shed, this time 20 feet by 10 feet. The floor-boards delivered were thirty feet long, fifteen inches wide and one and a half inches thick. Their weight made it impossible to lift them so, sitting on the ground, I dragged them the forty yards to the shed site. The design of the building was as before, and I reared another fifty hens from day old chicks. If you kept more than twenty hens, you had to register with the Egg Marketing Board and sell them your eggs. This proved to be a massive swindle set up by the Government to protect commercial egg producers. No doubt the last thing that they wanted was for good, large, fresh, free-range eggs to reach the consumer at a reasonable price, and the Board was clearly designed to prevent this happening. All eggs not required for personal consumption had to go to the Board, which paid two pence for a clean, perfect, large egg, and that was half the retail price. Any blemish, however small, such as a stain, or oversized, such as a double-yolked egg, reduced the value to a halfpenny. What one might receive from the Board would not meet the feeding costs. Once the system and purpose of the Board became apparent, it had a deleterious effect on my hens, who almost stopped laying, except for the odd tray of small, stained eggs which went, as a token levy, to the Board for a few pence. I learned another valuable lesson – the interests of business have the ear and support of Government. What they do may be legal within the framework of the law, as they decree it, but within the wider sense of understanding it is just common theft. Those in authority are always bleating about tax-evasion, the dishonesty of the individual citizen, the fall in moral standards and crime, yet they fail to recognise that half the problem is caused because people watch their dishonest antics and copy them, on the principle of 'what is good for the goose is good for the gander'. My father always said that only the dishonest could become rich, and it seemed that he was right.

At work, one of my minor tasks was to service the Smallholdings Committee which controlled the letting of small agricultural units. The Committee was composed of councillors who were all farmers, and the meetings were always held at the Shirehouse in the centre of Norwich on a Saturday morning, commencing at midday. This arrangement was for the members' convenience, as it enabled them to visit the cattle market during the morning, and then attend the meeting while their wives shopped in the city. Unfortunately for me, this ruined my Saturday as they were in no hurry to conclude the business of the meeting, knowing that their wives would be kept occupied until late in the afternoon. It was infuriating having to sit there while they frittered the time away discussing grain prices, fertiliser supplies and their own personal difficulties. There came the day when I wanted to get away early to go to Yarmouth, and I wracked my brains for a means of speeding up the proceedings. The meeting was in a small room and, on entering, I noticed how hot it was with the radiators turned up full. Then I had a good idea. I took the control knobs off all the radiators and removed the handles that opened the windows. When the councillors arrived they complained about the heat, and their futile attempts to open the windows or turn off the heating threw them into great consternation. With their jackets off, shirts unbuttoned, and sleeves rolled up in the sweltering heat, they set about the business of the meeting with determination. By half past twelve they were finished and glad to seek the fresh air outside. It must have been the shortest meeting ever of that Committee, and they were grateful when I assured them that I would sort out the heating problem. By 1.30 p.m. I was fishing happily off the North Beach at Yarmouth, having caught the flood tide.

But they were not a bad bunch of men. Every year the Chairman hired a coach and the whole Committee had a day out, ostensibly to inspect smallholdings, one year in the east of the county and the next year in the west, and I went with them. We did inspect some smallholdings, it is true, but we also spent two hours in a village inn for a cold lunch and a lot of beer. Half an hour into the resumed afternoon tour there were urgent calls for a halt. Eventually the driver found a quiet little lane and stopped. Hurriedly everyone alighted from the coach and, lining up alongside the verge, commenced to relieve themselves into the ditch. It was then that, round the bend fifteen yards away, three or four cows appeared, being driven by a middle-aged lady. Having started to urinate, they could not stop and carried on. 'It has turned out a nice day', the lady said, conversationally, as she passed, as if seeing twenty men lined up peeing into a ditch was just an everyday occurrence. Looking over their shoulders, they agreed with her as they continued to urinate. However ponderous the County Council might be, I found that there was always something to laugh about.

Having visited my parents one Saturday in late September 1961, I was on my way home when fate intervened again. On a whim, a sudden impulse, call it what you will, the thought occurred to me that it would be interesting to visit the Yare Hotel again. It had always been crowded, especially on Saturday nights, being the hub of the town's night life. It came as a surprise to find it virtually empty. The seething throng of boys looking for girls and girls looking for boys, the drinking gangs and the wild bands of party-goers of yesteryear, had all vanished, probably married with families or moved on. The younger set, if there were one, had no doubt established another haunt. Standing at the bar, surveying the desolation of that big room, I was taken unaware when a familiar voice spoke behind me. It was Julie. She looked thin and ill. I bought her a drink. She was very upset, telling me that Sam had left her for another woman and had taken the boy with him. I told her that he could not just take the boy, and asked her what she was doing about it. But all of her old spirit had gone and she seemed defeated. I wondered whether the call of the wild had reached her again and, once more, she was touring the pubs seeking the excitement and adulation of other men. Perhaps Sam had thought that the boy was unsafe with her. Who knows what the situation was? Julie had never been very forthcoming about her life.

'I am fed up', she said, 'perhaps I ought to kill myself'. I wanted to help her, but I was no longer free. We are not masters of our own destiny, but victims of circumstances. In an attempt to ease the tension, I said, jokingly,

'That is a good idea'. We had another drink and chatted for a while, during which she seemed to cheer up. Then she said she was going to get some fish and chips and go home. It was getting late so we said goodbye.

On my next visit to Yarmouth, a fortnight later, a woman stopped me in Northgate Street to ask whether I knew that the Irish girl I used to go around with was dead. I was stunned. She told me that there was an item about it in the local newspaper. Later, I read the paper. The Coroner's report said that Julie had died as a result of a mixture of alcohol and sleeping pills. The verdict was accidental death. My mind went back to all the good times that we had shared, the laughter, the fun, her warmth, vitality and zest for life. Suddenly it had just been snuffed out. I cried for her, for the wild instincts that had marred her happiness, for the life that she might have had, and for the perverseness of nature.

A few weeks after Julie's death I went into the Sceptre pub on South Quay, goodness knows why, as it was not my sort of pub. Only after buying a drink did I see Sam standing at the other end of the bar with a couple of other men. He wore his usual idiotic smile.

'It's alright', he shouted to me, 'I gave her a proper burial'. He laughed, as if he had cracked some huge joke. What was the point of saying anything to him? I drank up and left.

While Julie had been alive I had given little thought to the boy. I supposed he could have been mine, but I was content that he was with his mother. Now, he was very much in my mind. The seeds of guilt had germinated and were beginning to grow.

In the hurly-burly of life there is rarely time to stop and think about what happened yesterday, but after Julie had gone I thought deeply about the sequence of events that, for her, had ended so tragically. No doubt many people had contributed to the circumstances that had led to her death, but I had to recognise that I may well have played some part. In ending our engagement, perhaps I had been self-righteous and harsh, judging her by rigid standards that took no account of the frailty of her character. I had certainly treated her very badly after that time, and now I was sorry.

In the past my concern had always been about how other people were behaving towards me, but now I took a good look at myself, and did not like what I saw. Behind the broad smile and apparent affability lay a cold, hard, calculating personality governed by an inflexible self-discipline geared to selfish attainment. If adversity were supposed to make one a better person, it had not worked for me. I was a man at war with the rest of the human race. Whether it was being parted from my mother as a child and being deprived of affection for so long during my incarceration in hospital, or whether it was the need to concentrate all of my thoughts and energies on protecting myself in what had become a hostile society, I am not sure, but I had little regard for other people. Perhaps the change in attitude was not sudden upon finding myself disabled, but developed gradually with each upset encountered, making me just a bit more emotionally depleted and a little harder.

A quiet drink with Julie and her friend

Necessity made me use people, often just to get through the daily routine of living. Gradually, I had become like a sponge, soaking up kindness, affection and attention, and becoming selfish in the process. Looking back, I realised that I had behaved badly with all of the girls and women that I had encountered, treating them in a cavalier fashion. Even Rosalie I had arrogantly taken for granted. In contact with men, I was probably more at ease, dealing with them on a mind-to-mind basis, devoid of emotional or sexual overtones. But the exercise had been a revelation. I did not like myself. I was sorry for my conduct towards Julie, and the other women in my life, and now viewed many of the things that I did in my wild days with a mixture of regret and shame.

CHAPTER 13

Goodbye and Hello

At work changes were afoot. The Clerk of the Council, H. Oswald Brown, an austere Victorian figure, had retired, and was replaced by Boyce, an ex-naval Commander. Archie Way, the old Chief Clerk, had gone, and so had Mick Buswell. Their positions were filled by Lacey and Cook, two men who had grown up in the general office and who had no experience of our section. On the grounds that it would leave me more time to concentrate on the footpaths survey, Cook took over the Planning Committee from me, but I noticed that he needed an assistant, John, to do the bulk of the donkey work for him. I was relegated to the Western Highways Sub-Committee which had very little work to do.

Boyce was a likeable man, humorous and approachable, but his language was, at times, dreadful. Talking to me one day in his office he used the 'F' word as a noun, verb and adjective, all in one sentence.

'Does my language offend you?' he asked.

'No, sir', I replied, 'I grew up in quayside pubs'. He laughed, no doubt thinking that I was being humorous. Little did he realise that I was simply telling the truth.

The old adage 'no man is a prophet in his own country' could not have been more true than it was in Local Government. If you wanted to advance your career you had to move to a new authority. But opportunities were limited. I did apply for a post of Committee Clerk with the Bury St Edmunds Borough Council, and was short listed with five other candidates. In a pre-interview meeting with the Town Clerk it was explained that there was no other assistant, and the person appointed would be responsible for all committees and sub-committees, which met within a ten day period, some in the evenings, and their minutes would have to be compiled and circulated to the full Council that met a week later. The post also carried responsibility for all the administrative work arising from the functions of the committees. Also, the person appointed would have to do their own typing. For the salary on AP2, it looked to me like slave labour. When the interviews commenced, I told the other candidates that I had decided against the job and was going through the interview only in order to qualify for the out of pocket expenses of attending, which had already been incurred. Everyone laughed and said that they were of the same mind. The first candidate interviewed emerged from the room smiling, saying that he was confident he would not be offered the job because he had professed to be totally ignorant about everything. The next two candidates adopted the same strategy. When my turn came I was somewhat disconcerted to discover that the Deputy Town Clerk, who was on the interviewing panel, was a former officer of the King's Lynn Borough Council in Norfolk, with whom I had been in contact over planning matters for several years, and he knew me well enough to appreciate my true capabilities. The interview went too well for comfort. Finally, the Chairman, a big, heavy-jowled, man, asked if I would accept the post if it were offered. I told that I would want the top of the grade. Suddenly, he looked annoyed.

'Is that an ultimatum?' he thundered.

'Yes', I said.

We all waited half an hour while the panel deliberated, telling each other amusing anecdotes of our experiences in our respective authorities, until the officer in charge came out and announced that he was very sorry, but the panel had decided not to make an appointment. He looked puzzled as we all laughed happily in relief. Later, collecting our expenses from the cashier, he said 'no appointment then? You are the sixth lot that they have interviewed for that job'. We were not surprised. Who would take the post under the terms and conditions they had set?

Sometime later I applied for a similar position with the Kingston-upon-Thames Borough Council. The interview was to be at seven o'clock in the evening. I arrived at lunchtime and had a look around the area. Despite its promising sounding name, I found Kingston to be a dreary, one-road shopping area with dismal Victorian terrace houses behind. To kill time during the afternoon, I went to its small, run-down, cinema and watched an uninspiring naval war film, then had a drink in an austere pub on the main road before making my way to the council offices. If there were other candidates, I did not see them, and it was with amazement that I found myself ushered into the packed Council Chamber. I was to be interviewed by the full Council for a minor administrative post. I thought, 'this is going to cost the ratepayers a lot of money in terms of members' attendance expenses'. So there I sat, alone, facing the entire Council. Had there been a spotlight on me I might well have thought that I was on stage at the London Palladium. The questions were about my local government experience, and generally uninspired. Eventually, a very large, burly, man in his late fifties, rose to his feet. Adopting the stance of prosecuting counsel, he said, in an adversarial tone, 'So you were responsible for the survey of public rights of way in Norfolk'. I agreed. 'Well tell me, why is Norfolk one of the few counties that have not completed the survey?'

I explained that Norfolk was a large rural county and that the Council had relied on the many parish councils to provide the details of rights of way in their area. This information had been difficult to extract from the parish councils and this had delayed progress.

'Why was it difficult to get such simple information from the parishes?' he persisted.

'I suspect', I told him, 'that with many of the parish councillors being landowners, whose land was affected by public rights of way, they were reluctant to co-operate'.

The words were hardly out of my mouth before the whole Council was in uproar. Most fell about shrieking with laughter, and many shouted comments to the man who had asked the question. It seemed obvious that he had some personal involvement with public rights of way, and my remarks had some special significance for the others, who knew what that was. For a moment he glared at me, his eyes bulging in his head, his face purple with rage, then he sat down. I did not get the job. But I knew that when they all laughed. Local government does not like comedians.

The train back to London was empty, and it was raining when I arrived at a deserted station. Outside was a single cab. The last train for Norwich would have already gone, so I asked the cabby to take me to a clean, but modest, hotel. We trundled through the dark, empty, rain-swept streets for a while. Slowing his speed to a crawl, the cabby indicated a shady looking hotel across the street.

'What about that, Guv?' he said, 'They provide a girl as well as a bed'. Remembering my previous visit to London, and knowing how dangerous the place was, I said that my need was for just a bed, and could he find a decent hotel.

'If you are here just for the night, Guv, you might as well enjoy yourself. They will give you a good time', he persisted.

'You mean a good dose of the pox!' I said. 'No thanks. A decent hotel please'.

He then dropped me off at a very large commercial hotel that seemed to have dozens of floors and hundreds of rooms. My room was large, well-furnished, spotlessly clean, and comfortable. I had a good night's sleep and an excellent breakfast, all for thirty shillings. A cab outside the door took me to the station, where I arrived in good time to catch the Norwich train. It had been an interesting experience.

As I had said, the procedure for carrying out the survey of public rights of way was flawed from the beginning by relying on information being supplied by parish councils. In the end I completed the survey only by undertaking my own documentary researches. Needless to say, on publication of the draft maps there were many objections. Hearings of these objections were convened locally, and, with the local county councillor acting as chairman, the various interested parties could state their cases. This involved not only the landowners and parishioners, but bodies such as the Ramblers' Association, British Rail, and the public utilities, gas, water, electricity and telephones. Having arranged a hearing, I had to attend with a solicitor, who made a decision, based on the legal evidence available, as to whether there were sufficient grounds for retaining a path on the map. These hearings were shared between the legal staff so, on a rota basis, I went with the Clerk, Deputy Clerk, Senior Solicitor, Assistant Solicitor and the Junior Solicitor. The interesting thing was that, with the exception of the Junior Solicitor, they all discussed the evidence with me and sought my opinion.

The hearings usually lasted the best part of the day, which meant that we had lunch out. One hearing was near Watton, and on this occasion I was with the Junior Solicitor. There were two hotels facing each other across the main street. One looked a well-kept establishment, but he chose the other, telling me that they did really wonderful meals there. The restaurant area was in converted stables, and looked as run down as the rest of the place. A very elderly waiter in a worn, and stained, black suit came forward to take our order. The solicitor studied the menu carefully, as if he had just been handed a complex legal document. With slow deliberation he ordered a lamb chop, creamed potatoes and cauliflower something or other, to be followed by apple something with cream and coffee. I said that I would have the same, except tea instead of coffee. After some time the meal arrived – a very small, very fatty and very cold lamb chop, a small lump of cold, greyish, potato, and a spillage of something that was supposed to be the cauliflower. It was disgusting, and I was glad the portion was so small. The dessert turned out to be a small piece of apple pie, with a hard crust, and a smudge of cream. The waiter then produced the tea and coffee, and returned, saying, 'Would sir wish for some cheese?' He had a board about nine inches square on which were three small pieces of cheese, each about one inch square. They were dry and wizened. The solicitor studied the board thoughtfully.

'I will try that, please', pointing to what looked like a small cube of candle wax. The waiter smiled benevolently and with a small silver knife, cut a very thin sliver from the cube.

'Biscuits, sir?' The solicitor beamed as if he had been awarded an honours degree, and took two small biscuits from a tiny dish held by the waiter.

Nibbling his little biscuits and miniscule piece of cheese, he said to me, 'I told you that they did wonderful meals here'. I managed to keep a straight face, wondering whether he had perhaps been reared on pig-swill.

But he and I did get one good meal, although it came from a most unlikely source, a Councillor who was a notorious drunk. I had once encountered him at a meeting of the Broads Joint Advisory Planning Committee, held in the afternoon in the Grand Jury Room at the Shirehouse. He was sitting in the middle of the tiered seating at one end of the room. Halfway through the proceedings, while Lady Somerleyton was speaking, he clambered to his feet, with the help of the back of the seat in front of him and, red in the face with drink, shouted, 'It's all fucking rubbish!' Then he collapsed back into his seat and promptly fell asleep, snoring gently. Nobody batted an eyelid, and Lady Somerleyton carried on speaking as if nothing had happened. Now, this same Councillor was to chair a footpath enquiry. He arrived half an hour late and only slightly drunk. Halfway through the morning he asked whether we had made arrangements for lunch and, when we said that we had not, announced,

'You're going to have lunch with me. Boy, go ring my wife and tell her that there will be two more for lunch'.

I did his bidding and, when the hearing finished, we followed him home. It was a lovely house set in lawned gardens. He pointed out the nesting boxes on the trees, and took us to the kennels to see his dogs. Returning to the house, he pulled out a crate of light ale and expertly started to uncap the bottles. By the time I had managed two bottles he had downed six. His wife was tall, dark-haired and attractive, with a wonderful personality, but only about half his age. She put on the table a large dish of roast pheasants and partridges, with Yorkshire pudding and tureens of potatoes, cabbage, cauliflower, peas and carrots, all beautifully cooked. With a white napkin stuffed in his collar, the Councillor asked the Solicitor what he wanted. When he said 'pheasant' the Councillor just spiked a whole pheasant with a carving fork and put it on his plate. Hell fire, I thought, I will never eat a whole pheasant, so I said 'partridge'. The Councillor, not to be outdone, spiked two partridges and put them on my plate. He gobbled away, every few minutes pouring himself another glass of beer. I managed another glass, so as not to be impolite. While we ate, the Councillor talked about shooting, and I told him about the wildfowl on Breydon and my punt. Feeling left out of the conversation, the Solicitor said that where he came from they had ducks.

'What sort of ducks?' the Councillor asked.

Hopelessly out of his depth, the Solicitor said lamely, 'Just ducks'.

'You don't know what you are talking about', the Councillor said and continued his conversation with me. Later, he and his wife waved us farewell at the gate.

'That was one of the best meals I have ever had', I said to the Solicitor as we drove away.

'He is just a rude man', he snarled, white with temper. Two days later I passed the Councillor in the Council car park and said brightly, 'Good morning Councillor.......'. He glared at me as if he had never seen me before in his life, and walked past without a word. Excessive alcohol certainly plays strange tricks with the mind.

The administration of the Western Highways Sub-Committee involved accompanying the Deputy Clerk of the Council to the meetings in King's Lynn every month. On the day of the first meeting, one of my older colleagues said, 'You will need your raincoat'. It was a glorious, sunny, day without a cloud in the sky. When I said that rain was unlikely, they all laughed, explaining that the coat was to put over my head so that I could not see the danger of his fast driving. Walking with the Deputy alongside the office block to his car, the windows were full of grinning faces. I suspected that it had nothing to do with the raincoat gag, but arose from the incongruity of our appearance, for he was over six feet tall, and elegant, while I was a dumpy five feet five.

I liked and had great respect for the Deputy. He was not only well educated, but cultured, polite, considerate, good humoured and charming. When I was an office boy, he was the only man who ever apologised for the late signing of post. The meetings at King's Lynn started at 11 a.m. and were usually over in half an hour. The Deputy would then park on the Quay, arranging with me to leave at 2.30 p.m. This enabled me to have a leisurely look round the market, have a pint in the Queen's Head and lunch at a big restaurant called Ladyman's. The Deputy lunched at the Globe Hotel. He always asked what I had had for lunch, which cost no more than 2s.9d, and compared it to what he said was an inferior meal at The Globe at ten times the price. He did not say so, but I knew that he felt it would be infra dig to eat in common restaurants. The wistful way in which he spoke suggested that, in a way, he was envious of my freedom from the confines of a social class whose code demanded obedience to a complicated set of rules of behaviour. He never mentioned his upbringing, but he seemed quite naïve about ordinary life, once asking me what herring were like, as he had never eaten one because many regarded them as coarse, common, food.

One day, after a footpath hearing, he took me for a drink in a nearby pub, where we were joined by the Estates Manager of British Rail, who had also been at the hearing and, after discussing one of the paths concerned, he asked whether the Deputy would join him for lunch, adding 'without him', meaning me. The Deputy gave him a devastating smile and said, 'I do not think so, I am lunching with Mr Dix'. And so he did, treating me to an expensive salad lunch at a high-class hotel in Blakeney. Good breeding shows itself in men as well as in racehorses. We seldom returned to the office before 4.30 p.m., often taking the pretty route home via Litcham. He would point out the various county seats, and tell me who owned what, and who was related to whom among the county gentry. It was a delightful day out once a month, but it illustrates the leisurely pace of life in the County Council.

This leisurely attitude was endemic in the Council and emanated from historic working conditions, when the office hours were 10 a.m. to 4 p.m. In practice, these were still the work hours of many staff, whose first tasks of the day were to read their newspapers, discuss the previous evening's television programmes or, if it were Monday, to review Norwich City Football Club's recent performance. Week after week my colleagues analysed every move made by their hero, Roy Hollis, who was the captain and centre forward. They did not believe me when I said that he must have improved since I played against him, because then he was no match for me. This had no relevance for them, but for me it was a sad truth.

Usually, I completed my work-load just after 4.00 p.m. and then sat smoking and reading until the office closed. If Percy, who sat in front of me, was also finished, we chatted. This apparently irritated John, Cook's assistant, who sat alongside us. He came in precisely on time each morning, hung his jacket on the back of his chair, and started to write. He kept his head down until lunchtime, and repeated the same performance in the afternoon until closing time. Eventually he could contain himself no longer, saying sarcastically, 'It is all right for those with no work to do'. Smiling at his annoyance, I pointed out that if he used shorthand typists instead of laboriously writing it all out, he could be finished by lunchtime. When he made further remarks, I told him that if I put my mind to it, I could do both his job and mine. Shortly after this he went on leave.

When someone was absent it was customary for other members of staff to deal with any urgent matter that might arise. On this occasion, after completing my own work, I cleared his desk as well. While doing this I noticed two large piles of papers requiring the making of statutory orders: tree and building preservation orders, planning enforcement notices, and so forth. During the fortnight, I cleared these also, so that by the time he returned his desk was empty, except for the telephone. He sat lost with nothing to do. Where were all his papers he demanded to know. All done I told him. He spent the next half hour checking in the filing room. Returning, he asked how it had happened. With a big grin, Percy said, 'Derek did it all, and he was still lighting his pipe by half past four'. We never heard any more caustic comments from him. I had learned another lesson – people who appear to be working hard are not necessarily industrious, it could be that they are just inefficient.

I was eager to advance myself, but it seemed as if fate was against me. When I secured a grade of Clerical II, the union did a pay deal which amalgamated Clerical I and II into a new Clerical I, and I was back on the bottom row. When I achieved APT (Administrative, Professional and Technical) Grade 2, again the Union did a deal to amalgamate APT 1 and 2 into a new API. It was like snakes and ladders.

By early 1963, all the older administrative assistants were on APII, I was on API, and the other assistants on Clerical I. The wages were not bad, but they were not good. Council policy appeared to be many hands on low salaries. It was like being one little cog in a big wheel. There was no way forward. The cost of living was rising and it was becoming difficult to manage on the money I was getting. The crunch came when it was announced that staff were to be regraded. Those on APII went to APIII and those on Clerical I went to API. The effect of this was that everyone in the department was regraded except for me, and the people that I had left behind had caught me up yet again. I went to see the Chief Clerk who explained that it would be tidier to have just two grading levels in the section. When I pointed out that my position in the department had been adversely affected and that there was now no recognition of my qualifications, he said that qualifications were just pieces of paper and meant nothing. Remembering the hours of study, I reminded him that he had urged me to obtain those qualifications to secure promotion. He denied that he had ever suggested that I should study. I was now becoming angry.

'Look, young Derek', he said, 'Mr Boyce thinks highly of your work'. That was the match that lit the fuse.

'I am not young. I am thirty years old, and I have a wife and young family to support', I told him, 'and it is no good me saying to the baker that I think highly of his bread. He will want paying'.

It became obvious that there was no point in arguing further about the matter. For too long I had been drifting in the soft balmy air of a leisurely life in the County Council, and the time had now come for action. Returning to my desk I picked up the Local Government Chronicle, and the first advertisement I saw was for an administrative assistant with a knowledge of Town and Country Planning, with Norwich City Council, grade APIII. My application was posted the same day.

Within a week I joined three other candidates for interview. One was a big, good-looking chap, about my age, from Cornwall. He was very self-assured and it seemed a safe bet that he would get the job, but he returned from his interview saying that he had become embroiled in a disagreement with the Town Clerk about what constituted middle-distance running. Mick Buswell had always advised me not to be too specific about outside interests and, during my interview, I was careful to talk about routine family commitments taking up my spare time. After a short wait, I was called back to the interview room and offered the job. The other candidates, gave me their congratulations, but the man from Cornwall squeezed my hand so tightly that it was bruised for a couple of weeks after. Returning to the County offices I wrote my letter of resignation, giving a month's notice. It brought to an end fourteen years with that Authority. My only regret was that I had not moved sooner.

The Senior Solicitor told me with a smile, 'You will soon go through the experience of feeling like a ghost'.

He was right. Day by day, and little by little, my responsibilities and work were handed to other people. Work matters were no longer discussed with me and, within a week or two, it became clear that although physically present I was no longer part of the office and, although friendly on a personal basis, my colleagues no longer saw me as one of them. Drifting aimlessly about the office with no involvement, I did indeed feel like a disembodied spirit.

The Senior Solicitor was a Welshman. He was an unusual man whom I liked and respected. More scholar than solicitor, he was the only person I knew who could read the old Quarter Session records of the early sixteenth century. He once read to me the transcript of the witchcraft trials in Yarmouth. When he first arrived, I had taken a set of minutes to him for approval and he had just flicked the pages over before signing, apparently without reading them. But the next time I presented him with minutes he again flicked through the pages, but this time he handed them back saying that there was a spelling mistake on line eleven of page three. I felt that there was something unusual about him when I saw him reading a book while we were waiting for a meeting to start and noticed that he was just slowly turning the pages. Later, when I asked him about this, he explained that it was rapid sight reading. As children at first have to break a word down to read it, but later recognise a whole word, so, by the same process, it was possible to take in a whole sentence at a glance, then a whole paragraph, and finally a whole page. I practised the method and eventually learned to read short paragraphs, but never managed to digest a whole page. However, this was not his only accomplishment. He must also have had a photographic memory. I once encountered a very tricky legal problem involving rights of way interrupted by watercourses, with the complication of manorial rights and drainage responsibilities. When I went to seek his help he was reading. Quickly I gave him a snapshot view of the problem. He paused very briefly and then said something like, 'You will find two cases in the All England Law Reports, volume eleven, page two hundred and twenty-two, Rex v. Smith, and volume twenty-one page three hundred and ninety-four, Saunders v. Greene'. He resumed reading. He was absolutely correct. I wondered whether Cullingford at school might also have had such a similar gift that gave him total recall of whatever he had read.

The day came when I walked out of the County Offices for good. Truly it was the end of an era. In the space of two days it was goodbye County Council, hello City Hall.

CHAPTER 14

City Hall

If the County Council had been overstaffed and leisurely, the City Council was the complete reverse. The Town Clerk was a small, dynamic man, who walked briskly to the office, ran up two flights of stairs, was at his desk before the office opened, conducted business at a cracking pace all day and seldom left until well after the office officially closed. He expected each member of his staff to do likewise.

The Town Clerk's department occupied most of the second floor of City Hall and my office was just to the left of the main entrance looking out over the market place, with the ancient flint-faced Guildhall to the left and St Peter Mancroft Church to the right. On my arrival, I was greeted by my typist, Margaret, an intelligent-looking young lady, wearing a sombre tweed skirt, brown cardigan, flat shoes and no make-up. The Chief Clerk then conducted me around the building introducing me to everyone, so that by the time we returned to my office I had a bewildering impression of faces, the names of which escaped me.

The Chief Clerk told me that in addition to the Planning Committee, I would also be responsible for the Finance Committee and the Property Committee. As he was leaving the room he paused to add, 'And by the way, you have a Finance Budget Committee this afternoon at 2.30 p.m. Don't worry, Tommy will go with you.'

The set up was that each Administrative Assistant was solely responsible for his own Committees, so there was no liaison between Admin Assistants, which meant that no one took messages or did your work if you were absent. Left alone with Margaret, she told me that the three filing cabinets in the room were mine and she would do my filing. I looked at some of the papers on the desk, many of them were forms, the like of which I had never seen before. I asked her if she knew what they were. She said she did not, because my predecessor had never discussed work with her. Searching for clues, I opened a draw in the filing cabinet. It was empty. All the draws were empty.

'Where are the files?' I asked Margaret.

She said that my predecessor had destroyed them all when he left! I went into a cold sweat, as fear and anxiety gripped me. No files meant no precedents to guide me. I was in a strange situation, with a mass of unfamiliar work and nobody to advise me. The Chief Clerk had mentioned how he and my predecessor had been good friends. I wondered about that. Admin men rely on records and their care and maintenance are instinctive. If this man had gone to all the trouble to destroy the whole system it could only mean that either he had something to hide or was carrying out an act of revenge.

At 2.30 p.m. Tommy Thompson took me along to one of the Committee Rooms on the first floor. Members of the Council sat on one side of the table and the Officers sat facing them. Tommy drew me a plan, indicating the names of everyone there. After a few minutes he said, 'Are you alright?'

I said, 'Yes', whereupon he got up and left. The meeting went on all afternoon. Most of what was being said was in financial jargon that I did not understand but I took notes, as best I could.

Returning to my office, my head ached from the whirl of unintelligible things I had heard and my pages and pages of notes looked like gibberish. I found the previous year's budget finance meeting in the Minute Book and took it home with my notes. By the early hours of the following morning I had compiled something, even though I did not know what it meant. After Margaret had typed it up, I asked Tommy about who was the friendliest man in the Treasurer's Department. He gave me a name and I went to see this officer, explained my difficulties and pleaded for his help. He was very kind. Not only did he lick my minutes into shape but explained to me in simple terms what it was all about.

With the Planning Committee I was on familiar ground, and soon adopted to the new style. The Property Committee was hectic. The Council, heavily Labour controlled, was attempting to do its own 'Nationalisation' and was seeking to purchase every city centre property that came onto the market.

There were numerous Sub-Committees to arrange and clerk and their minutes had to be dovetailed into the schedule of the main Committees. In turn, the main Committees minutes had to be ready for the monthly full Council meeting. In addition, items of special importance had to be accompanied by a comprehensive report setting out every minute detail relevant to the subject and the Committee's reasoning leading to their recommendations with, where appropriate, a full financial appraisal appended to the report.

All minutes and reports in draft were circulated to the Chief Clerk, the solicitor involved, the Deputy Town Clerk and finally the Town Clerk. Each made their alterations in different coloured ink. I often found it amusing that after the first three had made alterations, the Town Clerk would change it all back to my original text.

When everything was approved, Margaret had to cut foolscap stencils for printing. She was fantastic, being very fast at shorthand, very fast at typing, had perfect layout and was totally accurate. Without her calm, quiet, efficient presence, I would have gone under. As it was, the volume and complexity of the work demanded my all, so that sometimes I worked through the lunch hour without realising the time. I took work home and struggled with it until late at night, and kept a notepad and pencil by the bed. In the morning, the pad would have cryptic messages on it that I had jotted down during the night. I never remembered writing these nocturnal notes and it was as if my sub-conscious worked while the body slept.

Gradually it became like a crazy nightmare world, where my brain was totally absorbed in wrestling with the work problems and I became oblivious to everything else, relying on Gwen to look after my birds, the garden and the chickens, whose number I had fortunately reduced. Within six months I was mentally exhausted and when I took some annual leave in late August I knew I was ill. Away from the office there was time to think about myself. It was clear that this pace could not continue or there would be serious consequences and I resolved to ease up, even if everything went up the wall and they sacked me.

But my big effort had cracked the problem, so that on my return to work I discovered that I was no longer a drowning man fighting to reach the surface but was at last able to see about me. There was still the swimming to be done to keep afloat but there is a big difference between swimming and drowning.

By the end of the year the Chief Clerk told me that the Town Clerk was very pleased with my work and was regrading my post to AP4.

Soon after my arrival at City Hall the Chief Clerk had told me that there were two big social events in the department's calendar. One was the office party, held around about Christmas, which was always a 'big do' and the other was a social evening with the police. The latter came first, during the summer. It was a male only occasion held in the police canteen, which formed part of the City Hall complex. We duly assembled about 7.45 p.m. and immediately I became aware of a very sombre atmosphere for what was supposed to be a social occasion. There were no smiles or friendly greetings. A huddle of burly policemen stood at one end of the bar and their representatives stepped forward to suggest that we pick teams to play against them at snooker and darts. In a brooding silence we solemnly played the respective matches. The police kept together and watched us suspiciously. All attempts at friendly, social, conversation were met with an impassive brief response. Just after 10.15 p.m. the overall results of the snooker and darts matches were announced. A police spokesman said what a splendid evening it had been, which he felt sure had been enjoyed by everyone. We all wished each other goodnight and we left.

The much-heralded office party took place just after Christmas at a hotel in the city centre. It was held in a large room, about the size of a small dance hall, with a large private bar attached. With just thirty of us present we were small islands in an ocean of open space. The Town Clerk, Deputy Town Clerk and the two solicitors took up a position at the bar, where they spent most of the evening talking shop. The nine typists stood in a group at one side of this vast hall, the administrative and legal assistants stood about awkwardly, holding a glass of orange squash and wondering what to do next. The three little office girls sat in a row on the opposite side of the hall to the typists and looked very isolated. As nobody else seemed to include them into their groups, I went and joined them. There was considerable relief when the Town Clerk came into the hall to welcome everyone and the cloths covering the sandwiches, sausage rolls, cakes, jelly and blancmange were removed. At least now there was some positive activity, even if it was only the sampling of food and making appropriate comments about its quality. Eventually somebody succeeded in getting the record player to work and the Town Clerk danced with two or three of the typists. One or two other couples took to the floor, but the dancing soon petered out and the Town Clerk, with his legal cohorts, retired to the bar again. In deference to the Town Clerk's strictly teetotal views, everyone restricted themselves to soft drinks but, in the security of the shadowy outer edge of the hall and while the dancing was in progress, I managed to fill up the little office girls with gin and Babychams. Soon they were very merry. Their shrieks of laughter attracted the attention of the younger male officers who came to join us, but our unseemly behaviour kept everyone else at bay.

At about 9.45 p.m. the word went round that it was snowing heavily and, with the prospect of a difficult journey home, the party was brought to an early conclusion.

An office party is always a dubious enterprise but, for a small department, with a tiered structure in which everyone is conscious of their position, the expectation that a strict code of conduct within the defined pecking order can be abandoned for a few hours each year, fails to understand the differing perspectives of senior, middle and junior staff. Only wild mavericks, who belong nowhere, can run free on such occasions. If I had a jaundiced view of the proceedings it was probably because I was comparing them with the licentious activities of Saturday night parties in my wild days.

When the elections were held, the assistant organising them said that he would like me to be a presiding officer. 'To make it easy for you', he said, 'you can have the polling station at the Guildhall, just across the road. There are only eleven hundred on the register.'

Polling day arrived and with the help of a polling clerk, I opened the door of the Guildhall at 7 a.m. Until about 10 a.m. it was very quiet with just a few voters coming in. Then a woman, who wore a uniform and looked like some sort of nurse, arrived with two elderly ladies, both in fur coats. She tried to explain to them what to do. They told her off in an imperious way and, after much hassle, we finally managed to elicit their names and issue ballot papers. One took hers and went into the polling booth, the other made a beeline for the door. The nurse caught up with her and another big argument ensued, during which she said that she did not have to put it in the ballot box. In fact, she might decide to eat it. While this fracas was in progress, the other lady left the polling booth and walked briskly over to one of the radiators against the wall and attempted to push her ballot paper through the grill in the top of the radiator guard. I reached her just before the ballot paper disappeared. When they left we heaved a sigh of relief but a quarter of an hour later the nurse returned with two more ladies.

'Name please?' the poll clerk asked.

'Trixie.'

'Your full name please?'

'Just Trixie.'

'Her name is Teresa Mondale-Williams,' the nurse said.

Turning to the nurse the lady said, 'You mind your own business, I am talking to the girl.'

By both myself and the poll clerk positioning ourselves each side of the booth and pointing out the ballot box in the centre of the room, we managed to prevent any more radiator postings. So it went on throughout the day, the nurse arriving every fifteen minutes or so with two more ladies. In all we had two further attempts to post in the radiators. Three said they had put their vote in the box but did not do so. One tore up her ballot paper into tiny pieces and scattered them on the floor and one put something in the box and then handed me the remains of her ballot paper. She had neatly torn off the candidate she wished to vote for and posted that section. Gently, I told her that her chosen candidate would not be happy unless she put the other pieces in the box. She gave me a charming smile and put them in the box.

At the close of poll I returned the ballot box and documents to City Hall and was greeted by roars of laughter.

'How did you get on with the ladies from the nursing home?'

'How many votes did they stuff into the radiators?' More laughter rocked them. I uttered a few, well-chosen expletives.

'Don't worry Derek, we won't send you there again. We always give the newcomer the Guildhall.'

Although the invalid car was a boon to me, it did nothing for Gwen and the children stuck out in the suburbs, and it seemed imperative to buy a car now that I could afford one. So, during the spring of 1964, on the advice of a colleague, I went to a garage on Constitution Road and settled for a Mk1 Ford Consul at £200. It seemed huge. It was another month before the hand controls were fitted. Learning to drive was going to be a problem. Fortunately, my old colleagues from the County Council kindly rallied round and, between four of them, accompanied me every evening. Cruising was easy enough. A hand bar just under the steering wheel gave acceleration by squeezing, and braking by pushing down. It was the clutch control that proved the obstacle, seeming to require the use of a third hand. In the end, my left foot proved capable of operating the normal clutch pedal and, with the column gear lever, changing gear became easy. The one remaining problem was the three-point turn on narrow residential roads, where the car kept rolling off the road camber into the kerb. I came home every night with my shirt soaked in perspiration from the concentration and effort. At last one of the boys solved the problem, that being to apply the handbrake at the end of each manoeuvre to leave a hand free to change gear.

My driving test was at 12.30 p.m. Everything went fine until coming down St Giles and the steep hill at the side of the Guildhall. A large furniture van stopped, as I thought held up by the traffic lights at the bottom of the hill. In fact, he had stopped at a shop to unload furniture. I had to back up the hill to get sufficient space to go around him. 'That has blown it,' I thought. So for the rest of the journey I just drove normally, weaving in and out of the many cyclists going home to lunch. When we arrived back at the test centre the examiner said,

'Well you can certainly drive!' He wrote out my pass certificate.

Now I was able to take the family out. We went to Yarmouth, often to the beach, and toured most of Norfolk and Suffolk. Later I took them to Retford to stay with their grandparents. I got on well with Gwen's father. We spent hours sitting in his 'office' smoking, drinking whisky and talking.

It must have been about 1965 that I fell out with the press. There was a Senior Reporter on the local paper who specialised in local government affairs and it seemed sensible to keep him abreast of major Council schemes so that by the time they came to fruition he would have a precise understanding of the issues involved. This enabled him to give a comprehensive and well-balanced report and ensured that the Council had full and accurate reporting of their proposals. He never jumped the gun and the system worked well. As with most things in life, it is the little, unexpected events that cause the most trouble. So it was in this case. The Council were appointing a City Planning Officer. The reporter telephoned me.

'How many applications have you received?' he wanted to know. It seemed an unusual request and, as personnel matters were sensitive, I asked why he wanted to know. 'You have not received any then?' he queried.

'Don't be daft, of course we have,' I said, still wondering what it was all about.

'So you are inundated with applications?' he persisted.

'No. We have received the usual number of applications that you expect for this type of position. Anyway it is not of public interest is it? You are not going to publish anything are you?'

'Oh no, we were just wondering,' he said.

That night the *Evening News* carried a banner headline, saying that, while the Council had received some applications for the post of City Planning Officer, they had not exactly been inundated by applications. The facts were true but the slant was an innuendo that the post had not attracted much interest.

By nine o'clock the next morning the Leader of the Council was on the phone, blowing steam. I explained exactly what had happened. Within minutes the Town Clerk asked me to see him and told me several Members of the Council had contacted him to complain. I went through it all again. He then spoke to the Leader of the Council briefly.

'It's all right,' he said, 'he says that you are not the only one to be tricked by the press but be more careful in future.' I rang the reporter and expressed my feelings on the subject.

'Sorry, it was my editor who insisted,' he said lamely. Whenever I hear people saying to press men 'no comment', they have my sympathy. The press do themselves harm in the long run by breach of trust for a short term gain.

I did not particularly like the new City Planning Officer as a man, and he appeared to have reciprocal feelings about me. As a planner he was brilliant and I greatly admired his work. He persuaded the Council that they should not destroy the historic old city to accommodate the motor car, propounding the theory that more roads just meant more cars. In fact he advocated that congestion in the city would force people not to bring their cars into the city but seek other means of transport. Just before pedestrianisation of town centre streets became fashionable, we had already carried out such a scheme on London Street, a narrow, winding street leading off the Market Place. It happened almost by accident. A collapsed sewer resulted in the closure of the road to vehicular traffic for several months and, despite the shopkeepers' initial fears of losing business, more people took the opportunity to shop in a street devoid of traffic and their sales increased. Consequently they welcomed the proposal to make the street for pedestrians only and the scheme was put into effect without any objection.

However, he did not always win. With the city expanding rapidly, like additional skins growing on an onion, both the City Council and the County Council, whose area was being invaded, decided on a joint exercise to try and establish the best rationale to plan for growth, without creating just a dense and expanding residential belt around the city. The City and County Planning Officers were commissioned to produce a report. In due course they produced a large glossy document, foolscap size and an inch and a half thick. It seemed as if all the Town Planners went to the same institute and were all taught the same pro forma for producing reports, for they all followed the same format. First there would be a section spelling out where the place was and its salient features, as if local people did not know this already, then the problem would be set out at large, followed by all the 'ifs and buts', concluding with a recommendation that further research would be needed to examine the issues raised in the report. The report on Norwich was no exception. The Chairmen of the City and County Planning Committees, together with the two Planning Officers and the Clerks of both authorities, met in the Town Clerk's office to consider the report. I was there to make a record of the proceedings.

The Town Clerk's office was a large, square room. At one end was his desk with a wastepaper basket at its side and at the other end was a small conference table at which we all sat. The meeting started quietly enough with the Chairman of the City Planning Committee welcoming everyone to the meeting and thanking the Planning Officers for the speed with which they had produced their report. Before anyone could speak, my old boss, Boyce, from the County, held up his copy of the weighty report and said,

'This tells us nothing. We all know the problem but it offers no solution. It is a load of fucking rubbish!'

And with that he heaved the report high into the air. It curved in a graceful arc right across the room and landed with a thud in the Town Clerk's wastepaper basket at the other end of the room. It was a beautiful shot and had a dramatic effect. There was a moment of shocked silence. Then the two Planning Officers, red in the face with anger and embarrassment, started spluttering their protests. The elected Members looked uneasy. Boyce looked at me with a merry twinkle in his eye and I did my best to contain my mirth. For a moment or two there was pandemonium but the Chairmen mumbled their agreement that the report did not reach any conclusions that they could discuss. As the meeting broke up in some disorder, the two Planning Officers beat a hasty retreat for the door, with Boyce shouting after them,

'You two had better get something bloody sorted.'

As far as I know that was the end of the project. Going down the corridor, Boyce caught me up.

'Happy here Dix?' he asked affably. I replied in the affirmative. 'Good,' he said with a big smile and strode off leaving clouds of pipe smoke in his wake. I wondered what on earth I could put on paper to summarise that meeting.

If Planning Officers made mistakes, so did Planning Committees. There was the classic case of H.M. Stationery Office who proposed moving to Norwich. For their new complex they proposed to redevelop an old part of the city slap across the ancient thoroughfare of St Augustine's. Quite separate from the planning impact of any development on this site, the design of the buildings and materials of construction were hideous. The Architects' Panel, composed of representatives from all the firms of architects in the city, who considered all planning applications and gave the Planning Committee their views, were scathing in their comments. I conveyed their comments forcibly to the Committee and the planners vehemently opposed the scheme also. But then the hoary old argument about bringing jobs to the city was brought to bear and permission was granted. Only when the buildings were erected did the Committee appreciate, too late, the mistake they had made. The northern part of the historic city had been destroyed and supplanted by this grotesque monstrosity. Members ranted and wailed. The Chairman said,

'We should have listened to Mr Dix, he pleaded on his knees for us not to allow it.'

In an attempt to relieve the tension of work I thought it might help to engage in some new activity and so I signed up for a course of evening classes on 'Painting for Pleasure', which was designed to be an introduction to oil-painting. The class comprised one young man, several women in their thirties and the remainder were elderly couples. In all there were over twenty of us. The tutor gave us some general advice about the application of oil colours and set us a piece to paint each week. They were not a very sociable group and apart from saying good evening on arrival and good night on departure, they studiously avoided any sociable conversation. The only occasion when there was any sense of community and discussion occurred late in the year when the tutor said that he thought we were all ready for a 'live study' and, if we would all chip in two shillings each, he would engage a professional model for the next session. The following week everyone was agog with excitement, speculating on whether the model would be a male or a female. The thought of a nude male put the young women into a spate of nervous giggling and the possibility of a nude female aroused the men to a state of animated expectation.

At last the tutor arrived with the model, a dear, plump little lady aged about seventy. Fully clothed, she sat on a chair for two twenty-minute sessions and a final ten-minute period. She really was a professional, for her pose was consistent and she moved not a muscle. She could have been carved out of stone. That evening I had taken a large canvas with me and I painted a full length portrait, portraying her exact likeness in the traditional manner. As we neared the end of the session she came around to look at everyone's work and, as we were about to leave, she asked if she could borrow my painting to show to her grandchildren. I was pleased to give the picture to her. At one of the last sessions of the course I arrived late. The subject was a large shallow dish of fresh herring and from the outer fringe of the group I could barely see them. I was tired, not in the mood for painting and did a slapdash job. The tutor looked pleased and said he thought it was the best picture I had painted. Clearly he was in the avant-garde brigade and interpreted bad workmanship as an exciting new surrealist form of expression. I did not propose to go down the route of degenerate art, mindful that during the whole year I had never seen the tutor with a paintbrush in his hand.

I felt that in this group I was the odd man out and so did not sign on for the following year. But I was keen to advance my painting and studied on my own. At one stage I attempted a large nude study of Gwen and, to discover the painting of flesh techniques of the Old Masters, I visited the library. Coming out of the library with an armful of books I met the Town Clerk. 'You are going to be busy,' he said pleasantly. He opened the top book which was full of nude figures and quickly proceeded to the second book, which also depicted naked bodies. He looked shocked and made a quick retreat. The next day the Chief Clerk asked me what I had been up to as the Town Clerk had asked him whether he thought I was sexually perverted.

For me, City Hall was all work. Many days there was no time to speak to anyone, except about business matters. When occasionally I met colleagues in the corridor it was surprising to learn what was going on. Everyone seemed to be having an affair with someone. One senior officer, well into his fifties, had thrown the job and absconded with his twenty-year-old secretary. Another colleague, also over fifty, confided in me about his miserable married life and told me he had often had his girlfriend visit him. He explained, with great glee, that he had a key to the public gallery of the Council Chamber and when she visited he took her there for sex. When I suggested to him that it was a risky undertaking, bearing in mind that the Town Clerk was a deeply religious man with firm views on family life and due decorum, he laughed. There was just one occasion, he said, when in the middle of their intercourse, the Lord Mayor had come into the Council Chamber to show it to a visiting party of foreign students.

'What did you do?' I asked him, visualising the drama of the incident.

'Well, we pulled ourselves together pretty quick and I called out good morning to the Lord Mayor, saying that we were both on the same errand, as I was also showing a visitor the Council Chamber.' He again laughed with glee at the memory of the occasion. It seemed incredible. He did not look like a man to indulge in such a wild venture but, sometime later, I actually saw him going into the public gallery with a very staid-looking woman of about forty, who was, no doubt, his lady friend.

I found trouble without looking for it. This time it was another election. True to their promise that the Guildhall venue was a once-only experience, the electoral team assigned me a polling station at a school on Colman Road. There were well over two thousand on the register and we were kept busy. In the middle of the afternoon an elderly lady came in to vote and then asked if she could have a ballot paper for her husband, who was outside in a wheelchair and could not get up the two steep steps. Through the open door he was visible sitting at the bottom of the steps. With one of the two polling clerks, I took the register to the door and went through the standard procedures to issue a ballot paper to him. He took the paper and voted. He handed me the folded ballot paper and, keeping it in his sight, I took the ballot box and dropped it in. He and his wife said 'Thank you,' and went. I thought no more about it but by 9.30 a.m. the next morning the Chief Clerk came to tell me that a delegation from the Labour Party were closeted with the Town Clerk, complaining bitterly about the illegal action I had taken in giving a vote to somebody outside the station. I told the Chief Clerk the situation and suggested that, as the polling station embraced the entrance as well as the hall, the whole complex was the 'polling station' and, as Presiding Officer, it was within my discretion to determine precisely where in the station I wished to issue ballot papers. There was nothing in the rules requiring a voter to use a polling booth to mark their paper, nor prohibiting the presiding officer from touching the paper after the vote had been marked. For example, if an elderly, infirm person had dropped their paper on the floor accidentally, there was no reason why polling staff could not pick it up for them. People often put ballot papers in the box without pushing them right through the slot and there was nothing to prevent polling staff pushing the paper to clear the slot. There had been no breach of secrecy, no breach of the rules on election procedure, so what was the complaint? The Chief Clerk said it all arose because the man in the wheelchair was a Conservative. I just laughed, saying,

'How the hell do they know that? After handling the ballot paper, even I do not know how he voted. Anyway, what is the point of their complaint, their candidate won with a comfortable majority, didn't he?'

The Chief Clerk must have relayed all this to the Town Clerk for I heard no more about it. But the incident illustrates the pettiness of local politics. It reminded me of the fact that despite long discussions on politics and current affairs with my father, over many years, I never discovered his political allegiance, if he ever had one. In my time I have been variously accused of being a right wing fascist and a left wing communist. The fact is that I am neutral, believing just in good ideas and common sense. A good idea is a good idea whoever proposes it. In my view, party dogma produces a blinkered approach to problem-solving.

With the passing years the next generation were growing up and I watched them with great interest. Grace came home for a holiday with her eldest son, Talib, who was about six years old. When I announced my intention of visiting a shop to buy some fishing tackle he pleaded to accompany me. Knowing what an excitable little boy he was, I was uncertain about my ability to control him and asked whether he would be good. 'Oh, yes, very good, very, very good,' he said, bouncing up and down with excitement at the prospect of coming with me. Just before we entered the small shop, that I knew was packed with gear, I warned him again that he had to be quiet and well behaved. He looked appropriately subdued. By the time I had traversed the three or four paces to the counter there was a crash behind me and I turned to see him with a bunch of eight-ounce spiked lead weights in one hand and reaching up to a high shelf for more. After replacing the articles to the shelf I took him firmly by the arm to the counter, only to discover that he was now reaching out with what seemed to be three arms and five hands, grabbing packets of traces and opening them with amazing speed. Taking these from him and putting them back on the rack, my attention was attracted by the shouts of the shopkeeper. To my horror I discovered that Talib was now entangled in one hundred yards of nylon fishing line. To placate the shopkeeper I bought the tangled mess, and was able to order my other items only by wrapping both my arms round the wriggling, squirming, little Talib. On the way home he smiled disarmingly at me and said,

'You see, I was a good boy, Uncle Derek.'

The following Easter Ivy's second eldest son, Robert, and her daughter came to stay with my mother and, when they were joined by Rowena and Annette, on our arrival, it became clear that the boy was bored with the female company. He leapt at my offer to take him to a football match, the local Derby between Yarmouth and neighbouring Lowestoft. It was a bright, sunny day when we arrived at the Wellesley recreation ground and I took a seat right up against the small, wicket fence, dead on the half way line. As the ground started to fill up Robert became very agitated.

'We can't stay here Uncle Derek,' he said in a worried tone. I pointed out we would have an uninterrupted view. 'Yes, but what about when they start to throw things from the grandstand?' he said looking nervously at the stand behind us.

'People don't throw things here,' I answered him. By now he was verging on panic.

'Where is the fuzz?' he asked, desperately looking around him. I laughed, telling him we did not need the police at our matches. His look of disbelief was only intensified when he saw the visiting team's coach parked next to the stand. 'They will wreck it!' he said.

Despite all my words of reassurance he spent most of the match apprehensively waiting for an outbreak of violence, which of course never occurred. I understand that on his return home his main topic of conversation was the match. Not the game, but the fact that it was played in total absence of trouble. I thought it was a terrible indictment of modern life when normal behaviour is regarded as abnormality.

Some of the family in 1962.
Derek, Gwen, Grace, Zuheir, Barbara, Albert,
Rowena, Dad, Talib, Annette, Mum, John

By 1966 the large chicken shed had been emptied and converted into a bird room to house twenty-one breeding pairs. The garden, after its massive input of chicken manure, was flourishing, at City Hall I was on top of the job and life was hectic, but even.

181

It was about this time that the Chief Clerk walked into my office, threw a file on the desk and told me the Council had bought St Faith's airfield from the Ministry of Defence. They had in mind developing it as a civil airport and hoped the County Council might join in the venture.

'I will leave it with you. See what you can do' he said, and hurried out.

After preliminary talks, I wrote formally to Norfolk County Council, who welcomed the proposal, and quickly established an Airport Joint Committee. They agreed that the first step was to get an Airport Manager and, in due course, Wing Commander Courtney was appointed. He had been a Battle of Britain fighter pilot and left his command of the RAF fighter station in Fylingdales to take up the appointment. I liked him, and we worked well together. He certainly got on with the job. The day he took up his position we went out together to the airfield. The cracks in the runway had weeds growing three feet tall, the control tower was a derelict shell, and all the hangars at one side were empty. He looked at the scene and asked how we should proceed. I told him that I knew nothing about aviation but all about local government and how to get through the red tape.

'You just tell me what you want done,' I told him.

'I don't want the hangars or surrounding land. I want the runway cleared and repaired and the control tower renovated,' he said.

Returning to the office I spoke to the Estates Surveyor about the hangars and the City Engineer about the repair work. Within a week the Committee had agreed plans for the work and within another couple of weeks the hangars were being let as industrial units, the start of Fifer's Lane Industrial Estate; the runway was cleared of weeds and repaired and renovation of the control tower started. In the meantime we had meetings with the Ministry of Defence to remove some equipment they had left behind, meetings with RAF Coltishall, the nearby fighter station, to establish flight procedures and advertised for air traffic control personnel. Within no more than six weeks from the start we were open for light aircraft.

To operate public services we would have to have a terminal building. Courtney told me, with some anguish, that the Planning Officer had contacted him saying he would do a layout.

'I don't want planners delaying us,' he said.

'Leave it to me,' I told him, and wrote a polite memorandum to the Planning Officer pointing out that the airport was a joint commercial project and that the Airport Manager was in the same position as any private developer. When his plans for development were ready they would be submitted for any planning permission needed, in the normal manner. He may have taken umbrage, but it worked and kept him out of our hair. The development proceeded apace, thanks largely to the Chairman of the Joint Committee who gave authority for work to be carried out. Within a few months Courtney rang me.

'Our first commercial plane has landed. Come down.' I went to see a Fokker Friendship standing on the runway and had a look over the plane. Courtney was delighted. 'You have been a tremendous help to me Derek, I'll take you up for a spin.' As he spoke I noticed two men wheeling a small aircraft onto the runway, its flimsy wings flapping up and down.

'That is very kind of you but I'm afraid I have to get back to the office for a meeting,' I said. One lesson well learned was that caution helps survival.

Very soon Norwich Airport was up and running. My job of midwife to the venture had been completed with its successful delivery, and now my involvement with it declined. Courtney threw a party at his house, to which Gwen and I were invited, and we had a very enjoyable evening. Usually, I shunned official 'get-togethers'. Each Christmas the Lord Mayor invited senior officers and administrative staff working closely with the Council to a sherry party. I had to go but made my escape as soon as politeness would allow. The Town Clerk organised an evening at his home once. I found an excuse for not being able to attend, only to discover he had postponed the event to a date which would be convenient. There being no way out, Gwen and I went. I always felt ill at ease at such events. Forced small talk was not my forte.

In the late summer of 1967 we received news that Grace's in-laws were in England and were proposing to visit my parents. They duly arrived, accompanied by two car-loads of handsome young men who were sons, nephews or otherwise related. It was noticeable that, apart from Grace's mother-in-law, the party was all male, which was a disappointment as it would have been interesting to meet a young Iraqi woman. As it was, there were too many people for us all to sit down to a meal together in our small living room and, while the main family members joined us for lunch, the front room was used to accommodate the remainder. The father-in-law was a fine looking, cultured, man in his late sixties, with the quiet charm of one used to wealth and power. He spoke English fluently and I knew immediately that here was a man that I could like and respect. Mother-in-law was a large, pleasant lady but, she not speaking English or I Arabic, it was difficult to make meaningful contact with her. Half way through the meal she said something to me in Arabic, which one of her sons translated for me.

'My mother says she likes your daughter (Annette), whom she thinks would make a good wife for my younger brother, and is prepared to pay you three camels for her.'

This came as a bit of a shock as I had never thought of Annette as a disposable asset. Mindful that I did not understand their culture, and in no way wishing to give offence, I had to think quickly for, in the ensuing silence, they all awaited my response.

I said, with a big smile, 'Please tell your Mother that, though I am very honoured by her generous offer, I have absolutely no use for camels here in England, but I would be happy to settle for two belly-dancers.'

Those who understood English started to laugh and when the young man translated my reply to his mother she roared with laughter. Everyone now seemed happy and jolly and no more was said on the matter. The young men settled down to play cards in the front room, and even squatting in the hall. After lunch I and my family left, but I understood that later in the day Grace's in-laws and my parents went out together for a walk along the seafront and enjoyed each other's company. I know that after that encounter my parents felt much happier about Grace's marriage to an Iraqi. It seems that when ordinary civilised people meet, racial differences are not an issue. I preferred Grace's husband to a great many Englishmen I knew.

That same year a post with Coleshill Council was advertised. The job entailed fighting planning appeals to protect the green belt between Coventry and Birmingham, and the salary was twice what I was getting at Norwich. I applied and was requested to attend for interview on a

Monday afternoon. Gwen accompanied me and we travelled on the Sunday. Coleshill was surrounded on all sides by motorways. Gwen said it was a glorified traffic island. The red, boggy, earth and blighted vegetation did not present the open rural landscape that I had expected, and the price of property looked astronomical. We sat up half the night in the hotel bedroom debating whether to take the job if offered. I was still undecided by the morning. When we went to the car park I could not see the car and panicked. Gwen finally pointed to a pale yellow car. It certainly looked like our car except our car was dove grey. As I rubbed the bonnet the yellow liquid came off. Whatever was in the atmosphere had come down with the dew during the night, covering everywhere.

'If you want to breathe that stuff, you can come on your own,' Gwen said.

The council offices were new, bright and friendly looking. I told the Chief Clerk that my call was just to say I would not be attending the interview as we had looked the area over and did not think we would be happy living there. He said that I had brilliant references and was the ideal man for the job. In fact I was the only candidate they had selected and if I would change my mind they could offer more money. Finally he was persuaded that it was not the job or the money but the location that was out of the question. We motored back to Norfolk at a leisurely pace and as soon as we reached the sea, I parked. Walking along the beach, in the clean, bracing, sea air, we agreed that in future no job, at any salary, would tempt us away from the coast.

If the City Hall regime was mundane, many of the people in it were anything but ordinary. One of my colleagues, who occupied the next room, looked perfectly normal but he had his foibles. When under pressure and the telephone rang he would throw the instrument on the floor. Later he repaired the damage so that the whole thing was nothing but a mass of sellotape. It had been thrown many times and there appeared to be no one piece bigger than a sixpence. His typist was a very beautiful red-head. Although the office walls were just about sound-proof, one day I heard her screams that went on and on. Reluctant to intervene I decided to keep out but, as the screams continued, eventually went to see what was wrong. She was standing in the corner near the door surrounded by smashed eggs on the floor. He was sitting at his desk throwing eggs and shouting 'catch!' He looked slightly amused, she was laughing hysterically. He had used three boxes of eggs and still had two more on his desk. Just after lunch one afternoon there were shouts of 'Sieg Heil' coming from the street. Looking out of my window there he was, cruising slowly past the front of City Hall in a huge, open car, painted dull khaki, the exact model used by Adolf Hitler during the war. Crowds returning from lunch were on the pavement giving the Nazi salute. He smiled serenely at his admirers as if he were Adolf Hitler.

If that was not bizarre, the action of the Medical Officer of Health certainly was. Complaining that the lights in the committee rooms were atrocious, he always brought a candle to the meetings, which he would ceremoniously light with a match, and read his reports by holding them in the candlelight. Nobody said anything and everyone just smiled condescendingly.

Not quite so funny, at least not for me, was the Assistant Solicitor who took over planning from the Deputy Town Clerk. A bumptious young man, always in a hurry, always rushing about, he was just an inept muddler. When he attended meetings it took a porter with a trolley to cart his load of files and law books. The slightest issue raised would send him diving on the floor searching through numerous files or books. 'You look in there' he said on his first visit, thrusting towards me three volumes of the Planning Encyclopaedia. I reminded him that my job was to follow the proceedings and take notes. Anyway, by the time he had found what he wanted the meeting had moved on to other matters. He once became very excited by a firm of developers who proposed to build a big complex spanning St Benedict's Street. I was with him when he met them.

'If the Council provides the site, we will get somebody to design the scheme and somebody to build it and somebody to manage it. The Council will have a percentage share of the profit.'

'And what will you contribute?' I asked them.

'We supply the expertise,' they said.

I told the solicitor it was a very dodgy proposition and I did not like the characters involved. He blustered and told me it was nothing to do with me. I did a company search. They had a share capital of just one hundred pounds. When he reported to the Committee the Members asked whether the company was sound. He waffled and prevaricated until they became exasperated. The Chairman looked at me.

'What do you think, Mr Dix?' I told the Committee of the company's financial position and the Chairman said, 'next business.' The Solicitor was furious.

'Why did you not tell me they only had one hundred pounds?' he asked.

'Because,' I replied 'it had nothing to do with me. Why did you not do a company search?'

But he had one good quality. He was infallibly wrong. Ask him for a legal opinion and whatever he said the real answer was the exact opposite of his view. On the whole, members of the City Council were quite ordinary, decent people and I thought that they did a good job for the citizens of Norwich. There was only one man I did not like, and he was the Chairman of the Finance Committee. My first day with the City Council had commenced with a budget finance meeting and it was a similar meeting that nearly ended my employment with them. Inflation was beginning to bite and spending committees had been asked to economise and prune their budgets for the coming year. These draft budgets were then scrutinised by the Finance Committee to see if any further cuts could be made to meet the Council's overall budget target. Bearing in mind that millions of pounds were involved, cuts of thousands of pounds would be required to make any impact. Eventually we came to the Social Services Committee's estimates.

'What is this item for provisions?' the Chairman asked. It was one of the homes for the elderly.

'That is for food,' the officer said.

'Old people don't need a lot of food. We could cut that by ten per cent,' said the Chairman. He then asked about a small item of two hundred pounds or so.

'That is for tobacco and sweets,' the officer explained.

'They should not smoke and sweets are bad for them. We can cut that right out,' the Chairman said, 'and do the same for all the homes.'

By now I was thinking what a mean bastard he was. Next it was the children's homes. The Chairman was now wielding his axe with a vengeance.

'Children don't appreciate good food. If you cut out the meat and bought cheaper basic food I am sure we could save on this item. Let us try a twenty per cent cut, and of course they don't need sweets.'

The officer interrupted to point out that the item also took account of giving the children a day out to the seaside twice a year.

'Well, just leave enough in to give them one day out a year', the Chairman said testily.

Now whether it was my own experience of poor hospital food, the pettiness of the whole thing, or just the lack of understanding and humanity being displayed for the elderly and children in care, I know not, but a sudden rage seized me. I was half out of my chair when the City Treasurer's arm was across my chest forcing me back into my seat.

'Don't be a fool man!' he hissed in my ear. I liked the City Treasurer. He was a big, quiet, friendly man. With great effort I took control of myself and the moment passed. Whether I would have actually punched the Chairman's teeth down his throat, I am not sure, but in that moment of unbridled rage the possibility could not be entirely discounted. As the Committee moved on to other items the Treasurer turned to me with a big smile and whispered in my ear, 'Don't worry old chap. Things like that, which they take out, we put back under a different heading.' I hoped that he read in my returning smile my understanding of his humanity and appreciation for his timely intervention. So life at City Hall continued on its routine way.

Visiting my parents in late February 1968, I entered the house with the usual question of how they were.

'I am going to die', my father announced. He did not look ill and I thought he was perhaps just depressed by the weather and not being able to get out of the house. Despite my banter, he was adamant. When I left that evening he seemed normal and I dismissed the matter from my mind. When I visited again a week later I found him very ill in a single bed in the downstairs front room.

'What is wrong with him?' I asked my mother. She looked worn out and was weeping.

'I don't know. He said he felt unwell, took off his artificial leg and said he wouldn't need that any more. The doctor has been but he did not say what was wrong.'

Father looked pale and very tired. He said he was in no pain but just felt very weak. Finally, Mother was persuaded to go to bed and I sat with Father all night until Mother came downstairs at about 4.00 a.m., saying she felt much refreshed after a few hours' sleep. During the morning Father shaved himself and, after a wash, seemed a little brighter. He wanted to talk. There was an item on the radio about the American economy and, although desperately ill, here he was talking about global economics. He said he fancied fish and chips, although he ate very little. By the afternoon, water was draining away from him at an alarming rate. The doctor called and said Father's body was just worn out. My brother arrived at lunchtime and one or both of us stayed at the bedside. At 11.30 p.m. my brother said he would sit up all night and suggested that I went home to bed so that I could take over again in the morning. I said goodbye to Father. He was still lucid.

'Keep out of the tripe houses,' were his parting words. It was with a very heavy heart that I set out for Norwich, deep in thought. The bushes at the side of the road seemed to be flashing past. I looked at the speedometer. The needle was flickering over the ninety miles per hour mark. I forced myself to concentrate on driving. At 7.00 a.m. I rang my sister-in-law to find out the situation.

'I'm sorry Derek, your father died at 1.30 this morning,' she said.

I reached Yarmouth at about 9.00 a.m. and found that the house had a strange sense of deep peace about it. My brother said,

'Do you want to see him?'

We went into the front room and pulled back the sheet to reveal a wizened little face that looked over a hundred years old and remarkably like my grandmother. This heap of skin and bones was not my father. Wherever he was, if he still existed, it was certainly not in the remains on the bed. We buried Father in the cemetery at Caister-on-Sea on a bright sunny morning. At the graveside, my mother looked out to where the sea sparkled in the sunlight.

'Well, at least he has a good outlook,' she said.

I realised that reality had not yet caught up with her. Ivy and Roy had come home for the funeral and took Mother back to London with them for a few days. After seeing them off, I parked on White Horse Plain off Northgate Street and did some hard thinking. Father had said life was for living, yet I seemed to be spending mine working. Work, promotion and money suddenly seemed to be unimportant.

I loved my father very dearly. He was a real man. Despite my education and professional experience, he had always been the 'governor'. When it came to common sense and being worldly wise, he was the man and I the boy. Of all the men I had met, it was he alone who had my total respect. When I hear men speak disparagingly of their fathers and say they cannot get on with them I realise how lucky I have been. If I could have picked any man in the world, rich or poor, to be my father, I would have picked my dad. As we grew older, my brother and I called him 'the old man'. People thought we were being disrespectful but he gloried in the title, for he knew it was a term of endearment.

It was not until mother returned from London that the full impact of Father's death struck her. Her grief was unbounded. We all cope with grief in different ways; she tried to mitigate her loss in work. Always industrious in home decorating, she now set about decorating every room in the house simultaneously. The house was in total chaos, with furniture piled up, step ladders, buckets of water, paint and paper everywhere. I found her standing on a step ladder, splashed with ceiling white and covered in dirty water, washing a ceiling and crying bitterly. She wanted no assistance. She just wanted to tire herself out so that sheer fatigue would numb and overcome her conscious mind and blot out her grief. It was a heart-rending sight but we just had to leave her to work it out.

My reappraisal of life consequent upon Father's death was profound. Living in Norwich had been virtually an exile. The sprawling, characterless, suburbs seemed like a desert or, as a teenager on the radio had described them, 'a cemetery with lights'. At the City Hall I was at the heart of city life, playing a small part in its present administration and future development, yet in my heart I was not part of the city; even after working there for twenty years, the people, however friendly, seemed like foreigners. I knew at last what I wanted. I wanted to go home.

During the months that followed, every avenue was explored for employment in Yarmouth but without success, until, in January, an advertisement appeared in the Local Government Chronicle for an administrative assistant with the Great Yarmouth Borough Council, to be responsible for the Town Planning and Highways Committees. It was on a lower grade, AP3, but it seemed like a gift from the gods. The Town Clerk was most put out when I asked to use his name for a reference.

'Are you unhappy here? Is something wrong?' he asked with concern. I said there was nothing wrong, I just wanted to go to Yarmouth. 'But you are committing professional suicide!' he exploded. 'You won't like it. You will be awfully bored. I don't understand. What is so special about Yarmouth?'

I could have gone into a long diatribe about the futility of constant work pressures, the treadmill, year after year, of sitting in my small office worrying about meeting deadlines. Instead, trying to encapsulate my feelings, I said, 'I just want to sit on the beach and watch the seagulls fly.' The look on his face told me that he thought I had gone completely insane. For six weeks there was no reply to my application, so I telephoned. A Welshman, who said he was the Deputy Town Clerk, answered.

'We have been very busy, we have had a ship in.'

It seemed a strange excuse but eventually I was called for interview. The interview was scheduled for 9.15a.m. but it was 10.30a.m. before I was ushered into the Town Clerk's office. There was the Town Clerk, Deputy Town Clerk, Assistant Town Clerk and the Assistant Solicitor. The Assistant Solicitor asked me one or two questions about Town Planning law and then advised the rest that I did know about Town Planning. The rest of the interview was like a comic opera. They wanted to know what the City Council were doing about various matters and, once I had told them, they then discussed the issues between themselves. This went on until 1.15 p.m. when, after asking me to leave, they called me back in less than five minutes to say I could have the job. The Assistant Town Clerk took me to the municipal buildings behind the Town Hall to see the Medical Officer of Health. He gave me the briefest and quickest medical examination I had ever had, thrust a small rusty enamel jug in my hand saying 'put a urine sample in this and leave it in the gents under the sinks.'

'Will it be alright?' I queried doubtfully.

'Oh yes, yes, I'll pick it up after lunch.'

When I related the circumstances of my interview to my colleagues in City Hall, they fell about laughing, saying I had made it up. When the day of my departure arrived, they packed the pub opposite City Hall to see me off and gave me a fishing rod as a leaving present. My only regret in leaving City Hall was that I had to leave Margaret behind. We had worked closely together for six years and, during that long time, there had never been a cross word between us. In fact she had never even shown the slightest sign of irritation, despite the terrible pressures of work. We had both adopted a completely professional attitude to the situation. Although we saw more of each other than we did of our respective spouses, no word was said out of place and there was absolutely no physical contact whatsoever. Yet, leaving her was as painful as a divorce. I think she must have experienced a similar feeling, as she seemed upset by my departure, saying,

'That's right, desert me. You will soon forget about me.'

'I'll send you a Christmas card,' I joked, although I did not feel like joking. Perhaps my leaving was for the best. Perhaps, although I would not allow myself to even think about it, I had become fond of her. Not romantically in love, not sexually lusting for her but, nevertheless, there was a very deep affection.

CHAPTER 15

Yarmouth Town Hall

My return to Yarmouth in March 1969 was a home-coming. At last I was back where I belonged. My forced departures in 1937, 1940, 1948 and 1959 were behind me and for the first time in many years I felt settled, peaceful and at home. During the week I stayed with my mother, returning to Hellesdon at weekends and sometimes for a Wednesday night to break up the week for Gwen, who again had the birds to look after. The bungalow at Hellesdon was put on the market and every evening I searched the Yarmouth area for a new residence. Gwen wanted a big garden, but modern bungalows had no more than a few square yards. It was May before I found what we were looking for and it happened almost by accident. Several times I had passed a semi-detached bungalow with a frontage of no more than twenty-five feet and discounted it as useless, but a mass of honeysuckle in full bloom between the building and the garage caught my attention and I stopped to have a look at it. Pushing through the tangle of the overgrown bush, there came into view an ever-widening plot of waist-high grass stretching for yards to a sycamore tree, a pine tree and a large hawthorn hedge. The total plot was a third of an acre.

A reputable firm of Norwich solicitors was engaged to carry out the conveyancing. I emphasised to the solicitor the importance of not selling one property without the positive purchase of the other. He smiled patronisingly, as if to say 'don't teach your grandmother to suck eggs'. Later he had me sign contracts for sale and purchase at the same time. The moving date was in late June and two days before the move I called at his office. He explained that he had not yet been able to complete the purchase of the new bungalow because the vendor could not be contacted. When I asked what my position was he said blandly that I would have to vacate the Hellesdon bungalow because it was now sold, but it would not be possible yet to move into the new bungalow. It seemed to me that private solicitors are even bigger idiots than some in local government. Despite his advice, there was no option but to move to the new premises, which we did, as I had the key to the back door. We had been in occupation for about a fortnight when a car containing what was obviously an estate agent and clients drew up outside. Taking the bull by the horns I said,

'The place has already been sold. Have you the front door key?' He looked surprised and handed it to me. 'Don't you people talk to each other? I have been round half a dozen agents looking for this key.'

Full of apologies he left. It was another two months before the solicitor completed the formal conveyance. What he had expected me to do with my family for two months because of his ineptitude is beyond imagination. The whole conveyancing business seems a farce and there is no reason why a central registry could not deal with property ownership in the same way as car ownership.

A local man scythed the grass and even Gwen was satisfied with the garden. A local carpenter built me a large bird shed, taking only three days from the day of order to its completion, and in no time at all we were settled in our new home.

If the pace at City Hall had been very fast and hectic, Yarmouth Town Hall was by contrast very slow and leisurely. It was almost like being on holiday. The work seemed like child's play. The staff were all friendly and the atmosphere relaxed. My only problem was a typist, shared with a colleague. She did very little work for him and had made her mind up to do no work for me. The Chief Clerk, who was well into his sixties, said he could do nothing about the situation because typists were hard to get. What little work I had was typed only by my pleading with other girls in the typing pool to each do bits for me. How I longed for Margaret! Thankfully the wretched girl left in a month or so. The first week at the Town Hall an officer in the Planning department rang me to say that a firm of builders were doing a housing development and would be happy to let me have a house at cost price. I thanked him and refused the offer. The same officer was also disgruntled when I checked planning consent forms against the Committee's minutes and found that some passed for signature did not appear to have been submitted to the Committee for approval. A woman from that department said, with a grin, to me,

'You have got yourself a bad name in a short time, haven't you? They call you the honest Local Government Officer!'

Not all the irregularities were designed. Some arose because of a lack of respect for legal niceties or a desire to get on with things, like the instance of 'one way' traffic signs that suddenly appeared on a street without any legal order being made. I told the Borough Engineer that they would have to come down, explaining that if a motorist were prosecuted for violating the signs, his solicitor would be bound to ask to see the order authorising them. We would then have to admit the signs were unauthorised and we would all look stupid. He took the signs down immediately. My colleague, Sid Walker, told me I should not have taken on the Borough Engineer.

'You've made a very bad enemy there' he said.

It was not true. The Borough Engineer was always very pleasant and friendly to me and frequently sought my advice on procedural matters to achieve objectives that he desired.

By mid-September I had my fishing rods out and went fishing in the harbour's mouth three or four nights every week. It was ideal for me, being only five minutes travelling time from home, and there was no danger of me falling into the river with the quay wall being some three and a half feet high. As we moved into October the number of anglers increased until we were standing shoulder to shoulder all along the quay and pier head. Sometimes there were at least four hundred of us. Each man had his own favourite spot. So, seeing the same group of men frequently where I fished, we became quite friendly. Waiting for the fish to come in on the tide we had long conversations.

'Do you work?' one asked.

'I have a little old office job,' I said, not daring to tell them it was at the Town Hall. Their comments about the lazy tea-drinking Town Hall staff and the stupidity of Councillors would be unprintable.

'With all of us about, you would think the fools would open the public toilets across the road at night, wouldn't you?' said one.

'It is like the light outside my home,' said Jack, 'been out for months but they do nothing about it.'

'Look at that bollard they've stuck up, stopping traffic coming straight along the quay. Now you have to come out at that blind junction,' said another.

Back at work I took up these matters. A couple of nights later, the fishermen remarked on the fact that the toilets were open and the bollard removed.

'Do you know what?' said Jack, 'They actually came yesterday and put a new bulb in my light!' They all laughed.

'Somebody must have heard you Jack.'

They never suspected that the 'somebody' was the little disabled chap in a funny black and white woolly hat and a filthy dirty torn raincoat, that they fished with. They had very good ideas on traffic management, environmental improvements and planning matters. Many of these were transmitted to the council in various ways and some were implemented. I often wondered whether Councillors talked to their electorate or, rather, whether they listened to them. Perhaps Councillors would have benefited by going around in disguise.

I liked to fish the last couple of hours of the flood tide and, if that occurred between 1.00 and 3.00 a.m., then that is when I fished. Alone at the quayside, under a canopy of stars, with great rolling, heavy, waves coming in from the sea, it was idyllic. It certainly knocked the spots off life in the Norwich Suburbs.

On the whole, life settled into a tranquil round of gardening, bird-breeding, the Cage Bird Society and autumn fishing. The only spot of bother was the Assistant Solicitor who had his finger in the Planning pie. Whether he resented the fact that I knew more about the subject than he did or whether there were other reasons, I am not sure, but he became aggressive, sarcastic, and sought to find fault where none existed. Actually he was quite a clever young man but he was extremely lazy and many of the problems he encountered were due to his failure to prepare for Committee properly. Things came to a head when a letter arrived from the Ministry of Housing and Local Government seeking an explanation to a complaint they had received about a garage development in the town. I knew that it was one of the dodgy consents that had been issued by a person in the Planning department and it would have required a lying 'cover-up' reply to satisfy the Ministry. I refused to write such a letter. He said a lot of hard words and I decided that in future I would not assist him by pointing out his mistakes. Within a couple of months he had fallen into so many holes of his own making, which normally I would have helped him out of, that he was in deep trouble. He left for private practice. His replacement was a nice, jovial young man. On his arrival he suggested that we went out for a pint together in the evening.

'I know nothing about Planning' he confessed.

'That's alright,' I told him, 'I do. Providing you leave me alone and don't start lording it over me, I will see that you don't put a foot wrong.'

'You are on. Have another pint,' he said. He became a good friend and he, I and Maurice, a legal assistant, went out drinking on most Friday nights.

One of the Senior Councillors was Alderman Ecclestone. He was shrewd, a good tactician and spoke eloquently. Very sharp and caustic in his comments, he played a dominant role in the Council. However, he sometimes suggested actions that were not strictly within the Council's powers. In Committee I had to point out that the proposal was *ultra vires* or against the Ministry guidelines. Alderman Ecclestone used to become very irritated by this. Once he said,

'Stop telling us what we can or cannot do. There are miles of open countryside between us and the rest of Britain and here we do what we please.'

Members thought that a good wisecrack and laughed heartily.

'Of course you can do as you please,' I told him, 'but my job is to draw your attention to the relevant points of law and procedures.'

'Yes, yes, we know all that' he said testily.

Shortly after that episode the Town Clerk invited me to his office for 'a cup of tea and a chat'. He was a nice man but a bit timid and indecisive. He talked round and round various subjects and I began to wonder what it was all about. In the end he said,

'If you like it here, stop crossing Alderman Ecclestone before he asks me to sack you.' I just laughed.

'Do you mean you want me to let the Committee do something illegal?'

'Well, no, but just try not to cross Ecclestone too much.'

Early in 1972 the Chief Clerk retired. Two legal assistants and an administrative assistant, all older than myself and employees of the Council for years, applied for the post together with a young administrative assistant, a pushy young chap from Yorkshire. A number of people from other departments applied also. There seemed to be nothing to lose, so I put in an application too. On the morning of the interviews Taffy Griffiths, the deputy Town Clerk, came into our office. Taffy was a small Welshman with a puggy face and a great sense of humour. He possessed the rare quality of being able to be 'one of the boys' and still retain the respect of the staff. Yet he was the strong man of the Council and the lynchpin of the department. I had sat next to him in Committee on several occasions. If a Member was talking nonsense, he would say in what was supposed to be a whisper, no doubt audible throughout the room, words like 'prat' or even more vulgar names. Now he stood in front of my desk grinning. 'You've had it boyo! The appointments Sub-Committee is Alderman Winter, Councillor Mrs Batley and your old enemy Ecclestone.'

The interview was brief. Mrs Batley asked if I was happily married. While I hesitated, Alderman Winter interjected,

'What sort of question is that to ask a married man?' They all laughed and I did not have to make any response.

When all the candidates had been interviewed, they called me in and told me I had the job. Ecclestone smiled warmly and said confidently,

'I know Mr Dix will make an excellent Chief Clerk. He has the necessary strength of character.'

Taffy said he was mystified as to why Ecclestone had been my main supporter. I was now on Senior Officer grade and earning much more than I had at Norwich, but the duties of the post looked awesome, with direct responsibility to the Town Clerk for every function of the department, except the strictly legal work. Briefly, this entailed the administration of the Council and all the Committees and Sub-Committees, electoral registration and elections, local land charge searches, licensing, the Mayoralty and civic functions, budget control and of course typing, filing and the general office. However, my immediate concern was how the rest of the staff would react, some of whom were much older than myself and had been in the department for several years. It was a difficult transition from being one of the boys one minute and boss of the whole outfit the next. I knew from my own experience that staff hated change and dreaded new bosses who threw their weight about. I resolved to just let things tick over as usual until everything settled down. The only immediate change was one of fundamental attitude to the job. The retiring Chief Clerk advised me to see myself as a buffer between the staff and the Town Clerk, but I saw the post as a bridge rather than a buffer.

Changes that were instituted came about slowly, not by my peremptory commands but by the decisions of the staff. Over a period of time talks were held with each section of the department about procedures and inter-section working arrangements, during which staff were asked for their views. Ideas were discussed and changes, if any, were introduced by the staff themselves. Many problems were resolved this way and everyone seemed happy. The test of my position arose in October. A General Election had been called but there was a problem because the County Council had failed to produce the new registers of electors. The Town Clerk took me with him to County Hall to see if there was any way around the difficulties. There was no solution offered. On the way home the Town Clerk was very glum. I told him that we would have to just amend all the old registers manually.

'But there isn't time' he said, 'it's a mammoth task.'

I told him I would ask the whole department to come in on Saturday to do it. He looked at me as if I were mad. With the exception of one typist who had arranged to go away for the weekend, all the staff agreed. I walked into the office at 8.00 a.m. Saturday morning and was greeted by cries of 'good afternoon' and 'we guessed you had overslept'. The whole of the staff were busy on the registers. All rank went by the board as they mucked in together. By midday the task was complete. By their happy and ready response to my request, I knew the staff were saying that they had accepted me in my new position. The Town Clerk was surprised and relieved.

'How did you manage it?' he asked.

'By appealing to their loyalty to you, sir, and the department, but in return they will expect help when they are in trouble.'

I watched him turn this over in his mind as he said, 'Yes, of course.' If he was thinking that I had driven some sort of hard bargain, he was right.

Uncle Arthur had died in 1971 and the following year Aunt Nellie came with her nephew to spend a weekend with one of their old friends in Gorleston. She came to see me and stayed for the Saturday afternoon. She was still the same dear old Aunt Nellie but small, thin and frail. Most of the time was spent in reminiscences of the happy times we had enjoyed together when I was a child. A few tears were shed when we said goodbye. I rightly guessed that it would be the last time I was to see her, for a few months later she passed away peacefully in her sleep. That she played a major role in my development there can be no doubt. Ingrained in my character is the appreciation of order, tidiness, cleanliness and being nicely dressed. Her quiet authority for such things was instilled from the very beginning and thus she stamped her mark on me for the rest of my life.

The rest of that year, and the early part of 1973, passed without incident and all seemed to be going well. Then, on my way into the office after lunch, my legs gave way and I fell heavily. My right knee took the impact and within minutes there was severe swelling. I did not think too much about it as I had sustained a similar injury when falling down a flight of stone stairs at the County Council. The doctor came and said it needed resting. With rest, the swelling diminished but came up again as soon as I put weight on the leg. Days of resting it turned into weeks. I despaired of it ever getting better. Gwen had booked another holiday in Norway; she now went off every year. It started with Devon, the Lake District and Scotland but now she was smitten with Norway. My mother came to look after me when Gwen left. Apparently my doctor was also on holiday and a young doctor called to see me. He decided that I needed to be on the leg, but with support, and prescribed making a sort of cast for the leg by alternate layers of thick cotton wool and tightly wrapped bandages around the leg from thigh to ankle. My mother applied the bandages as directed and I stood up. As the leg took my weight a horrendous pain shot through the knee and I screamed for her to take it off. Within an hour the aching pain subsided and the swelling started to go down. By the next morning the knee looked almost normal and, although tender, I was able to get about. By the time Gwen returned a week later I was already back at work. I suppose it never occurred to the doctor that my trouble was a dislocated kneecap. During my working life I was never ill. Any sick leave was always due to injury from falling.

It was at this time that a new Councillor was elected. He and his father were both canary breeders and, when younger, he had in fact been my assistant secretary at the Cage Bird Society. He had also worked in the direct labour section of the Borough Engineer's department and, it was understood, had been obliged to leave. A rabid Labour Party supporter, he now had it in for officers. Shortly after his election to the Council he stopped me in the street to tell me that I was on the 'death list'. I just laughed and did not even bother to ask him what that meant. A young married woman, Councillor Torne, was also a newcomer to the Council. When I was fishing one evening he came along the quay with Councillor Mrs Torne and they stopped to chat.

'I live only just across the road' she said, 'I am now going to make a cup of coffee, I will bring you one across'. She did just that. In fact several evenings over the next few weeks she would appear with a small flask of coffee. While I fished, she would sit on the wall and we would talk about Council business. No other subject was raised and after about half an hour, she would say goodnight and leave. It seemed a normal, friendly act on her part and I assumed she just enjoyed chatting about the Council. The Town Clerk asked to see me one morning and started a familiar round-the-bush sort of discussion, which meant he had something to say but could not find the right words. In the end I said,

'If you are trying to tell me something I am not getting the message.'

He went a bit pink and looked embarrassed, then blurted out,

'Are you having an affair with Councillor Torne?'

I stared at him in surprise and told him about the coffee supply.

'That is hardly an affair is it?' He looked relieved.

'Well there is a lot of talk among the Councillors.' Strangely the coffee visits stopped. I had an idea that somebody had hatched a little plot. After all, I was on the death list.

The next attempt was more subtle. The Town Clerk came into my office and told me that he had been approached by Alderman M..... who had asked whether I could park my invalid car elsewhere than outside the Town Hall, because it looked unsightly. This time I was upset. I pointed out that the parking facilities were, as he well knew, at a premium in the vicinity of the Town Hall. I had thought that the two bays reserved for disabled drivers at the front of the building were there expressly for people such as myself, and what did Alderman M..... expect, a limousine? The Town Clerk looked uncomfortable, mumbled that I would have to sort it out with M....., and left. The situation looked bleak. The nearest public car park was beyond my walking distance and the limited parking on the quay near the Town Hall would mean crossing a busy three-lane road. In good weather it would be extremely hazardous and when there was ice and snow, or even a strong wind, downright impossible. Making it from the car, where I now parked, just across the pavement to the door was sometimes very difficult and frightening because my balance was so poor that the wind just blew me over. Situated where it was in an exposed position, the Town Hall seemed to catch and funnel the wind, turning even a good breeze into half a gale. If parking near the entrance was denied to me there was no way I could continue working at the Town Hall. While I was wondering what to do, a friendly little Councillor came to see me and I mentioned the matter to him.

'Well it is appalling. Disgraceful. What are you going to do?'

'If I have to pack the job in because of it,' I told him, 'you can be sure the *News of the World* will hear about it. It would look good wouldn't it, "Alderman forces disabled man out of job because he cannot bear the sight of his Ministry of Health invalid car".' Half an hour later Alderman M..... was on the telephone.

'No, no, Mr Dix, the Town Clerk must have misunderstood me, all I said was that I thought the Ministry should have given you people a better looking vehicle. There is no question of you not parking where you like. I am very happy for you to park outside the front of the Town Hall.'

I repeated the conversation to the Town Clerk,

'Lying devil,' he said, 'anyway you won that one!' He looked relieved, as he usually did when trouble was resolved.

Alderman M..... was a big man, arrogant, domineering, with a loud voice and he thought he was very clever. To me he seemed not very bright, but devious and unscrupulous. In fact he was a typical bully. Any Councillor who dared to disagree with him was guaranteed to receive a scathing personal attack. The verbal abuse would refer to him being ignorant, or small, or divorced, or a newcomer with no knowledge of the Council, or failing in their business life, or being young, or not being able to control his wife, or being bald, or deaf, or anything that came to hand. When personal abuse failed to silence an opponent, there were even threats of violence. There was one occasion when an Independent Councillor stood his ground in the Council Chamber and refused to be intimidated. Alderman M..... went into a rage, threatening to get him after the meeting. When the meeting ended he made a beeline for this Councillor. I was talking to another Councillor when he rushed between us thrusting us both violently aside. The Councillor was sent staggering and I managed to clutch onto the seating or I would have been thrown onto the ground.

Alderman M..... was, I suspect, one of those people who are frightened of disability. In the same way as animals have an instinct to turn against one of their kind who is sick or injured, he was not civilised enough to counter such primitive reactions. One thing is certain, he had always avoided me like the plague. Whether it was my disability or whether it was because I was not frightened of him is a moot point, but it suited me because I disliked him. Even when a Labour swing at the polls brought him into power as leader of the Council our contact was rare and brief. We never actually clashed on Council business because I circumvented him. Such was the case when I was reporting to a Committee on a request by the Port and Haven Commissioners for a contribution to repair the quay heading at South Quay. I told the Committee that the responsibility for quay maintenance lay with the Commissioners and, with long stretches of quay heading falling into disrepair, it would be a costly business if the Council set a precedent by giving financial support to such work. The Council had never made such a contribution before.

'He is wrong!' roared M....., glaring at me, 'We made a contribution eight or nine years ago!' Members cringed in their seats and looked to me for a reply.

Thinking quickly I said, 'If Alderman M..... recalls such an occasion, I am sure he must be right. Perhaps the Committee would like to defer the matter so that I can ascertain what level of contribution was made on that occasion.'

The matter was deferred. Reporting back at the next meeting, I told them, 'Alderman M..... is quite correct. The Council did make a contribution to port works in the past, but that was a shared scheme in connection with the erection of a flood protection wall, rather than actual quay heading repairs.

'There you are! I knew I was right!' Alderman M..... said triumphantly beaming at everyone. The Chairman reminded members that the current request was not quite in the same category as a flood protection scheme and the request was refused. Alderman M..... did not question the decision, still glowing in the euphoria of thinking he had won the argument.

Council business was not all so prosaic. One Councillor was full of bright ideas.

'Why,' he asked, 'don't we combat vandalism to bus shelters by building them so that they can go underground. All you would need is a post in the pavement with a button. Anyone wishing to use the shelter could push the button to hydraulically raise the shelter above ground and, when they do not need the shelter, they can push the button and it would go down again below ground.'

This was greeted with howls of laughter. It made me laugh also. 'Well don't you think it might be a good idea?' he asked pleadingly, looking at me.

'It's a brilliant idea,' I said, 'but I can just visualise two old ladies sitting in the shelter when a gang of yobs come along and push the button!'

Daft ideas were not the sole prerogative of Councillors. Officers also came up with ludicrous schemes, like the proposal by the Social Services Officer who wanted to canvass the town to discover elderly people who might need assistance.

'I have arranged for the milk delivery companies to deliver a questionnaire to every house where there is an elderly resident,' he told the Committee, 'and the next morning they can put them out with their milk bottles for the milkman to collect.' I started laughing.

'What's wrong with that?' the Chairman asked.

'Nothing,' I said, 'provided it is not a very wet or very windy day.' Members rocked with laughter at the thought of milkmen chasing pieces of paper while trying to deliver the milk. In the end it was decided that Councillors would seek out the elderly in their wards and, where necessary, assist them to complete the questionnaire.

CHAPTER 16

Reorganisation

For the craziest scheme of the century, the supreme accolade must surely go to the Government, for its weird and wonderful measures for the reorganisation of Local Government in 1974. In one stroke it reduced local democracy, created a plethora of District Councils with few functions of importance, greatly enlarged the local bureaucracy at considerable cost to the rate-payer and threw the whole of Local Government into chaos.

The Great Yarmouth County Borough Council became a District Council with an enlarged area, taking in rural parishes to the north and south of the town. But major services such as Education, Social Services, Highways and Strategic Planning went to the County Council, together with minor services such as Libraries and Museums. What was left was 'Toy Town' functions. Generous retirement hand-outs were offered to Chief Officers and in one fell swoop we lost virtually every head of department and deputy head. The result was that departments were now controlled by men who had been originally number three in the department. Some were up to the job but many were not. So far as our department was concerned, the structure had been headed by the Town Clerk, who also had the role of overall Chief Officer responsible for co-ordinating Council policy, Deputy Town Clerk and Assistant Town Clerk. The new structure was Chief Executive Officer, with the same responsibilities as the former Town Clerk, Borough Secretary, who was deputy to the Chief Executive Officer for departmental matters only, Assistant Secretary (Legal) and Assistant Secretary (Administration).

With the early retirement of the Town Clerk and his Deputy at the change-over, the former Assistant Town Clerk became Chief Executive Officer, the only remaining young solicitor became Borough Secretary and I applied successfully for the post of Assistant Borough Secretary (Administration) on Principal Officer grade. The post of Assistant Secretary (Legal) was not filled for many months because there were no qualified solicitors available.

Although the Council had fewer functions and there was in consequence less work, all senior staff found themselves on higher grades and, of course, with more money. The greatest task was to find something useful to do. But there were problems ahead not envisaged by of this shake up in the organisation of Local Government. One of these unforeseen consequences was in the area of personal relationships. In a stable organisation, vacancies occur spaced over a reasonable period of time and are filled by people approved by the senior staff. This means that new personnel have a fair chance of being acceptable to their boss. No such niceties were possible in the mêlée that ensued at reorganisation when officers were rolled out cheek by jowl like dice from a dice-box.

From the outset I had the distinct impression that the Chief Executive Officer and the Borough Secretary did not exactly hit it off and I became 'pig in the middle'. All too often instructions given to me by the Borough Secretary would be countermanded by the Chief Executive Officer and, in carrying out specific instructions from the Chief Executive Officer, I usually found myself at variance with the Borough Secretary. I thought ruefully of the old saying, 'no man can serve two masters'. In the end the Borough Secretary confined himself more or less to legal matters and I found myself dealing almost exclusively with the Chief Executive Officer on the Council administration functions, but I knew that the Borough Secretary's resentment of the situation was crystallising into a personal grudge against me. Yet there was nothing I could do about it. At times matters arose where the Chief Executive Officer did not want to get involved and the Borough Secretary seemed reluctant to step into the administrative field, so I was left to my own devices. In fact there were occasions when they both took annual leave at the same time and I was left in sole charge of the department. I wondered what the doctor who wanted to put me in a home to do basket-making would have made of my success in local government.

I did not know what to make of the Chief Executive Officer. Most of the time he seemed inscrutable, playing his cards close to his chest. He was neither friendly nor unfriendly and we had no serious disagreements. At times I think I irritated him by pushing a point of view too hard, but any reproof on his part was very gentle, usually in the form of poking fun at me. He was a master in the art of diplomacy and keeping the ship on an even keel. In the turbulence of the Council-and-Officer relationships a good deal of mud was slung, but he had a happy knack of letting it pass over his head. When controversy raged he just would not get involved. It was like watching a professional boxer in the ring whose nimble footwork frustrated all of his opponent's attempts to land a punch. He seemed to have the ability to analyse a situation dispassionately and take a strategic decision to sail on a favourable wind. Although I was happy working for him, it was with a sense of caution, for it seemed unwise to take liberties with someone who was an unknown quantity. He surprised me one day in an officer's meeting when they were agreeing a course of action which I thought was not quite legal. He just smiled with amusement at my objections and said,

'The law is for observance by fools and the guidance of wise men,' which everyone thought was very humorous. That was his style, the gentle, witty rebuke.

On another occasion when I was pursuing a certain course of action he indicated that he thought I was heading in the wrong direction. He was obviously very concerned and opposed to what I was doing but he did not get steamed up or make a big issue of it, he simply said, 'A word to the wise is sufficient, is it not?' I did not argue but accepted the criticism and complied with his wishes. This did not mean that we did not discuss matters or that he prevented me putting my point of view, but he was the boss and the final decision had to be his. At an Officers' meeting an issue was under consideration where everyone, including the Chief Executive Officer, was in favour of a proposed action. Only I was opposed to it and outlined the dangers of what they were doing. A few days later my prognosis was proved correct and the whole scheme became a mess. As I entered the Chief Executive's office that morning he greeted me with the words,

'If you dare to say, "I told you so", you are fired.' That is what I liked about him, his humour in adversity.

One thing that did puzzle me was that although he called everyone by their Christian names, he usually referred to me as 'Mr Dix'. But then I noticed that most of the Council's senior officers did the same thing. It seemed as if people were saying that I was not one of them and by using the surname they were politely distancing themselves from me. I mentioned the matter to one of my senior assistants who said he thought they were showing deference to my superior intellect, but of course we both knew he was joking.

When everything was settled we looked much the same as before. We lost just one junior administrative post. If we had a comfortable workload in the past, it was even more comfortable now. Most of our efforts were now directed at cajoling the County Council into maintaining levels of service in matters that we had previously undertaken ourselves. If we were confused, so were the public. As services deteriorated and complaints came in, the public thought we were fobbing them off when we kept saying, 'Sorry we do not deal with that any more, you will have to contact Norfolk County Council.' But the change did generate work, even unnecessary work, such as elections for County Councillors. Then there was the nit-picking over parish matters and parish council elections for the rural areas we had acquired, but the dynamism and thrust of an autonomous local authority had gone.

The constant haggling with the County took time but was not productive. I knew from my fourteen years with the authority that they took scant notice of anything District Councils said. But we had to play the game and in the early days a number of officer meetings were arranged between the County Council and the District Councils. I went to one of these to represent the Yarmouth Council. The room was packed with people standing in groups when I arrived. A young man conducted me around introducing me to various people. One group were Senior County Council Officers.

'This is Mr Dix from Great Yarmouth,' he said. Two or three shook hands with me. Another said in a loud voice,

'Oh I know Mr Dix very well. He and I once shared the same mistress.' Smiling, he shook me warmly by the hand. The rest of the group looked on in shocked silence. So it was he who had been Josephine's boyfriend all those years ago. It is funny how the past keeps catching up with you. What was most extraordinary about the post-reorganisation was that it was not only officers who fiddled about with detail, so did the Council. They spawned dozens of sub-committees to deal with the minutest details. One Council meeting started at 7.00 p.m. and ended at 3.00 a.m. For eight hours I sat there listening to absolute twaddle. Yarmouth had always been political but now it was even more so. Many fancied they were in the House of Commons. With no meat to digest, they had long political debates on national issues. At the end of that long session Councillor M....... (Aldermen were abolished in the reorganisation) declared that it had been a good meeting which had sorted things out. The 'Minutes' took me less than five minutes to dictate the next morning. They had passed no more than three resolutions, and these related to minor routine matters.

Every year a group representing all departments interviewed youngsters applying for some dozen posts of supernumeraries. It became evident that fewer and fewer boys were applying and the offices were filling up with girls. It also became evident that the best applicants were coming from a school in the nearby town of Lowestoft. Councillor M....., as Council Leader, decreed that we should only appoint youngsters from the town, a marvellous decision that would in the long term lumber the Council with a number of second-rate staff. Girls were a problem. One bright young thing was causing problems and I asked to see her. She flounced into my office and sprawled into a chair, saying,

'If you are thinking of telling me off you can forget it. Nobody tells me off!'

I told her there were two options. She could either discuss the problem with me or she could go over to the Treasurer's and pick up her cards. We discussed the problem but it had no effect. A week or two later she sat at her desk with glazed eyes, stoned out of her mind with drugs, and had to be taken home. A few weeks later she resigned her position. I always requested staff, never ordered them, to do things. I said to one young girl in the general office,

'Would you take this letter over to the Planning Office please.'

'Why can't you take it yourself?' was her reply. Her supervisor looked aghast.

'He is not asking you. He is ordering you to do it.'

The girl looked surprised. The problems arose from the new Borough Secretary, whom I considered to be weak. He asked a girl to make him a photocopy of a letter.

'I'm busy. You'll have to do it yourself,' she snapped. And he did. Other Officers also took advantage of him. We had the whole printing operation passed to us, although we did not have the space to accommodate it properly. The Treasurer also talked him into letting our department be the guinea pig for a new computerised word-processing system. We spent days with the equipment out of action and had I not kept the old typewriters, the work of the department would have been at a standstill. When the system was first installed he asked me how many typists we could dispose of. He was most upset when I told him none. He did not seem to be able to grasp the basic fact that work still had to be typed, that the increased speed of output was minimal, and that it was just a little less laborious for the typists. But what hurt him most was when he discovered that new electronic office equipment has a built-in obsolescence. After a time, spares for repairs are unobtainable and the equipment is then just so much junk. He inspected one system and said,

'It looks alright.'

'Yes' I told him, 'but it no longer works.'

He was not alone on the information technology trip. The Council installed a new main computer that was claimed to do everything, except dance. The weekly budget control returns came in a two-inch-thick wad of concertina paper outprints, which contained the details of the whole of the Council's transactions with indecipherable codes, from which it would be impossible to determine any particular item relative to one's own department. I kept a simple manual system of our expenditure and was the only officer who was in command of his budget. Other officers, who had been tearing out their hair, followed suit. The computer never resolved the problem. What the uninitiated fail to recognise is that if you have super advanced technology, you have to have staff with the necessary experience to operate it.

The classic example of the craze for technology was brilliantly illustrated at an officers' meeting. A matter was being discussed during which the figures twelve times twelve arose. Quick as a flash the Treasurer took out his pocket calculator, tapped away and announced for everyone's benefit, 'one hundred and forty four'. It was funny but in a way also tragic. The thought occurred to me that if a man who lies in bed all day loses the use of his legs, would a man who relied on information technology lose the use of his brain?

Although the reorganisation of Local Government was for me the salient feature of 1974/75, there were other events that pinpointed those years as a time of change. Rowena had left home in 1973 to live with Bruce, a charming man, but fourteen years her senior. Annette, having left school, had done a year of further education in shorthand and typing and obtained a job as a typist with a large firm of timber importers, but walked out of the job after two weeks, saying she did not like audio typing because it hurt her ears. She had always been a shy, retiring, little girl but now she left home to share a bedsit with two of her young friends, funded by the Government's misconceived social security allowances. Having permitted the country to become over populated by immigrants, for whom there were no jobs, they presumably felt obliged to sustain the consequent unemployed by generous hand-outs from the public purse. All they did, in reality, was to destroy the work ethic in young people and give them a false impression of an easy existence. Away from parental influences it was not long before Annette spread her wings and took off.

It is one thing to enter the adult world from the security of a sound home base and a steady job, but it is quite something else to hitch a lift on the winds of fortune. For a time she flitted about the country like a dead, dry, leaf caught in the currents of a draughty courtyard. Never knowing where she was, or what she was doing, was a matter of great distress to me. The telephone on my desk would ring and I would hear her voice, 'Hi Dad, this is Annette.' Those simple words created enormous suspense, as I tried to guess her reason for calling. If I had caused my father anxiety, I was being repaid with interest, but you cannot put an old head on young shoulders and all I could do was advise.

My concern was that she would follow in my footsteps towards a wild time. For I had learned the dreadful truth that while running wild and breaking convention has the deceptive appearance of independence and freedom, it is all too often busy forging the chains of remorse, regret, and sorrow to shackle one for the rest of life.

While I was coping with these changes, Mother, at the age of seventy-five, decided to go off alone to see Grace in Baghdad. From her glowing accounts of her visit to Babylon and meeting and lunching with nomadic Arabs in the desert, she had a wonderful time.

Suddenly I began to feel old. In one sense I was old because now all the staff members in my department were much younger than myself, but something else was happening.

Bird-seed always came in half-hundred-weight bags. I used to pick them up and carry them to the shed, now I had to drag them. My strength had declined. Then came the day when, having been working in the garden, I found it difficult to get back to the house. Leaning heavily on a rake I managed it, but for the first time since I was a child my legs just did not seem to work. I had to admit that my walking distance was decreasing, I was not as nimble on my feet as years ago and I tired more quickly. But in my current mode of life I could still manage fairly well.

A sort of plateau had been reached. I was not seeking further promotion at work so it was just a matter of keeping the job ticking over. The children had left home. I went to see my mother several times a week, bred birds, decorated the bungalow and went fishing. You might say that I was reasonably content.

Life does not stand still. For some years Mother had been on tablets for diabetes. Now, at the beginning of 1980, she developed circulation problems in her legs. One foot went very dark in colour and she suffered great pain. The doctor had told her that she would have to have the leg amputated. She told me that the doctor had given her two tablets and said that if she took one she would sleep for a day but if she took both of them she would never wake up again.

'So, what are you going to do?' I asked her.

'I gave them back to him,' she said.

My heart sank. He was a good doctor and his action told me what lay ahead. Within a few days she was in hospital. That evening I went to see her in the women's surgical ward. It was a grim place, with beds full of old ladies awaiting surgery, and the image of the place was not helped by a middle-aged, ginger-haired, little nurse running around in a badly blood-stained apron. Mother was standing by the window. I persuaded her to come and sit down.

'Who are you?' she asked. 'You're not Derek. My Derek is going to come and get me out of this place. I'll smack your face if you talk to me.' Mother looked wild and demented.

I went to see the Ward Sister and told her that Mother was crazed with pain. She said she knew that. They had been with her all afternoon, fearful that she might throw herself out of the window.

'Well can't you give her a pain killer?' I asked.

'Yes,' she said 'but it might kill her.'

'For God's sake,' I told her, 'she is nearly eighty years old, she is going to have her leg cut off. What difference does it make?'

'If that is what you want,' she said. I told her to go ahead with the injection. By the next evening Mother was lying peacefully in bed and back in her right mind. The evening after that she told me they had withheld the drugs to make sure she understood the form they wanted her to sign consenting to the amputation. The operation was carried out the next day. My brother visited that ward once and promptly fainted. I went to see my mother every evening, both at the hospital and the convalescent hospital. She was remarkably cheerful.

By late summer she had to be discharged from hospital. My brother telephoned me at the office to say he had found her a place in a home some twenty-five miles away. I went out to see her. It was a dismal place, with a pungent odour of urine everywhere. Two days later I managed to get her moved to a local authority home in Gorleston, within a mile of where I lived. This place was modern, clean, friendly, and she had good company. I went every evening to see her. She would have been well looked after and comfortable there but she had this great urge to return to her own home. I tried to reason with her but to no avail. In the end I had to get the builders in to do substantial work, constructing a ground floor shower and toilet unit and raising the kitchen floor, so that everything was on one level for her wheelchair. She went home in August.

Rowena had left Bruce for another man, Ian, and they were married in September. Grace and her younger son came over from Baghdad and, with Mother in a wheelchair, attended the wedding. We were all there; it was to be the last time that we would all be together.

My poor mother never did master the knack of standing on a primitive artificial leg and remained confined to the chair. She did have a mysterious weekly visitor, a complete stranger called Iris.

'Who is she?' I asked.

'She just came to the door and said would I like a chat. She is a lovely person.' Mother thought highly of Iris and obviously enjoyed her visits. But my worst fears were now realised. Apart from Iris, her home help for an hour, an occasional visit from a neighbour and seeing me for a couple of hours in the evenings, she was alone and isolated. To make matters worse she started to be pestered by somebody ringing her doorbell in the early hours of the morning. She complained to the police but the nuisance continued. I went to the Police Station but could get no sense out of the desk officer. I told him that if he was unable to do anything about it I would sit outside in the car and watch for the culprit myself.

'You must not do that.' he said. 'You are likely to cause a breach of the peace.'

'We already have a breach of the peace,' I told him. 'I am going to do it and if there is a breach of the peace you will have to be there, won't you?'

I parked my car farther down the road that night. It was difficult to see clearly in the dim street lighting. About 1.30 a.m. a man stopped at the house. He looked up and down the street and I was sure he had seen me. He came away and walked along the road. I started the car and cruised very slowly alongside him. It was the son of a near neighbour who had moved away years ago. He always had been a strange fellow. We eyed each other as I passed. The nuisance visits ceased.

My brother and his family had arranged to spend Christmas Day with Mother and my family all gathered at Rowena and Ian's for the day. About 11.30 p.m. there was a telephone call from my brother saying that Mother was unwell, that they would be leaving in half an hour, could I go over. Mother was in bed and complained of a headache. She finally went to sleep but I spent the night in the lounge and kept an eye on her. The doctor said she had had a mild stroke. My brother took over supervision from me at midday on Boxing Day and we arranged to do twenty-four hour shifts, with the change-over at midday. After a day or two the strain and lack of sleep started to show. The doctor tried to get her admitted to hospital, without success. We tried to get help but none was available. My brother said in disgust,

'We might as well be back in the sixteenth century, boy. It's going to be just you and me.' I telephoned Ivy in London to see if she might give a hand.

'I'm tied up for several days,' she told me 'we have a lot of social events connected with the Labour Party and the Lambeth Council.' She obviously had her priorities mixed up. However, Mother seemed to enjoy being looked after by her sons. We had quite hilarious times, like the occasion when I was trying to lift her and fell into bed with her.

A specialist came to see her.

'Can you add up?' he asked her.

'Of course' she replied.

'What is three plus four?'

Mother hesitated, 'Five.'

'What is five minus two?'

Mother hesitated again 'One.'

He smiled. Later he explained to me that various parts of the brain had different functions. That part which dealt with calculations had been affected. Otherwise Mother seemed very normal.

Ivy finally arrived, with Roy, on the 8th January. Mother seemed downcast at the change-over but my brother and I really did need some rest. The next day she was taken to hospital after having suffered another stroke.

Ivy and Roy went back to London. I went with Gwen to see Mother in hospital. She was unconscious and she died that night.

'Make sure I am dead, before you bury me,' Mother had always said. True to my promise I went to see her corpse in the undertaker's chapel of rest. I had great difficulty identifying her. In life she had never worn make-up, but now the undertakers had painted her face and she looked like a fifty-year-old tart. We buried her with Father at Caister. A very beautiful, gently spoken lady came over to me to offer her condolences. She introduced herself as Iris. I now knew who she was. She was the wife of a prominent member of the Local National Front Party. With all the bad press coverage that party receives, the fact of the matter was that, in time of need, they provided a valuable social service that no other party bothered to undertake. I shall always have a feeling of great gratitude to this gentle and compassionate lady.

After the funeral we went back to Alderson Road. Ivy and her family started going through Mother's things. There was nothing more I could usefully do for Mother now so I went back to work at the Town Hall, conscious of the fact that had Mother taken the doctor's two tablets nine months earlier, she would have saved herself a lot of pain and distress. She had said in the end that she wanted to die and that I should not mourn for her. I was glad for her that she was out of the world, for I had noticed that her other foot was turning a dark colour and knew that, had she lived another month or two, she would have faced another amputation. But losing your mother, who has been a kind, dear, loving and caring person, is an emotional blow. The mind does not fully comprehend the finality of death at first. A month or two after her passing, a Council meeting finished early, around about 7.45 p.m. Good, I thought, I can nip down and see Mother. I was in the car heading for Alderson Road before I realised that she was not there any more.

CHAPTER 17

The Country Retreat

While I was in the throes of looking after Mother during her final year, Gwen was broadening her horizons. In July she had gone for a holiday in Iceland and was spending an increasing part of her time oil-painting. She revealed a rare talent for art, selling many of her paintings through commercial outlets, commissioned work and exhibitions.

Rowena seemed to be ensconced safely in a good marriage, and my only concern now was for Annette. She was never in one place for long and created endless difficulties for herself. Late in 1981 she returned home with the announcement that she was going to marry a tall young man of Scottish/Irish descent. They secured tenancy of a Council house in Norwich and I saw little of them. They had a daughter in the following year.

Neither Gwen nor I really liked the bungalow at Bradwell, which had always been intended as a temporary stop-gap while we found something better, but the years had quickly slipped away and our inertia had resulted in a long stay. The spur for a move came when a bad smell started to pervade the bungalow. Whether it emanated from the adjoining premises as a result of a new central heating system having been installed, we failed to discover, but the search began for a new home. We inspected many quaint thatched cottages, renovated farm-houses, and new houses and bungalows, yet we found nothing to suit us. In desperation we designed a house with the idea of building something more to our liking. Then Gwen spotted an advertisement for a modern house in the country. On a cold, wet, dreary day in February we went to see it. As we entered the large hall I was surprised to see that the layout of the house was almost identical to the house we had designed to build. Entering the large kitchen, we looked out of the patio window onto what was virtually a small field.

'Do you want it?' I asked Gwen.

She simply said, 'Yes'. The remainder of the inspection was no more than a formality.

The house was situated down a narrow road, which was no more than a metalled cart track, in a small rural village that rose gently out of miles of open marshland. From the roof I could have seen Caister, where I was born, and at night the lights of Yarmouth twinkled on the horizon. It was deathly quiet. The village, which only recently had been connected to water and electricity supplies, reminded me of Keyworth when I was a boy. We moved in on the 1st of April, 1983. There was over half an acre of rough land to turn into a garden. We believed that we had found Shangri-la and would be happy in the peace and quiet of the countryside, and yet still keep in touch with Yarmouth and the sea, which was no more than a ten minutes car-ride away. But perhaps the moving date should have rung a bell, for very soon our supposed Heaven turned into Hell.

The property had an early nineteenth century farmhouse, that was being renovated, to the south, with an old stable building running along the boundary as far as the rear of the house, a short length of wall, and then a twenty-feet tall mixed hedge of holly, hawthorn, and many other trees, extending to the end of the plot. On the northern side was a pair of semi-detached late eighteenth century cottages. The boundary ran against a small brick outbuilding, then a hedge of conifers, separating us from the cottage garden, which gave way to the unfenced rear boundary of a bungalow and, beyond that, a large hawthorn hedge at the rear of two large Council houses.

The trouble started when I engaged a local landscape gardener to plough the land. After cutting three furrows he abandoned the work, saying that the elderly gentleman in the bungalow had accused him of trespass on his land. The next morning, being a Saturday, I took a spade to help me over the rough ground, to where the elderly man was hovering in his garden. I said,

'You are just the man I want to see. What do you think you are doing interfering with my contractor?'

'He was on my land,' he said.

'Well how far does your land extend?' I asked. He did not reply. I stuck the spade in the earth towards him, saying,

'Is it here?'

'I am not sure,' he said.

'How long have you lived here?' I asked.

'Forty-five years,' he said. I told him that after forty-five years he ought to know where his boundary was. I started to dig a trench in a straight line towards him until I reached the extent of his cultivated land, where I uncovered the stumps of a hedge that had been cut to ground level. The stumps ran in a straight line across the bottom of his garden. 'Well this is the boundary, isn't it?' I asked.

'No,' he said agitatedly, 'I planted that hedge well inside my land.'

I told him that as it was the only visible sign of a boundary, I considered it to be the boundary, and I put in some posts my side of the hedge stumps.

'The bungalow belongs to my brother-in-law. I will have to see him,' he said.

The next morning I went to the bathroom at 5.30 a.m. and, looking out of the window, I was surprised to see the old man standing perfectly motionless at the corner of his garden nearest to me, staring silently at my house. When I went to the bathroom for a shave at 7 a.m. he was still there, standing in the same position and motionless. By mid-morning he had been replaced by another elderly gentleman, in the same place and adopting the same pose. And so it went on in a sort of shift arrangement throughout the day and until after dark, presumably until midnight. I just could not believe it. They were performing the ancient ritual of 'casting the evil eye'. When I did not

217

drop dead within a week, they resorted to more modern remedies and I received a solicitor's letter instructing me to remove my posts from their client's land. I spoke to the old chap again about the boundary, and he said that he was going to get a surveyor to measure his land.

'If you do that you will lose some land, as I am sure that my posts are well within my plot,' I told him.

But he was adamant. We both appointed surveyors. After much deliberation, they pegged out the boundary between us. As I had predicted, he lost another ten feet of land. Once the boundary was established I engaged a fencing contractor to erect a six-feet-high close boarded fence between us on my side of the pegs. Within a short time the old chap dropped dead with a heart attack. Perhaps it is true, after all, that black magic spells sometimes rebound on their originator.

At the same time as all this was going on, the renovation of the farmhouse next door was completed and the owner moved in, complete with tractors, sheep hurdles, dogs, loads of junk metal and drums of chemicals, with which he filled his garden. Our introduction came about on the Saturday morning after they moved in to take up residence. I discovered that my neighbour was a big, strong man, as he pushed through the hedge with a saw in his hand and began to saw it down. I went out to him and said, in a friendly way,

'Can I help you?'

'Yes,' he said gruffly, pointing to my concrete fuel bunker up against the wall, 'you can remove that for a start. I own a nine feet strip of land on your side of this hedge, and my buildings.' That knocked the wind out of my sails. I explained that my deeds showed ownership up to his buildings and to the hedge and, if he thought he had some claim to land, he had better consult a solicitor. He went back through the hedge, muttering to himself.

My predicament became clear when I discovered that my land had been owned previously by the man who lived next door in the cottage. He had given it to his son, who built the house that I had now purchased. The second cottage was occupied by this man's sister and brother-in-law, and it was their son who now occupied the farmhouse. It was even more galling to learn that my neighbour, who now claimed this strip of land, had actually assisted his cousin to erect the fuel bunker on my site before he bought the farmhouse. From what was now being said, I understood that there might have been all sorts of encroachments and disputes in the past, but I had bought the property offered for sale, and to which the vendor had claimed title.

A couple of weeks after our first encounter, I was resting on a chair at the side of the house, after doing some digging of the side garden near the stable buildings, when the man from the farmhouse came and sat on the front wall. He glared at me in a disagreeable manner, and then said, 'I'm fed up messing about like this. I'm going to smash this wall down and come through with my tractor'.

'Oh yes', I said, 'and what do you think I will be doing while you do that?'

He started shouting, and Gwen rang for the police. By now he had been joined by his mother and father, his son, and two or three other people whom I did not know. His mother shouted, 'We have been here for two hundred years and we know what is what'.

Somebody else shouted, 'Bloody foreigners! Why don't you go home?' By the time a police car arrived, half an hour later, they had dispersed. I explained to the police officer the cause of the dispute. He then went next door for over half an hour.

When he returned he said,

'He has no site plan, but I have read his deeds. It would solve the problem if you let him have the land'.

I was a little taken aback by this brilliant piece of policing, which seemed equivalent to saying to a person being attacked and mugged, 'It will solve the problem if you let them have your wallet'.

There was obviously no point in discussing the matter so I said,

'If he thinks that he has a valid claim he should go through the due processes of the law and take the matter to court'. As he left, it occurred to me that in the time it had taken the police to attend the incident, the mob could have lynched and buried us.

In a day or two a solicitor's letter arrived. I engaged a solicitor and they had a long exchange of correspondence. Part of the problem was that I could not understand the grounds of my neighbour's claim, but early one morning I awoke with the solution. My brain must have been working on it overnight. The clue was in his solicitor's last letter, referring to his client's site having a certain frontage footing as shown on the Ordnance Survey map. I knew the map was inaccurate because it misrepresented the distance between the stable buildings on one side of my site and the brick outbuilding on the other side, both of which had been existence for well over a hundred years. What the map did say was that my neighbour's plot was 0.44 of an acre. I measured his current frontage, multiplied it by the depth of his plot, and found that the calculation came to exactly 0.44 of an acre. My solicitor pointed this out to his solicitor and, after a long delay, there came a reply that their client had decided not to proceed with the matter.

Within a year the farmhouse was sold to a young couple. The land disputes had been resolved, but the events had blighted the property for me. Not only did I not feel at peace, because of the upset and aggravation, but it poisoned our relationship with the rest of the village. One or two people spoke as they passed, but only if they were alone. A shopping coach left the village just after 2 p.m. on a Wednesday afternoon, with the pick-up point on the main road, just around the corner from our road junction. As a group of villagers waited for the coach, they would be able to hear the phutter of my invalid car coming down the road so, by the time I turned the corner, all of them would have their backs to the road looking out over the field, and so would not have to acknowledge me. Once past them, my driving mirror revealed that they all turned round again to face the road. It happened every Wednesday. Even those who spoke to me when alone dare not break ranks with the rest of the villagers. I tried the local pub just once. It was downright hostile. It came as no surprise to me to hear that in nearby villages, a man from London who took tenancy of a pub, and another couple from away who took over the local shop, were forced out of business by village boycotts. We decided that we did not need the village and would stick it out. A gardening firm from Norwich came and ploughed, levelled and seeded the rear garden. We planted alder, birch and walnut trees at the far end of the plot, and turned half of the site into an orchard, with apples, pears, plums, gages, damsons and cherries. Elsewhere we introduced as wide a variety as possible of trees and shrubs, including oak, ash, rowan, robina friscia, prunus sargenti, Scots pine and many different conifers. Hazel sprang up naturally; so did wild cherry, plum and sloe. The heavy clay soil might not be ideal for flower or vegetable cultivation, but trees grew apace.

By this time, there was a dearth of fish and sea angling had declined rapidly. On a fine October evening, the Council meeting having finished early, I took the opportunity to visit the harbour.

Where a few years earlier fishermen had crowded the quay, there was now a solitary angler.

'How is your luck?' I asked him.

He turned around from watching his rod, 'Very poor,' he said.

We were soon discussing the good old days when fishing was worthwhile.

'I remember,' he said, 'an old crippled chap who used to fish here. He had a thick little old rod, like a brussel sprout stalk, but by golly he caught a hell of a lot of fish.'

'You mean me,' I said. He eyed my black suit, crisp white shirt and tie, and laughed.

'No. He was a scruffy old bugger. Always dressed in a filthy raincoat and smoked a pipe. Haven't seen him for a long time now. 'Spect the poor old sod is dead.'

'He wore a black and white woolly hat,' I said.

'That's right,' he agreed.

'It was me,' I told him. He shook his head.

'No. This old chap drove one of those little blue invalid cars.' I pointed to where my invalid car was just visible the other side of the bushes.

'I know,' I told him, 'I still do'. He stared at me in amazement.

'Good God, I would never have recognised you. I'm sorry.' We had a good laugh about it.

Rightly or wrongly, people judge by appearance, and clothes do matter. That is why I sent one of my assistants home to change when he arrived at work dressed in jeans, open sandals and a Mickey Mouse T-shirt. The public expect local government officers to dress in a certain way. To do otherwise would result in loss of confidence. In the days when I worked at the County Council, but was at Yarmouth Town Hall organising a cage bird show, a lady stopped me in the foyer to ask about a Council matter.

'Sorry,' I told her, 'but I do not work here.'

'Well you look as if you do,' she retorted.

Was it the suit, or had the job turned me into an official? It is remarkable how people in different occupations come to have some sort of common denominator. Do they grow together to adopt a common identity, or do people of a certain disposition gravitate to a particular job?

At the end of December that year Annette gave birth to a son, but it was no occasion for celebration. Her husband could not settle to a domestic life and their divorce, that seemed inevitable, occurred some months later. The following year, Ivy and Roy paid us a visit for a few hours, as they were having a short holiday in the area. I had seen little of Ivy over the years. She was so engrossed with her family, her teaching career and her public services as an Alderman on Lambeth Borough Council, that she had little time for anything else. It seemed that she had grown away from our family. Now, she looked thin and ill, but I did not realise how desperately sick she was. Her death from cancer a few months later came as a great shock.

Early in April 1986 I had another fall. It was a strange affair which happened on the landing on my way to bed. My knees took the impact, but then my body fell backwards, locking my legs under me. At my request, Gwen heaved me forward, but as my hands steadied me there was a searing pain in my left wrist. Using one arm, I managed to drag myself into the bedroom and, eventually, onto the bed. The doctor came the next morning, examined my wrist, and said it was a sprain. At first he appeared reluctant to give me a medical certificate as being unfit for work, but I pointed out that without the use of both hands I could not even rise from a chair, quite apart from the fact that my invalid car was controlled by the left hand. Using the toilet was a problem, but I found that by putting my elbow on top of the low flush cistern it was just possible to lower and raise myself from the seat. The wrist remained painful and unusable and it was a fortnight before I managed to get down the stairs. With lack of use, the muscles in that arm started to go flabby and wither.

The weeks passed but the wrist did not improve. When my doctor went on holiday, a young Indian doctor called to see me. He looked doubtful when he examined my wrist.

'I do not know what is wrong, but I am going to look it up in my books,' he announced. I admired him for his honesty. The next day he was back saying, 'I think you have broken a bone. I am sending you to the hospital'.

He was correct. The surgeon put the X-ray on the screen and pointed out the fracture to both bones in the wrist. He said that they had knitted together of their own accord and, as the hand was fairly straight, it was best to leave it alone. Eventually I was able to use the hand, but it was weak and painful for a long time and there was never a complete recovery.

Because of my poor balance and the increasing number of falls, I found it helpful to use a walking stick. My legs seemed to be getting much weaker and, at my request, the doctor made an appointment for me to see the orthopaedic surgeon. At the hospital I was shown into a cubicle and told to strip to my underpants and lie on the couch. Half an hour later the surgeon breezed in, followed by a young black woman, who was presumably a student.

'Well, what is wrong with you?' he asked. I told him that my legs were getting weaker and would not support me. 'Of course they won't,' he interrupted my explanation, 'over the years you have grown that great fat body! I can't do anything. Go to Weight Watchers'.

With a short laugh he breezed out again, followed by the black woman. As they left the woman's eyes met mine. Those dark, limpid, eyes were full of sympathy, and I knew what she thought about the consultation. It seemed to me that, whatever else had changed, orthopaedic surgeons were just the same as they were forty years ago. Could it be that they hand on their attitude to patients from one generation to another?

Anyway, I took his advice and during the next twelve months reduced my weight from eleven to nine stones, but it made not the slightest difference. Slowly but surely, walking became more difficult, and no longer was it possible to walk from my car to my desk in a continuous journey. I disguised my problem by stopping off at offices on the way, ostensibly as brief social calls, but really I was taking rests. Such techniques were not new to me as I had always had to stage-manage my conduct to minimise and conceal my incapacity. This was achieved in various ways, such as arranging to be the first to arrive and last to leave meetings, being seated whenever possible and taking up positions that would mask those parts of my body that I did not want noticed. I must have been quite successful for when the question of repairing the lift in the Council offices was under discussion and its requirement for members of staff who were disabled, a Councillor queried whether there were any disabled staff. He was told,

'There is Mr Dix'. He looked surprised.

'Mr Dix is not disabled', he said.

But I did not fool Councillor Adlington, the wife of a local doctor. When she was Chairman of the Public Health Committee she visited my office frequently to discuss the Committee's affairs. She took me by surprise one day by saying,

'You are much more disabled than people think, aren't you Mr Dix?'

She was a strong-willed, dominant, person who knew exactly what she wanted and we got along well together, but she did put me on the spot on one occasion. The Committee dealt with licensing and had discretionary powers over the showing of films in their area. A report had been received from the British Board of Film Censors suggesting the banning of a certain film which featured certain female acts of sexual deviation, which they described in graphic detail. Despite my attempts to gloss over the matter, she insisted on reading the report and said that it should be brought to the committee. When this item was reached during the meeting, she announced calmly,

'Mr Dix will read the report of the Censors to you.' We had three other lady Councillors on the committee, and I looked at her in amazement. She fixed me with a baleful eye, and I could see no alternative but to obey. It was as embarrassing as telling a really filthy joke to one's grandmother. The lady Councillors were pink in the face when I finished, and the male members looked uncomfortable. Councillor Adlington was as unperturbed as if I had just read a shopping list.

By the time of the 1987 General Election, I guessed that this would be the last General Election that I would organise. Sitting in the large Assembly Room, with its high windows looking out over the river and the huge oil-paintings of former civic worthies gazing down on the proceedings, the counting of votes was going smoothly, as usual. But in my mind I saw, not the ballot boxes, the counting staff or the candidates' agents and representatives, but row upon row of cages full of canaries, budgerigars and other exotic birds, as they were in the days when I organised the annual exhibitions in this room as a young man. All too clearly I recalled the faces of the old fanciers, all my old friends, most now long departed. It became a memorable but sad evening for me. I knew that an era was coming to an end, for it was becoming increasingly obvious that my legs were not going to carry me for much longer. But, as always, there were other unforeseen changes afoot.

It was a few months later that the Chief Executive Officer was relieved of his departmental responsibilities and the Borough Secretary became the departmental head. I feared the worst, for now the Borough Secretary would have free rein and no longer would we have the Chief Executive Officer to protect us from the worst of his excesses. To say that I and the Borough Secretary got on well together would be untrue. In fairness to him, he did make some attempt to have an amicable relationship with me, as I did with him, but somehow our chemistry just did not gel. Within ten minutes of us being together the détente started fraying at the edges. He would become increasingly peevish and sarcastic, and I would hide my feelings by becoming cool and detached. It seemed that neither of us could do anything about it, as that is just the way it was. In the end we behaved like actors delivering a dialogue in which they did not believe.

The root cause was probably our differing perceptions of what local government administration was about. I thought he was weak and ineffective, lacking the courage to stand his ground with other chief officers and the Council, and that some of his management ideas were ludicrous in the extreme. He seemed to be ridden by doubt and prejudices. What he thought of me, apart from an instinctive dislike, is anyone's guess, but I know that he resented my ability to manage committee meetings, handle other officers and, no doubt, he felt apprehensive about my positive approach to achieving administrative goals. From some of the things he said, I gathered that he suffered from some sort of inferiority complex, imagining that, being a northerner from Lancashire, he was in some way discriminated against in the south. As an East Anglian I am quite ambivalent about other regions and could never understand the north versus south attitude adopted by some northern people. I came across this ridiculous prejudice only once in the canary world, when I encountered a breeder in Derbyshire who would never sell a bird to anyone living in the southern counties. But for a professional man, who chose to work in the south, to echo such sentiments was unbelievable. He and I once interviewed candidates for an administrative post. After seeing all of the candidates, he asked me who was my choice and, when I named the man, said that he was surprised that I had selected a Lancastrian having regard to the anti-northern bias. Where the man came from was, to me, irrelevant. I refrained from telling him that he was the one who was prejudiced, neither did I mention that my maternal grandmother was a Lancastrian. How do you tell your boss not to be such a stupid prat?

He also had a bee in his bonnet about what he saw as a 'them' and 'us' scenario, 'them' being administrative staff, and 'us' being legal staff. At a meeting of departmental section heads he became quite agitated about it, saying that he was fed up with the feud that was going on between the legal and administrative wings of the department. 'Why can't you be more friendly to legal staff?' he asked me. I said that I had no idea what he was talking about, and told him that I and Maurice, the senior legal assistant, went out drinking together every Friday night, which seemed to me to be a fairly friendly relationship. He was lost for words but continued to be irritable. I came to the conclusion that he had preconceived notions that festered in his mind until he believed them to be reality.

It had been a difficult period dealing with him in his role as head of the legal section, and being my immediate boss, but with him now being the supreme head of the department I waited in some trepidation for the upheaval to come.

His immediate new initiatives were very trendy. All staff were requested to write a criticism of their supervisors who, in turn, were to make a critical appraisal of their section heads. I asked the Borough Secretary how far the exercise was to go; for example would section heads make a critical appraisal of himself? He smiled smugly and said that he did not think that would be necessary. The outcome was predictable. Those members of staff who responded did so on the basis that they felt they were not properly appreciated, otherwise they would be on higher salary grades. What was to have been an on-going procedure fizzled out. Then we had a monthly staff meeting. The general office was closed, typing and printing came to a halt, and administrative and legal desks were abandoned for the staff meeting. We had long and heated discussions about the drinks-vending machine not always functioning properly, and why female staff could not wear trousers in the office. The only business-related issue was a call for the Borough Secretary to sign his letters earlier so that they could catch the post. When the Borough Secretary suggested that refreshments might be provided at future meetings, to make the occasion more sociable, everyone applauded it, until they discovered that he meant the staff should supply the refreshments. I watched these proceedings with amazement, and doubted whether they would engender loyalty. More likely they would diminish respect and authority.

The weekly meeting of section heads was little better. There was the usual bickering about files not being up to date, and the counter claim that this was because certain officers kept back correspondence instead of passing it out for filing. The young Assistant Secretary (Legal), who was under, he said, intolerable work pressures, gave an account of all the charts with which he had decorated his room, showing the progress of various legal activities, indicated in different coloured inks. This was, he admitted, time-consuming, and he wondered if he might have a part-time assistant to carry out the work of updating the charts. The Borough Secretary expressed great enthusiasm for the idea, instructing everyone to keep such charts. He asked me why I had not thought of the system. I said nothing, but my mind went back to my boyhood days when I had proudly shown my father an exercise I had carried out relative to the canaries, listing the number of eggs each bird had laid, the number of eggs that hatched, the number of youngsters reared, with appropriate percentage calculations.

'Will all that produce even one additional youngster?' he had asked. I had to admit that it would not. 'Well don't waste your time', he said, 'go and do something useful – like finding them some fresh green food'.

I knew it was a waste of time and effort, but for a few months we produced charts showing the number of files made, put into storage, issued, and so forth, the number of letters, memoranda, reports and documents typed, and lists of all our other activities. The chart on the progress of Land Charge Searches illustrated what we already knew, that completion was being held up by delays in the Planning Department.

For more than a year I had asked the Borough Secretary to sort out the Planning Officer on this matter, without success. Now, I produced the chart and suggested that it provided the detailed information for him to take the matter up with the Planning Officer. He declined. It was, he said, perhaps inappropriate for us to continue the chart for land charge searches, as their progress was dependent on action by other departments. And that was a typical solicitor's response to an administrative problem.

It had always appeared to me that the major flaw in the local government system was the concentration of power in the hands of the legal profession. Virtually every local authority in the country is headed by someone with a legal background. This anachronism stems from the historical duties of the old Town Assemblies, where the Mayor and Burgesses administered not only the civic affairs of their communities, but also the judicial functions, and so needed a legal adviser. This carried on through the Town Clerks, and Clerks of the County Councils, who also had twin duties as Clerks of the Peace. Although the judicial role has long been divorced from the civil administration, the legal profession has clung tenaciously to a privileged position in local councils. Yet, in modern local government the need for legal advice is no different from that required by a commercial undertaking. How many of the companies listed on the London Stock Exchange are controlled by a solicitor? The answer is, virtually none. Unfettered by custom, ritual and the out-of-date practices that confine local government, the commercial enterprises are operated by people with managerial skills. In local government, not only do the reins of power lie in the hands of lawyers but, in many instances, second-rate solicitors, on large salaries, occupy positions that are no more than junior administrative posts. In rare cases there may be a solicitor with a flair for administration, but this runs against the grain, for the very nature of a solicitor's training militates against good administration which is about getting things done quickly and efficiently. Unfortunately, the solicitors' creed is, if possible, do nothing, and thereby avoid making a mistake. In practice this means much pomp and procedure, a good deal of rhetoric, and very little action. Anyone who has ever consulted a solicitor about anything whatsoever, will know the frustration of long-drawn-out, tedious processes that never quite reach a definite conclusion. If that sounds like a good description of local government also, I am not surprised. Stripping the legal profession of its domination of local authorities, and the introduction of commercial management skills, would probably reduce staff requirements by over fifty per cent, and improve services.

But perhaps the wider issue should be addressed of whether the small local councils should be abolished. They are in essence no more than a sop to so called local democracy. The reality is that matters of importance are controlled by central government, and the administration of routine services could be conducted much more efficiently by a regional authority. I recall expressing this view to my father after I had worked in local government for only a few years. His response was that I should not talk myself out of a job, but my subsequent many years of service in the County Council, City Council, County Borough and District Councils have only reinforced my belief that local government in its present form is outdated, inefficient, and should be scrapped.

On a day early in 1989, the telephone on my desk rang. It was Councillor M....., now chairman of the Personnel Committee.

'Are you thinking of retiring Mr Dix?' he asked.

I told him that such a thought had not entered my mind, and that I would wish to carry on working for as long as possible.

'I don't blame you', he said, and rang off. I wondered what he was up to now.

It was not a long wait to discover his intentions. A week or so later, the Borough Secretary called me into his office, together with my two principal assistants, to tell me that the Council had decided to reorganise the structure of the department into separate sections. In future, the assistant dealing with committee administration would take over full responsibility for the Council and committee administration, the other assistant would have full responsibility for elections, electoral registration, local land charge searches and licensing. I would now be responsible only for the Mayoralty, printing, typing, the general office and budget control. In short, I had been stripped of all my real work and power. It amounted to constructive dismissal.

The fact that I retained my title of Assistant Borough Secretary was meaningless, not that titles meant anything to me. What was more important was the retention of the grade. If the Council wanted to pay me a large sum of money to do a minor administrative job, and throw away the advantage of all my experience and expertise, that was their loss. Councillor M..... might have removed me from the Council Chamber and out of his sight but, if he thought that I would take umbrage and leave, he had made a grave error of judgement. I had never been a proud man and loss of status was not important to me, but I did miss the interest in running the Council, which had been my life for so long. Councillor M..... had once accused me of being born with a silver spoon in my mouth. Little did he know of my background. No doubt his bigoted mind confused intellect with class.

Who had actually engineered this move remained unresolved, but obviously the Borough Secretary must have acquiesced in the matter, even if he were not a major participant. If he had expected a violent reaction from me, he was to be disappointed. I made no comment whatsoever. Instead, I settled down to do the job now allotted to me to the best of my ability, for I knew, in any event, that my working days were numbered. My aim now was just to complete the necessary years of service to qualify for a full pension. I was mindful, however, that they had played a dirty trick. The local Labour Party were renowned for in-fighting among themselves for position and power but, when such tactics were applied to staff matters, where people's careers and livelihoods were seriously affected, it demonstrated their total disregard for rectitude.

The only other duty left to me was to advise the Public Health Committee. This came about, I believed, only because the Borough Secretary did not wish to tangle with Councillor B....., a formidable lady, who was chairman of that Committee. When Councillor B..... had joined the Council, a year or two earlier, her reputation had preceded her from her former authority. The Council grapevine had received the information that she was the scourge of all officers, and so it proved to be. In the same way as some people enjoy fox-hunting, she enjoyed officer-hunting. She had a keen instinct for recognising weaknesses and gaps in officers' explanations of their failures to achieve what was required of them, and pursued and harried them with great spirit and relish. She had a set formula for officer-crushing. First would come a light grilling to expose their tender parts, then a good roasting to soften them up, and finally their disintegration as their arguments, defences and dignity were torn apart. It was painful to watch. Never alone, always having another lady Councillor with her, she seemed to glorify in having an audience to watch her carrying out the punishment, like the woman at Keyworth who beat her son in my presence.

On one occasion, I was in the Chief Executive's office, together with the Borough Secretary, when Councillor B..... sailed in with a companion. With a very brief introduction of the purpose of her visit, she proceeded to berate the pair of them for some failure of action. They sat there taking it like two naughty schoolboys who had been caught out by the headmistress. After giving them a thorough verbal thrashing, she left. They sat licking their wounds.

Councillor B..... was an interesting personality. Physically very attractive, educated, articulate, well-spoken, quick-witted, intelligent and well versed in local government matters, there was nobody to match her. Oddly enough, she and I got on well together. Whether it was because I was not intimidated by her, or because I always played the game straight, or because she had decided to be kind to me, I never worked out, but she allowed me to take diabolical liberties with her, and get away with it. A few days before each committee meeting, the Chairman and Vice-Chairman have a briefing meeting with officers, so that they are fully conversant with matters that are to be discussed. On my way to such a meeting with Councillor B..... I passed the Borough Engineer, red in the face and looking harassed.

'Be careful,' he warned, 'she is in a hell of a mood this morning.' As I entered the committee room, she was sitting at the table, with the Vice-Chairman and a representative from the Treasurer's department.

'You're late!' she snapped, looking at the wall clock.

'Not so, Chairman,' I said cheerfully, 'that clock is three minutes fast.' She glanced at her wrist watch and saw that I was correct, but she still looked angry. 'Somebody upset you this morning?' I asked, giving her a big smile, 'You look even more attractive when you are angry'.

She tried to control it, but the urge was too great; she grinned. She probably thought, 'cheeky old devil', but the ice was thawed and the meeting proceeded happily. At another such meeting she was laying down the law about what should or should not be done, or else there would be trouble. I just laughed,

'What are you going to do? Tie me down and beat me with a bamboo rod?'

Quick as a flash came the return volley, 'You would enjoy that, wouldn't you?'

She smiled in satisfaction as she watched me searching desperately for a suitable reply and finding none. She had won that one, game, set and match. So, as I trudged through the drab business of administering the mundane details of the general office, meetings with Councillor B..... became the highlight of my calendar.

Just to turn the screw no doubt, the Borough Secretary decided to hand my office over to the Public Health Officer. I was consigned to a dark, dingy office at the rear of the Town Hall, which I shared with a junior clerical officer. He was a sociable young man, so at least I had somebody to talk to. It seemed strange to be sharing an office again after having spent nearly twenty years on my own. Within a few months he left and was replaced by a lady assistant. She was pleasant enough, but it was not quite the same. With a woman, I found that the conversational range was somewhat curtailed.

Eventually, I negotiated a deal with Rank Xerox, whereby we traded in our old large printing machine for two smaller models. This not only resolved our breakdown problems, giving us at least one machine in operation at any given time, but it also increased our capacity. The new machines would not fit into the office occupied by the old model, so they were accommodated in what had been a wide corridor, opposite to the room that I now occupied which, in turn, proved ideal for paper storage and print preparation. I and the young lady transferred to the former machine room, which just happened to be the room next door to my old office. The Borough Secretary did not look happy, but the logic of the arrangement was undeniable.

As the months slipped by, the Borough Secretary became increasingly petty and hostile, looking for any small fault within the general administration that he could criticise. I kept a low profile, for my completion of forty years contributing to the pension fund, and entitlement to a full pension, was nearly achieved. However, I did have just one wrangle with him.

One of my female assistants dealt with a matter that was strictly controlled by procedures set out in the Council's 'Standing Orders'. Returning from a meeting where this matter had been dealt with, she advised me that the standard procedures had not been followed. This breach of standing orders was very serious and I was surprised to learn that the Borough Secretary had also been at the meeting and, presumably, had allowed this to happen. Fearing that the matter might be called into question, and my assistant held responsible, I sent the Borough Secretary a note, which was standard practice, drawing his attention to what had occurred, and saying that I assumed he accepted, as the senior officer present, responsibility for what had taken place. He sent for me. Sitting at his desk, flushed with temper, he flung the note on the desk, saying that he did not accept it. Accept it or not, I told him, I had a copy on file showing that it had been sent.

'Don't you trust me?' he snarled. I thought that was pretty rich coming from a man who had recently connived in my demotion.

'I don't trust anyone,' I said.

'But I am an officer of the law!' he declared pompously.

'Yes,' I said, 'The House of Commons is full of officers of the law, and I don't trust them either'. For years I had tried to conceal my opinion of him, but now he would be in no doubt.

A week or two later I celebrated my fifty-eighth birthday and qualified for a full pension. My legs were very weak now and, for the first time since I was a child, began to give me pain. Being on my feet more during the last seventeen months, attending to office machinery, had not helped. Some days they were better than on other days, but there appeared to be a general decline in my strength. Walking was now slow and difficult. On the third week in September I took a fortnight's annual leave. I hoped that the rest might prove beneficial, but intuition told me that I would be unlikely to return. When everyone had gone home, I made my way through the now silent and empty offices, saying goodnight and exchanging pleasantries with the cleaning ladies that I passed, as was my usual practice. At the end of my leave my legs were no better, and the doctor gave me a medical certificate for absence from work. These certificates continued for a year, when I then sought, and obtained, early retirement on ill health grounds. By the time that I formally retired I had just about forgotten the Town Hall and everyone in it. During that year nobody had made contact with me, and it seemed clear that they had forgotten me also. So it was that, far from leaving the Town Hall and local government in a fanfare of trumpets, I just slipped quietly away into oblivion.

Many people who retire after a lifetime of work miss their employment and mope for their past glories. I discarded local government with no more emotion than I would for changing out of a dirty shirt. For me, there were still the canaries. Getting to the shed was sometimes a difficult and painful business, but once there I could manage them from a chair. For a couple of years I was able to cut the back lawn using my ride-on mower, but when that became too onerous I paid a young man to do it for me. Fortunately the layout of the garden involved little maintenance, other than the grass cutting, and the few flower beds near to the house had always been Gwen's preserve.

With my brain now cleared of all the trappings of local government law and practice, there was time to think of other things. One of those other things was the Stock Market. From my studies for the Chartered Institute of Secretaries examination I was well versed in reading company accounts and, during my time at the City Hall, I had clerked the Investment Panel which met regularly with stockbrokers to review the pension fund's equity portfolio, so I had some experience of the subject. At first there were a few mistakes, but eventually the successes outweighed the failures. I was soon to discover that the commercial world was even more dirty and corrupt than local government.

Despite all the rhetoric about regulation and fair trading, many of the practices might be legal, but they were still swindles. Individual small share-holders have no influence on the control of a company, and a closed circle of the elite form the boards of most companies, awarding themselves enormous salaries and share options with impunity. Takeovers and mergers are designed to benefit company directors, and all too often the shareholder is the loser. The fluctuation in share prices is artificially manipulated for the benefit of big players and stock brokers. For example – XYZT Holdings plc may be a top company, trading internationally and with a sound record. The shares are priced at £4.00. You might buy 1,000 at a cost of £4,060, including stamp duty and broker fees. The share price fluctuates and might rise to £4.10, but it is not possible to sell at a profit because after brokerage fees the return would be £4,059 – a loss of £1. The company then acquires two small companies, and eventually negotiates a merger with another large company to make it a dominant supplier of its product. The share price falls steadily, although the company is doing well, until it reaches £3.15s. Additional shares could be purchased at this price, but there is no guarantee that the price will not drop further. Suddenly there is a takeover bid at £3.30s. a share. This is accepted by the majority of shareholders and there is no option but to sell at this price and bear the loss. There is no way of knowing how many shares are being held which were acquired at particular prices and, whatever the current share price, this can be manipulated down to make the company an attractive proposition for a takeover. Directors with massive holdings acquired at discount prices can clearly gain from a takeover bid, and some will be rewarded for their co-operation with a seat on the purchasing company's board. But their real reward comes eighteen months later when they leave office with a generous golden handshake. By then of course everyone has forgotten XYZT Holdings plc, or their involvement with it.

Although I have been hit three times with these circumstances, fortunately the majority of companies are stable, and the fascination lies in pitting one's wits against fluctuating market forces to make a small profit. But, as with card playing, the rule is that if you cannot afford to lose do not gamble. With a tidy sum tucked away in cast-iron securities, I do not regard the money invested in the Stock Market as real money. It is more like playing a giant game of Monopoly. It seems a strange world when I think back to the struggle I had to save £165 for the deposit on my first bungalow, when now I can pick up the telephone and, in less than two minutes, spend thousands of pounds. It seems immoral that, for a year's hard work, I once received only £135. Now, if my judgement is correct, I can make hundreds of pounds in two or three days with two simple telephone calls. Of course, I could equally lose the same amount, but at least I sink or swim on my own decisions, free of the whims and prejudices of small-minded politicians.

If 1989 were a bad year for me, it was a disaster for my brother. After a brave and long struggle, Barbara died of cancer. A few months later Grace returned to England from Baghdad with her two sons, and shortly after her return her husband also died of cancer. Everyone seemed to be dying of cancer, yet the Establishment remained very quiet about the possible causes of this disease.

The autumn after I retired it seemed a good idea to go fishing. Since my fishing days in the 1970s, a flood defence wall had been erected, which meant that it was no longer possible to get a car to the quay edge. However, a concrete pedestrian ramp with rails had been constructed at the point of my favourite fishing spot and, once the ramp was negotiated, there was a distance of about only ten yards to the river wall. I built a wooden box to fit onto a four-wheeled shopping trolley which would take all my gear, and provide a seat. But I was nervous of going out alone in case my legs failed me. My first expedition was early in the morning just before sunrise, and Gwen came with me. It came as a surprise to discover how heavy the rod now felt. We caught nothing. With the confidence acquired on that first trip I ventured on the second one alone in the evening, and proved to be the only angler on that vast empty quay. The peace that used to exist at this place was now disturbed by a large amusement arcade just across the road, with blazing multi-coloured lights. Within a short time I was catching good-sized whiting. Then a gang of some dozen youths, accompanied by two girls, all aged about sixteen or seventeen, crowded onto the ramp behind me. At first there was a lot of childish horse-play then, with apparently nothing better to do, they turned their attention to me, shouting insults. A man aged about forty came along the quay and stopped for a chat. While we talked I caught two large whiting and it was getting quite exciting, although while landing one of them I nearly fell down. Fortunately I was able to save myself from falling by clutching onto the wall, but that was my big fear. If I fell I knew that it would be very difficult to get on my feet again.

Soon we were joined by a short, elderly, man. At this point the mob of youths returned and it was not long before the verbal abuse turned into stone-throwing at us. The elderly man said that he was going around the corner and would phone for the police. Some five minutes later a wailing police siren sounded farther along the quay and the youths scarpered, but the police car never made an actual appearance. The evening ruined, I packed up and went home before there was any more trouble. Two days later I tried the midday tide, but there were no fish. A young policeman stopped to see how I was doing.

'I would have been pleased to see you the other evening,' I said, telling him what had occurred.

'We get a lot of trouble from that crowd,' he said.

'Yes, but what do you do about it?' I asked.

'What can you do?' he replied as he walked away. If that was the police attitude I knew that it would be unwise to fish there again, so that was my last fishing expedition. I had enough to contend with trying to overcome the problems of my disabilities without the aggravation of an ignorant mob. Twenty years earlier, those lads would have been fishing themselves, or at least acting like young men rather than overgrown children.

On one of my earliest visits to this place on the quay in 1969, a group of young boys, aged about ten, were attempting to fish next to me. One was a very small, very puny, little chap. He had little idea as to how to cast his line, and a mighty heave resulted in his lead weight and flying hooks missing my head by inches, to wrap around the post beside me.

'Watch it young dynamite!' I said good-humouredly. He looked slightly abashed as his mates fell about laughing. Eight or nine years later, as I fished in the same place late in the evening, a very tall, well built, handsome young man stopped to speak.

'You're still here then? You don't remember me, do you?' I shook my head. 'I am Dynamite. Ever since you called me that, the name has stuck, and I am known to everyone as Dynamite'.

We had a good laugh about it, and I was pleased to see what a fine man he had become. What, I now wondered, would the rabble generation develop into? Technology might be advancing, but had the zenith of our civilisation passed, and was the moral fibre of our society disintegrating? The days when one could walk through the streets late at night without fear had long gone. Now, it seemed, one could not even fish from a public quay in the early evening without fear of molestation.

Two more years passed and my legs were now so unreliable that I was unable to walk anywhere. Even if I managed to park the car within twenty yards of the building where the Cage Bird Society met there was no guarantee that I would make it to the door, so I had to forgo that simple pleasure, as also going into shops or anywhere else. My legs would seem fine for a few steps but, without warning, they would go weak. On more than one occasion they failed me on the way to the bird shed, which is within ten yards of the back door, so that I had to lower myself to the ground and drag myself to the shed, and then climb onto bags of seed until my body was of sufficient height to regain my feet. Having to drag oneself along the ground is an object lesson in humility.

In the summer of 1997, my stick slipped on the slimy surface of the driveway as I was going to the car in torrential rain. I fell heavily. This time it was my right wrist that took the impact, and from the excruciating pain it seemed probable that it was another fracture. It took a long time to drag myself over the wet ground and into the house, where I finally managed to heave myself up the first two steps of the stairs on my elbows so that I could get to my feet. I did not bother to see a doctor, and after some weeks the wrist healed. I was now terrified of further falls, which seemed to be happening every couple of months, for each time it was like receiving a severe beating. With both wrists now seriously damaged, I resorted to two sticks to help me to get around the house, and bought an electric trolley to get me to the bird shed. More than sixty years had elapsed since I had taken my first steps after having been paralysed with polio and, as walking became increasingly difficult, I was aware that the circle was closing.

On my sixtieth birthday Rowena took me out for the evening, together with Gwen and Annette. We visited the Mitre. After nearly forty years it had changed very little. That is to say, the premises had not changed. But pubs are largely about people. The people I had known in the Mitre were no longer there, and the place was just full of memories and nostalgia. That was my only visit to a pub in the last seven years. Being generally confined to the house and the car limits my social contact but, when driving into Yarmouth to take Gwen shopping, occasionally I see Jap in the street and stop for a chat. He is still the same unchanged Jap I have always known. Recently I asked him if he still visited Breydon.

'Not often,' he said, 'it seems different. You would not recognise the place, Pirate.'

I reminded him of the summer evening we had rowed up Breydon, when a brilliant red and orange sunset had filled the sky, bathing the estuary in a golden light. The fluorescence in the water had glowered strangely, and dripped off the oars like greenish white luminous quicksilver, creating the sensation of being in a weird, fantastic, surreal painting. We fell silent, both remembering the event. Then Jap said,

'We shall never see those days again Pirate. We were looking at the world through young eyes.'

I knew what he meant. Our advancing years had destroyed the romantic view of the world. The magic had gone. It was our perception that had changed, not Breydon.

When the weather is fine I sit on a bench in the garden and smoke my pipe, just as the old men did in Keyworth. But, unlike them, I sit alone. All my old friends have gone. Some have moved far away, some were lost in the drifting tide of time and many, such as Gordon who came with me on the Broads holiday and my old drinking companion Maurice, are long dead. I see them now only in transient flashes of memory. They, like all the people who touched my life, come and go without conscious effort on my part. Past incidents spring to mind. Some make me wince with embarrassment, some make me laugh or smile, others bring unbearable anguish, filling my eyes with tears.

Looking back down the long years I wonder whether I could have done better. Somebody once said to me that in the game of life they thought I had been dealt a rotten hand of cards. Perhaps that was so, but how well had I played them? Life follows a crooked track, unaccountably twisting and turning, with every now and then a fork in the path. Without knowing what lies ahead we are forced to follow either one branch or the other. It all comes down to 'what if'. What would have been the result if I had not gone to the Grammar School? If Rosalie had married me would it have brought sublime happiness, or some unforeseen misery? How would life have proceeded if I had married Julie, or not married Gwen? What if I had taken the job at Coleshill, or not taken the job at Yarmouth? At each juncture I made a decision, for better or for worse, and the cards were played to the best of my ability, given the circumstances at the time. With hindsight, I recognise that many of the decisions were bad ones, and I have regret for things I did, but even greater regret for the missed opportunities.

From lying totally paralysed on my hospital bed as a little boy I had risen like a Phoenix, albeit a broken one, to make my laborious flight through the years. During the journey I met many interesting people. Some were cruel, some were ignorant or lacked understanding, the great majority were indifferent, but at every point along the way were individuals who displayed exceptional kindness. Without the assistance of these Good Samaritans my passage would have been difficult, if not impossible. Often it was the little acts of kindness that meant so much, like the five-year-old boy who, seeing my walking problems as I leaned heavily on my stick to leave the barber's shop, leapt to his feet to open the door for me.

On my journey through life I had managed to secure a reasonable education, to enjoy an interesting career, acquire sufficient money for my needs, meet good friends, experience family life, and make a name for myself as a Cinnamon Canary breeder, with my birds going all over Europe and even as far as Argentina. I had known joy and sorrow, pleasure and pain, success and failure. The passage had been eventful and edifying, seen through eyes looking for explanations and seeking to understand people and events, a few of which have been mentioned to illustrate the general tenor of my life. With determination and endeavour I had successfully mitigated many of the restrictions imposed by my disabilities and, with patience and good humour, dealt with most of the prejudice that I encountered. Whether I won the battle to lead a normal life is a moot point, but I believe that I put up a damned good fight.